In Her Hands

IN HER HANDS

THE EDUCATION OF JEWISH GIRLS IN TSARIST RUSSIA

ELIYANA R. ADLER

 WAYNE STATE UNIVERSITY PRESS DETROIT

15 14 13 12 11   5 4 3 2 1

Library of Congress Cataloging-in-Publication Data

Adler, Eliyana R.
In her hands : the education of Jewish girls in tsarist Russia / Eliyana R. Adler.
p. cm.
Includes bibliographical references and index.
ISBN 978-0-8143-3492-8 (alk. paper)
1. Jewish girls—Education—Russia—19th century. 2. Jewish day schools—Russia—19th century.
3. Russia—History—1801–1917. I. Title.
LC3585.R8A34 2011
371.076082—dc22
2010026279

Typeset by Maya Rhodes
Composed in Adobe Garamond and Serlio LH

To my parents

who gave me every educational opportunity

my father Leslie K. Adler

and my mother Leya Aum (1943–2001)

And thus in the education of women is included the source of education for the whole people; in their hands rests the fate of the next generation.

—Abram Iakov Bruk-Brezovskii

CONTENTS

ILLUSTRATIONS

TABLES

Acknowledgments

The process of taking a vague and untested idea, background material from numerous courses and books, and piles of primary documents and turning it all into a book is challenging, rewarding, and surprisingly lengthy. It has been a tremendous learning experience for me. I have also learned to rely on help from many quarters.

At Brandeis University I was fortunate to have Antony Polonsky as my advisor and both ChaeRan Freeze and Gregory Freeze as readers. Jonathan Sarna and Bernadette Brooten helped me learn how to be a historian. Fellow students, including Naomi Jacobs and Yohanan Petrovsky-Shtern, also enhanced my learning experience. The Ruth Spitz Memorial Fellowship helped to finance my graduate studies. I am grateful to Brandeis Judaica librarians Charles Cutter, Jim Rosenbloom, and Nancy Zibman for their ongoing attentions.

I began delving into this topic at the YIVO Institute for Jewish Research. I am grateful for Leo Greenbaum for pointing me toward the American Autobiography Collection. On subsequent research trips to YIVO, including one funded by the Abraham and Rachela Melezin Fellowship, I benefited from the expertise of Fruma Mohrer and Marek Web.

The bulk of research for this project was conducted at the Russian State Historical Archives in St. Petersburg. Galina Ippolitova helped me to navigate the archive. In St. Petersburg I also made use of the holdings of the Russian National Library. Advice from ChaeRan and Gregory Freeze, as well as local scholars Dmitri Elyashevich and Anatoli Khaesh, helped me to manage this first foreign research trip. Grants from the Department of Near Eastern and Judaic Studies and Women's Studies Program of Brandeis University helped me to pay for it.

On a more recent trip to Vilnius, Lithuania, to conduct research on a related topic, I found several relevant documents and texts at the Lithuanian State Historical Archives and the Library of Vilnius University. I am grateful to Galina Baranova and Snieguole Misiuniene for helping me to isolate materials in advance. My colleague Sarunas Liekis provided much appreciated logistical support. This trip was generously funded by the Abram and Fannie Gottlieb Immerman and Abraham Nathan and Bertha Daskal Weinstein Memorial Fellowship in Eastern European Jewish Studies of the YIVO Institute for Jewish Research.

I have been truly blessed to complete this project at the Joseph and Rebecca Meyerhoff Center for Jewish Studies at the University of Maryland. Through a two-year post-doctoral fellowship at the center, an additional year as an Ephraim Urbach Post-Doctoral Fellow, and subsequent years as a visiting assistant professor, I have had the bounty of library and human resources. In particular, I would like to thank the two directors during my tenure, Marsha Rozenblit and Hayim Lapin, and colleagues Maxine Grossman, Benjamin Jacobs, Miriam Isaacs, Sheila Jelen, and Rachel Manekin.

Over these years friends, colleagues, and journal readers and editors have taken the time to look over pieces of this work. I owe a debt of gratitude to Carole Balin, Tova Cohen, Ben Ekloff, Avraham Greenbaum, Paula Hyman, Sheila Jelen, John Klier, Rebecca Kobrin, Rachel Manekin, and Marsha Rozenblit for providing comments and suggestions. All errors are entirely my own. I acknowledge the publishers of *East European Jewish Affairs*, *Polin: Studies in Polish Jewry*, and *Studies in Jewish Civilization* for granting me permission to reprint material previously published in a similar form within their pages.

Although the initial phases of internal and external review were fraught with difficulties and took longer than anyone could have foreseen, it has been a pleasure to work with the dedicated staff at Wayne State University Press. My thanks go to Kathryn Wildfong, as well as the other professionals at and associated with WSUP for conscientious, sensitive, patient, and enthusiastic help.

My family has been a source of inspiration and support in this project as well as in life. This book is dedicated to my parents: to my mother, who had faith in me to choose my own educational path, and to my father, who modeled a love of history and intellectual engagement. My parents-in-law have consistently supported my unorthodox career path.

It takes a great deal of patience to be married to an academic. Thank you, Steve, for listening to my meandering ideas, for some inspired suggestions, and for supporting my decisions.

If there were a world record available for asking the most, the most varied, and the most interesting questions, I am certain that my children would win top honors. They truly exemplify taking education into one's own hands.

IN HER HANDS

INTRODUCTION
Education and Transformation

In the speech delivered at the opening of his private school for Jewish girls in Kherson in 1866, Abram Iakov Bruk-Brezovskii began with a paean to the history of Jewish education. "No one can rightly accuse our tribesmen of indifference to learning."[1] He then contrasted the supreme dedication of Jews toward educating their sons to the situation for girls: "Unfortunately, this concern about education, until recent times, extended only to boys; almost no attention was paid to the education of the female sex. True, in the Bible and the Talmud several educated women are mentioned, but they were outside of the norm of our people. The history of the Jews does not show even one communal educational institution for the female sex."[2]

Bruk-Brezovskii conceded that some might oppose education for girls: "There are people who think that education for the female sex, especially of the lower classes, is excessive and can even sometimes be harmful, because it cultivates a taste," but he saw no merit in their opinions. On the contrary, Bruk-Brezovskii viewed educating Jewish girls as a means of transforming the entire community: "And thus, in the education of women is included the source of education for the whole people; in their hands rests the fate of the next generation. For our Jews, the education of women holds yet another importance: only through them can we, little by little, supplant our jargon and imperceptibly acquire for ourselves the national language—an exceedingly important step toward internally and externally merging with the Russian people."[3]

1

Although Bruk-Brezovskii was not alone in placing the responsibility for proper instruction of children on women, he was one of a relatively small number of individuals who followed up on this belief by opening a modern school for Jewish girls. These schools, over one hundred of which thrived between 1831 and 1881, not only trained thousands of Jewish girls in secular and Judaic subjects, but also paved the way for the modern schools that followed them. Nonetheless, their story has largely disappeared from the historical scholarship. This work seeks to restore it to its proper place.

Shevel' Perel' opened the first modern private school for Jewish girls in Russia in 1831. His school, located in Vilna, the center of rabbinic Judaism in Eastern Europe, offered lessons in European languages, Russian, Yiddish, and the Jewish religion. Girls as young as eight years old could enroll for a two-year course of study. Fifty years later, in 1881, Perel's school remained open, although under the leadership of his son-in-law, Vul'f Kagan. It had expanded to include four years of study, over one hundred students, and a broader and deeper curriculum. Thousands of girls passed through Perel's school. Some, like his daughter Flora, stayed on as teachers; others taught elsewhere or went on to pursue further educational opportunities. All of Perel's students brought their knowledge of Russian language and culture, and their new approach to the Jewish religion, back with them into their homes. These girls' influence spread from their homes and school to the Jewish community of Vilna and beyond.

In telling the story of Perel's and Bruk-Brezovskii's schools, and the many others that followed, this book examines curricula, teachers, financing, students, public opinion, educational innovation, and how each of these changed over time. The private schools for Jewish girls that opened in the second half of the nineteenth century both reflected developments within Russian Jewish society and drove further developments. It is precisely in their capacity as both a marker of and a catalyst to change that these schools prove most useful in illuminating the Russian Jewish community at a time of profound transformation.

Indeed, change was a constant for Jews in nineteenth-century Russia. To speak in broad generalizations, at the beginning of the century the Jews were locally autonomous, Yiddish speaking, religiously traditional, and socially isolated. By the turn of the twentieth century, communal autonomy had given way to political activism on the world stage, the Jewish community had broken down into a variety of orthodox and secularizing groups, many Russian Jews were socially and linguistically integrating into the surrounding society, and millions of others were leaving their homes and families in an attempt to build new lives abroad.

Much scholarship engages the important intellectual and religious trends of the day, including Zionism, revolutionary politics, emigration, the rise of so-called ultra-Orthodoxy, and the tremendous literary flowering of the latter half of the century. Until recently, far less attention was paid to the lives of "ordinary" Jews and their active and passive involvement in the upheavals of their era.

Insofar as education comes into the story, it is typically as illustration or evidence. This study, however, seeks to place education at the center. The emergence of private schools for Jewish girls is thus viewed not only as a demonstration of the inroads of modernity into the Jewish community, but also as a crucible of educational experimentation. This approach reveals the importance of integrating this chapter within the greater narrative of Russian Jewish history.

Contours of the Russian-Jewish Encounter

At the end of the eighteenth century, due to the partitions of Poland, the Russian empire found itself greatly expanded in territory and ruling over a host of new ethnic and religious groups. Of greatest concern were the Poles, with their large population, relatively high educational level, grievances over their loss of autonomy, and allegiance to the Catholic Church. The Jews, although far less significant numerically, stood out due to their vastly different language, dress, culture, religion, education, and occupational structure. Prior to the partitions, Jews had been barred from residence in the Russian empire.[4]

One of the first acts of the Russian state vis-à-vis its new Jewish population was containment. Empress Catherine II (1762–96) established the Pale of Settlement to limit Jewish settlement to the areas where Jews already resided. She also sought to regularize the Jewish population by introducing estates. Most Jews registered in the urban estate while some members of the wealthy elite entered the merchant estate.[5] Her son, Paul I (1796–1801), initiated a project to collect and codify all laws regarding the Jews. His son, Tsar Alexander I (1801–25), in turn, completed the project and promulgated the 1804 Statute on the Jews. This piece of legislation appealed simultaneously to varied constituencies within governing circles, and consequently contained articles both restricting and encouraging Jewish acculturation. It thus included laws further limiting Jewish settlement alongside an invitation for Jews to attend all educational institutions in the empire.[6]

Both Tsar Nicholas I (1825–55) and his son, Tsar Alexander II (1855–81), initiated and oversaw efforts to transform the Jews into Russian subjects. In 1827 Jews were first drafted into the military.[7] The introduction of a State Rabbinate came in 1835. The crown rabbis, created to serve both bureaucratic and spiritual functions, in fact proved unable to supplant the traditional rabbis, leading to the development of a dual rabbinate.[8] Jewish boys had to begin attending a state-sponsored Jewish school system as of 1844. In 1847 the *kahal,* or self-governing institution of the Jewish communities, was abolished. All these pieces of legislation would have long-lasting, and often unexpected, consequences.[9]

The Tsar Liberator, Alexander II, is best known for emancipating the serfs and ushering in an era of Great Reforms. In the early years of his reign he introduced limited local government in the form of the *zemstva,* reorganized the judiciary, and brought needed reform to other areas of the Russian state. Although Alexander did not introduce radical legislation for the Jews, he nonetheless oversaw important reforms to the Pale of Settlement, censorship, conscription, and the state Jewish school system. This era of relative liberalization would come to an end with Tsar Alexander's assassination in 1881.[10]

Alexander III's (1881–94) own reactionary proclivities gained force from the widespread notion that his father's reforms had been a failure, and led to the "Temporary Laws" of May 1882 and a series of restrictive measures against Jews. Rather than try to make the Jews into proper Russian subjects, the government now applied harsh discrimination to encourage disengagement and emigration. As of July 1887 all Russian secondary and higher institutions were subject to strict quotas, with the enrollment of Jewish boys at secondary schools limited to 5 percent outside the Pale and 10 percent within it.[11] Although the law did not specifically mention girls, in practice Jewish girls were often barred from Russian schools as well.[12] These anti-liberal policies characterized the final rulers of the Russian empire.

The Russian Jewish encounter took place against the backdrop of the particular histories and cultures of each group and in the context of the arrival of modernity. New ideas about governance, citizenship, politics, nationalism, religion, gender, education, and every other sphere of life would shake the foundations of tradition among both Russians and Jews. These were compounded by new economic, strategic, and political realities. Just as it is crucial to view the development of the "Jewish Question" in Russia in the context of other issues and as one small component of the myriad of challenges facing the rapidly modernizing empire, it is also important to understand the growing interest in Russian education among Jews as part of a complex process of acculturation.[13]

The gradual move from traditional religious educational patterns toward more secular and Russian ones resulted from governmental policies, but also from economic realities, new opportunities, and new ideological directions. The Russian Jewish *Haskalah* (Enlightenment) posited intrinsic value in scientific study and in becoming good citizens of one's native land. To be sure, their major focus was on education for men, but, like Bruk-Brezovskii, some of the *Haskalah* thinkers realized that women also had a role to play.

The Study of Women's Education

Until fairly recently, scholars of Jewish history and of Jewish education have tended to work separately. In the works of Jewish historians, the subject of education is used to illustrate traditional patterns or as evidence of change. Scholars of Jewish education have often examined their topic in isolation, without attention to greater societal trends. Within Jewish studies, the history of education has often been viewed as distinct from the study of history.[14]

What has been common to scholars from both fields is their almost exclusive focus on the male experience. Zevi Scharfstein's authoritative work on Jewish education in the modern period is made up of three volumes describing in detail the educational experiences of Jewish boys in all the major Jewish communities for the past two centuries. There are a few passing references to girls, but only in the sections on the twentieth century are Jewish girls part of the narrative.[15] While no work on Jewish education fails to describe the central male institution of the *heder* (the one-room traditional Jewish school for boys ubiquitous in Europe), many fail to mention girls at all.

Historians of Jewish life in Eastern Europe, meanwhile, displayed a curious lack of curiosity toward women's education. In 1896, when there were still private Jewish girls' schools in existence, Leon Bramson, who had himself been involved in philanthropy and education, wrote an early history of elementary education for Jews in Russia. His interest was primarily in new educational endeavors, and he provided valuable information on the early private schools for Jewish boys and on the government's Jewish school system. Toward the end of his narrative he remarked that girls schools were a growth industry, having increased from 40 to 100 institutions. He noted that these schools found funding sources outside of tuition, and also that the Jewish subjects tended to be weak.[16] Bramson's two-page spread on private schools for Jewish girls would be their last appearance in historical scholarship for one hundred years.

When subsequent scholars of Jewish life in Eastern Europe referred to women's education at all, it was usually in a cursory manner. Louis Greenberg, writing in the 1940s, opened his lengthy description of the *heder* system with this observation: "In fact, there was practically no illiteracy among Russian Jewry, for almost every male—and in many cases females, too—could read the prayer book and the Bible."[17] Like many of his colleagues, Greenberg did not go on to explain how girls gained these skills.[18]

What emerges from the general historiography is a highly gendered understanding of education. Historians delegated education to the sphere of male experience, which inevitably treats male learning as normative and female education as marginal, exceptional, and beyond the pale. Even when authors recognized that normative patterns of education may have existed for Jewish girls as well, these were not considered a topic worthy of inquiry. It was thus possible for learned and rigorous scholars to mention that girls may have had educational training but not pursue the topic further.

Indeed, insofar as anyone has told the story of Jewish women's education in Eastern Europe, it has been the story of its "invention" by Sarah Schenirer. Frau Schenirer, as she was known to her students, founded the first Bais Yaakov school for Jewish girls in independent Poland following the First World War. The story of the humble Hasidic seamstress who devoted herself to a seemingly hopeless cause and ended up creating a successful school system still in place today is truly inspiring. It has been retold in a number of popular works and more recently revised by a couple of scholars.[19]

Schenirer was responding to the fact that religious Polish Jewish girls of her day attended Polish schools and thus moved away from Judaism. But the attendance of Jewish girls at general schools itself requires explanation. Jews in twentieth-century Poland sent their daughters to general schools not only in response to their immediate circumstances, but also because nineteenth-century Jews had made such a move possible. This work argues that the private schools for Jewish girls set in motion a series of educational sea changes that helped to open the possibility of Jewish girls attending secular and state educational institutions.

The prominence of social history in the study of the Jews of Eastern Europe, thanks largely to the pioneering approach of Jacob Katz, has made possible a sophisticated conversation about the place of education.[20] In particular, both Michael Stanislawski and Steven Zipperstein have opened up this field.[21] More recently, Simion Krieze, Steven Rappaport, Benjamin Nathans, and Mordechai Zalkin have provided detailed studies of aspects of Russian Jewish education.[22]

Exploration into the education of Jewish girls in nineteenth-century Eastern Europe is an even more recent phenomenon. Deborah Weissman, Shaul Stampfer, Shoshana Pantel Zolty, and Avraham Greenberg have all made important contributions.[23] Both Paula Hyman, as a historian, and Iris Parush, as a scholar of literature, have begun the process of providing an overarching analytic and narrative structure for the subject.[24]

My own work is informed by theirs, as well as that of many other scholars who have written about important aspects of the East European Jewish experience. Moreover, it would not have been possible without the opening of Russian archives after the fall of the Soviet Union in the early 1990s. The few scattered references to private schools for Jewish girls in memoirs and history books, even when combined with references from contemporary newspaper reports, were simply not enough to work with. Simion Krieze, a close reader and tireless researcher of published sources, was able to show in his 1994 dissertation that there existed private schools for Jewish girls, but it was the archival resources that made this in-depth study possible.[25]

Sources and Methods

In the archives of the former Ministry of Education I was fortunate to locate hundreds of files of correspondence between would-be educators and the ministry. Included are documentation on the educators, requests for permission to open private schools, letters of recommendation from local officials, financial statements, educational plans, inspection reports, and requests for funding. However, not all the files were equally complete, such that in many cases the information available about individual schools and principals is not parallel.

To some degree, I was able to fill in these gaps by further archival research in the files of the Vilna office of the ministry in both Lithuania and New York, and with the use of published almanacs of state employees held in the Vilnius University Library and the New York Public Library. However, the very fact that some yearly reports submitted by Jewish schools to the Vilna Jewish Teachers Institute and publications of the tsarist Ministry of Education are available only in New York says something about the fortunes of documents in a region wracked by wars and revolutions. The data I collected on the northern regions of the Pale are better but are still incomplete, and even if I had been able to conduct further research in archives in the Kiev and Odessa regions, the data would remain uneven.

Throughout the text I have been careful to distinguish between facts about individual schools and conjectures based on these facts. Wherever possible, I have included charts based on parallel information to give a sense of the range and spread of various data. In some cases I was able to use surviving copies of yearly almanacs published by regional and local authorities that include names, educational background, salary, and years of employment for state employees to supplement other information. But of course the full runs are no longer extant and information varies from region to region and even year to year.

Other sources used in this project include contemporary periodicals, educational materials, and memoirs. The periodicals produced by the Russian Jewish community express their unique ideological stances via content and language choice. Although during the late nineteenth century most of these periodicals fell into the progressive camp, they still differed from one another. News reports about newly opened schools, programmatic articles on Jewish education, opinion pieces about women's roles, and advertisements have all proved useful for this research.

By the turn of the century, there were even periodicals specifically devoted to Jewish education. Jewish educators in that era of innovation also produced textbooks, how-to manuals, and works about education. Additionally, a few Jewish organizations sought to gather data on Jewish education. Although much of this material falls outside the chronological boundaries of this study, it has nonetheless been useful in reflecting on the earlier period and in demonstrating the transformations in Jewish education.

Whenever possible, I have tried to include qualitative examples from memoirs and even fictional writing. There is by now a vast literature on the challenges of reading autobiographical writing.[26] Recent scholarship has even moved this conversation into the realm of Jewish studies.[27] In this work I use memoirs to illustrate or support points rather than to prove them. In addition, some of the memoirs used come from an autobiographical writing contest, rather than published and polished sources, and thus avoid some of the pitfalls associated with the genre.[28] Fiction is employed sparingly, and for the purposes of mining the authors' opinions rather than avoiding them.

I aim, throughout this work, to be transparent in my use of historical sources. With a book such as this, based primarily on unpublished and obscure documentary findings, it is of the utmost importance to provide the reader with information, both in the text and in the notes, about the provenance, character, and quality of the sources available. I have endeavored to do so while maintaining a smooth narrative flow.

Structure

The narrative arc of this book is chronological, although the chapters are thematic. Part 1, consisting of chapters 1–5, follows the emergence and development of the new private schools for Jewish girls. Beginning with the historical circumstances that enabled their creation, and moving through staffing, financing, and academic matters in the schools, these chapters introduce the schools and how they changed over time. Part 2 looks at the interactions between these new educational institutions and the society in which they functioned. We see both how the schools responded to changes taking place around them and how they in turn influenced their environment.

Modern educational institutions emerged in the Russian Jewish community as a result of both internal and external pressures. The first chapter examines the Russian Jewish Enlightenment, or *Haskalah*, as well as legal and societal forces that helped to bring about change. Russia as a whole, and the Jewish community in particular, underwent major transformations over the course of the century. Advances in education for Russians, for women, and for Jews inform this chapter.

Chapter 2 outlines the implementation of the state-sponsored school system for Jewish boys, and what effect it had on private education for Jews. Although neither the *maskilim* (enlighteners) nor the Russian government placed the education of Jewish girls at the forefront of their concerns, their combined actions and interests provided conditions uniquely conducive to the development of modern private schools for Jewish girls.

Even ideal conditions, however, require enterprising actors. Chapter 3 seeks to profile the educators who opened the new girls' schools. We will see that a combination of ideological and financial concerns led this diverse collection of men and women, both Jews and non-Jews, to devote themselves to educating Jewish girls. Although their educational, religious, and professional backgrounds differed significantly, all of them worked to provide new educational opportunities for generations of Jewish girls.

In addition to devoted faculty and willing students, the new private schools required steady funding. The tuition that families were willing and able to provide in most cases was not sufficient to the needs of the schools. As a result, the principals developed methods to raise money locally, and identified other possible funding sources. Chapter 4 traces how the use of sliding-scale tuition, candle tax surplus, and Jewish communal subsidies illuminates the development of both the schools and the Jewish community as a whole. Although the first private schools aimed to enroll the daughters of wealthy acculturating Jews exclusively, expanding ideas and opportunities meant that they had to find ways to adapt to an increasingly diverse student body.

This was true in the academic as well as the financial sphere. Chapter 5 examines curricula in the new schools and how they changed over time. Whereas the first schools had relatively modest offerings and taught Yiddish as frequently as Hebrew, over time the subjects multiplied and Hebrew became a required subject. The study of religion and of crafts also gradually increased and developed. Although each school had its own distinct student body, faculty, and community, it is nonetheless possible to trace trends of greater breadth across all the schools.

Chapter 6 focuses on the students who attended the private schools for Jewish girls. In addition to narrowing in on the numbers and background of the girls, insofar as possible, it pays particular attention to how the girls utilized their training. The import of this question is strengthened by the prevalence of Jewish women in politics and education in Russia at the turn of the century.

Commentators at the time could hardly fail to notice the new educational opportunities afforded Jewish women, nor their prominence in public life. Chapter 7 examines how both the progressive and traditional voices in Russian Jewish society viewed these transformations. Whereas the concern of rabbinic leaders may not be surprising, the profound ambivalence presented in the modernizing Russian Jewish press reflects the complexity of gender and modernity.

Chapter 8 shows the many important ways in which the private schools for Jewish girls influenced later iterations of Jewish schools, students, and educators. Freed of the strict oversight of either the *heder* or the government Jewish schools, the private schools provided a unique laboratory for educational experimentation. Methods of teaching Hebrew and crafts, and of integrating students developed in these schools, would all be put to use in later educational institutions.

Taken as a whole, this work contributes a new chapter to the story of Jewish life in tsarist Russia, and suggests that this new chapter both engages with and alters the standard story. By looking first at how the schools emerged and developed over time, and second at how their active presence influenced the society around them, we see that Abram Bruk-Brezovskii, whose words provide the basis for the title, was correct in his proposition that the education of Jewish women would transform the entire people.

PART I

EDUCATION

1

EDUCATION IN AN ERA OF CHANGE

In 1804, shortly after large numbers of Jews first became subjects of the Russian empire, an ambitious statute granted Jews access to all Russian educational institutions. It also offered a vague threat that Jews' refusal to reform themselves educationally could lead to government intervention.[1] Given that the highly traditional Jewish community had no interest in secular Russian education and that Russia had little to offer in the way of primary and secondary schools, the statute remained largely theoretical. However, over time the situation would change. This chapter examines the developments that led to the creation of modern Jewish schools for and by Jews. In order to understand these developments, it is important to focus on the dynamics of the relationship between the Russian state and the Jews, educational trends in Russia as a whole, and educational changes within the Jewish community.

Education Policy and Practice in Tsarist Russia

Along with the rest of Europe, Russia experienced major advances in education during the nineteenth century. However, certain factors made the Russian situation unique. Historian James McClelland has memorably termed the expansion "erratic dynamism."[2] As we will see, while not governed by a rational and orderly approach, the advances were significant and ultimately opened up new opportunities for many sectors of the populace.

When Peter the Great (1682–1725) embarked on his grand plan to westernize and modernize Russia in the eighteenth century, he did so from the top down. In the field of education this meant that Russia was the only European state to establish its academy of sciences in conjunction with its first university and academic secondary school.[3] Even with the steady increase in secondary schools for the wealthy elite over the years, the educational system remained markedly top-heavy.

For the gentry class, whose custom had long been to bring tutors into their homes to teach their children, this was not necessarily a problem. However, the lack of lower-level educational institutions made it difficult for other classes to enter the educational system. This problem was further compounded by the development of education taking place under a variety of governmental bodies, often without the possibility of complementarity. Thus, for example, the parish schools run by the Holy Synod offered only a basic education, not covering the subjects required for entry into the prestigious academies run by the various branches of the military. Even the municipal schools under the Ministry of Education did not offer the Latin required for entry into the private gymnasia overseen by the Ministry of Finance.

Nevertheless, despite a system designed to serve the wealthiest sectors of the population and to maintain a divided social order, and the vagaries of educational institutions under the auspices of four separate government departments, educational opportunities for all sectors of the Russian population increased throughout the nineteenth century. To a degree, the trends in educational reform followed the general tenor of the reigns of the various nineteenth-century tsars, but even this organizing principle did not always hold true. The Ministry of Education (*Ministerstvo Narodnago Prosveshcheniia* [MNP], literally the Ministry of National Enlightenment) was indeed established during the relatively liberal early years of the reign of Tsar Alexander I. However, education only really began to advance under the far more cautious reign of his brother, Tsar Nicholas I. Tsar Nicholas and his able and long-serving minister of education, Count S. S. Uvarov oversaw both a consolidation of control over all levels of educational institutions and a broad expansion of the number of such institutions. Thus, whereas the student body in gymnasia grew from 5,569 in 1809 to 7,682 in 1825, within the first decade of Nicholas's reign enrollment had reached 15,476.[4]

Tsar Alexander II (1855–81) ushered in the era of Great Reforms in the first decade of his reign. Liberalization in a number of key areas, including a relaxation of censorship, led to societal expectations of more reforms to come. The introduction of limited local governance through the *zemstvo* institutions, as well as the 1864 Education Statute, would make elementary education far more accessible, for example.[5] Ultimately, however, Alexander retreated from making other, similarly bold decisions, and after his assassination in 1881 the government cracked down in a number of areas, particularly education.

The other systemic peculiarity of the Russian educational system worthy of mention is that by the 1870s educational institutions, and especially the universities, had become centers for popular unrest. It was thus that certain branches of the government, regardless of their views on education in theory, sought continually to limit both opportunities for higher education and the scope of the curriculum.[6] This trend was particularly pronounced in the crackdown following 1881.[7]

Over the course of the second half of the nineteenth century, a series of ministers of education sought to steer a course between creating an educated population capable of sustaining growth on the one hand, and avoiding the creation of an educated population capable of recognizing the enormous contradictions, inefficiencies, and inequalities of the Russian empire on the other. Dmitrii Tolstoi, who served from 1866 to 1880, stands out as an individual deeply committed to the continuation of the tsarist system but also aware of the tremendous potential of education. His policies included unswerving support for the classical curriculum offered in the gymnasia and cruel crackdowns on student gatherings in the university.[8]

Despite human and fiscal resources vastly inadequate to meet the educational needs of its enormous population, as well as vacillating and inefficient government support of the project of education, the nineteenth century saw a significant increase in educational opportunities for all Russians. Whereas in 1856 the state had but one elementary school for every 7,762 subjects, by 1896 the latter number was 1,499.[9]

Women's Education in Imperial Russia

The difficulty in pinpointing a coherent educational policy in the Russian empire is perhaps best illustrated by the fact that by the late nineteenth century Russia could boast more women in higher education than any other European state and at the same time a higher rate of female illiteracy.[10] Despite frustrations and reversals, options at both ends of the educational spectrum grew over the century.

Prior to the nineteenth century, aristocratic Russian girls were educated in the home. Although a few convent schools and Empress Catherine's pet project, the Smolny Institute in St. Petersburg, did exist, most wealthy girls learned literacy and the skills of running a home less formally.[11] By the nineteenth century the slow and steady growth of schools for girls took place largely outside government purview. Attendance at private finishing schools became more normative for girls from wealthy families.

Increasingly, women who benefited from education sought to expand educational opportunities for other women. By the time of Tsar Alexander II's Great Reforms of the 1850s, women's education had become an important topic of discussion in the journals and parlors of the Russian intelligentsia.[12] There was great hope that after ending serfdom, the tsar would turn to reforming Russia's educational system and to expanding rights and opportunities for women.

Here again, the reality was nuanced. Government decrees of the reform period opened up the possibility of widespread schooling for girls. Both private individuals and a variety of government departments, including the Ministry of Education and the Department of Institutions of Empress Maria, responded by opening schools in larger urban centers. By the mid-1870s more than 60,000 girls studied in public and private schools.[13] At the same time, the attempt to provide women with higher education was met with considerable resistance.

The first known female auditor in a Russian university came in 1859. She was followed soon by scores of other newly educated women seeking to expand their educational and professional horizons. Many students and most professors supported, or at least tolerated, the influx of women into the academy. However, as the legal backlash to the failed Polish Uprising of 1863 targeted the freedom of the universities, the opinions of the faculty had little import. Despite the fact that women were not implicated in the perceived unruliness of university students, they were no longer allowed to audit courses.[14]

The great hope of the early years of Alexander II's reign, and the disappointment at the abrupt end of the first experiment with women's higher education, were both essential motivating factors in the growing women's movement. Women of the nobility began to devote their energies and funds to providing vocational and other schools for the poor. At the same time, some young educated women turned to teaching as a profession while others sought avenues to continue their studies at home or abroad.[15] Education was a unifying goal of the nascent women's movement before radicalization split its ranks.[16]

As Christine Johanson has pointed out, however, the expansion of educational opportunities for women had remarkably little to do with the women's movement. Minister of Education Tolstoi eventually conceded to allow women's higher courses, albeit without degree-granting status, in response to a preemptive move by the Ministry of War. In 1868 Minister of

War Miliutin, whose ministry oversaw the Medical Academy, knew that the empire was dangerously short of medical professionals and began to accept women. Tolstoi responded by opening the public higher education lectures for women in 1869.[17]

During this same period, Russian women began to go abroad to pursue university degrees as well. By 1872 one hundred Russian women, among them twenty Jews, had completed degrees in Western Europe. This phenomenon led to a growing number of highly educated women in the empire but also to greater opportunities for expressing frustration with the regime. All the university towns frequented by Russians came also to house revolutionary and proto-revolutionary groups. In recognition of this serious issue, in 1873 the government recalled all Russian women. They had to either return immediately to their Motherland or risk losing the opportunity of ever returning.[18]

The following years saw ongoing shifts in the fortunes of women's higher education in Russia. The expansion in the number of students and in their political activism led to tighter controls over the women's higher courses and their enrollment. Tsar Alexander III tried to close the courses down entirely in 1886. Yet the revolution of 1905 allowed once again for growth.[19] Thus, although the autocracy never embraced women's higher education and certainly hindered its development, a small subset of Russian women were able to fulfill their educational dreams, as well as to enable educational opportunities for other girls.

Jewish Education on the Eve of Change

At the beginning of the nineteenth century, the Jews who found themselves in the Russian empire retained a traditional educational system that had grown out of the educational institutions that emerged in medieval Western Europe and developed further in early modern Eastern Europe. Jewish law mandated religious education for boys, and consequently Jewish communities had created and refined a normative educational experience for boys. As we will see, the educational experiences of Jewish girls were less regulated and straightforward.

All communities of more than a few Jewish families in Eastern Europe had at least one *heder* (pl., *hadarim*) or traditional school for Jewish boys. Additionally, larger communities often sponsored a school for the sons of the poor called a *talmud torah*. The vast majority of Jewish boys learned to decode Hebrew liturgy and sacred text in these institutions.[20] Most would not have the financial and intellectual resources to go on to the higher-level *hadarim* and *yeshivot* to gain a more comprehensive education in the vast body of religious literature, but nearly all gained familiarity with the basic texts and practices of Jewish life through their primary education. According to some reckonings, even as late at the First World War, the majority of Jewish boys in Russia still attended the *heder,* for at least some period.[21] There can be no question of the centrality of the *heder* in Jewish life.

While attendance at the *yeshivot,* or seminaries, was limited to the financial and rabbinic elite, these institutions also played an important role in Jewish communities. Most medium-size and larger Jewish communities supported a *yeshiva.* Householders were expected to house and feed the students, many of whom came from out of town. Although most community members did not directly benefit from the local *yeshiva,* they shared in its prestige and took part in its maintenance.

With the crystallization of the anti-Hasidic movement of the *mitnagdim,* in the early nineteenth century, the role of the *yeshiva* would further expand. For the *mitnagdim,* Torah study stood at the center of all human endeavors. It was the single most important way to serve the Divine. Over the course of the nineteenth century, rabbinic leaders built a number of grand *yeshivot* and significantly raised the status of Torah study and Torah scholars in their communities.[22]

Regardless of socioeconomic background or intellectual acumen, all boys could expect a *heder* education. Iris Parush and Shaul Stampfer have recently called into question the quality and even the true aims of this education. Whereas previous scholarship tended to assume a meritocracy whereby the brightest boys, even of meager means, would be shepherded through the system to reach their full potential, the reality may not have been so idyllic.[23] Most boys could never hope to study in a *yeshiva.* Nonetheless, Jewish society presented them with a clear educational path and hierarchy based on knowledge.

Traditional Education for Girls

For Jewish girls the path was less clearly defined. The responsibility to provide Jewish boys with religious instruction, according to Jewish law, falls not only on the father but, in the absence of the father, on the community at large.[24] Educating Jewish daughters, on the other hand, is a questionable enterprise. Early rabbis argued about the permissibility of providing Jewish girls with access to sacred texts.[25] The contours of this lengthy debate have been well chronicled elsewhere.[26] For our purposes, the salient point is that the education of Jewish girls fell outside of the official responsibilities of the Jewish community.

To be sure, all Jewish girls learned the fundamentals of Jewish religious practice, and the proper roles of the Jewish woman, in their homes. It is difficult to know exactly how this socialization took place, although some hints are available from memoirs and legal texts.

Running a Jewish home required both practical skills, like cooking and sewing, and knowledge of the prescribed religious doctrines and duties of women. One memoirist, Etta Byer, born in 1884 in Lida (Vilna province), described how both could be accomplished simultaneously: "Mother bought me a tiny thimble and we mended clothes or darned stockings. We polished the candle-sticks for the Sabbath. Mother was pleased with my work. We sang together all kinds of folk-songs, spirituals, the lyrics of the rabbis and the Chasidim."[27] E. Kushner, born in Ukraine in 1898, learned regularly with both her father and grandfather from a young age: "I do not remember exactly when I began to learn to pray. I know only that early every morning my father would teach me a new line, and by the age of four I had already learned a great deal by heart."[28] The children in her household learned more formally as well: "In the late afternoon my father would learn with the children. He, who had extraordinary aptitude, a sharp intellect and a good memory, used to believe that everyone was as gifted as he and could understand in a wink. Those children who understood him easily, he enjoyed teaching, and those who did not have strong desire, or to whom learning came a little hard, he would send to Grandpa."[29] In these and other memoirs it is possible to get a glimpse of traditional Jewish methods of socialization in the home. Girls shadowed their mothers to learn concrete skills and accompanying customs. Some Jewish girls also had access to more formal training in the liturgy and other Jewish subjects through male relations.

Avraham Ber Gottlober provides a more ethnographic depiction. Born in 1810 in Starokonstantinov (Volhynia province), he was married at the age of fourteen into a Hasidic family and moved to Chernigov. Years later, in his memoirs, he described the marital customs of his youth:

> After noon, in joy and celebration, the bride would immerse in the ritual bath. Older women danced before the bride, and brought her into the waters of the *mikvah,* to sanctify her to enter into the tradition of the covenant of marriage. Then they would teach her the secret of conception and how to make a blessing on the lighting of Sabbath and holiday candles, to

separate *hallah,* and in particular [how] to separate from her husband at the time of her impurity, and count the seven intermediate days as is written in the Written and Oral Torah. And they would use strong words in order to etch this into her heart. For only in this way would she, in this world and the next, find favor in the eyes of the Lord and her husband, and merit worthy sons and modest daughters.[30]

Thus, according to Gottlober, the laws of family purity, as well as the other commandments typically associated with women, were taught to a young bride by older women at the time of her marriage. Mary Asia Hilf, born in Teofipol (Volhynia province) in 1874, described her mother's introduction to the three women's commandments with only slight modifications. Her mother, married at the age of sixteen, learned the Jewish rituals of the home from her mother-in-law by example: "Granny Rifki's teachings ranged from the best way to prepare the sweet, white or Sabbath Chala [*sic*], a bread twist, to the blessing of the ritualistic candles with prayers and tears on erev Shabbes, or Sabbath Eve. And never did my mother forget the older woman's precepts and examples."[31] Either evocation suggests a mimetic tradition, passed down orally and without consultation of *halakhic* texts and authorities.

This scenario is supported by the *Arukh ha-Shulhan,* a nineteenth-century codification of Jewish law written by Rabbi Yehiel Mikhel Epstein (1829–1908). On the subject of Jewish women's education, R. Epstein confirmed that girls must be taught laws that apply to them. Later he discussed the manner in which this education took place: "We have never taught women from a book, nor have we heard that people actually do so. Rather, every woman teaches her daughter or daughter-in-law those well-known rules women should know."[32] Rabbi Epstein thus described and favored the informal matriarchal transmission of tradition he had seen around him while expressing some anxiety about new methods.[33]

These and other informal methods of socialization remained a stable part of Jewish life. Additionally, female literacy was not unusual in traditional Eastern European Jewish communities. The image of the pious elderly woman immersed in her *Tsene u-rene* or *tkhines* is a constant in contemporaneous literature and memoirs. The *Tsene u-rene,* a Yiddish work of biblical stories with *midrashic* and ethical enhancement, penned by Rabbi Ya'akov Ashkenazi in the seventeenth century, quickly became standard Sabbath reading for Jewish women. The scholar of Yiddish literature Khone Shmeruk

Studio portrait of Borekh Mortkhe Altschuler (1826–1916) of Minsk, a
teacher of Russian, Hebrew and Yiddish in Schedrin, and his wife, Alte, a
Yiddish teacher for girls and a *zogerke* (women's prayer-leader), Rechitsa, ca.
1900. (YIVO Institute for Jewish Research)

estimated that, between 1765 and 1850, a minimum of 210 editions of this book were printed in Eastern Europe alone.[34] The very size and number of printings is indirect evidence of women's literacy in Yiddish. Similarly, the *tkhines,* or women's supplicatory prayers, although difficult to quantify because of the inexpensive printing techniques, were ubiquitous among Jewish women.[35]

No statistical data on Russian Jewish women's literacy from the early nineteenth century exists. At the same time, publication data and literary tropes suggest that Jewish women reading in their vernacular was not unusual. Yiddish, the spoken language of East European Jewry, is a largely phonetic language, relying on Hebrew characters, and would not have been difficult to learn. Many of these women may have been introduced to Hebrew reading skills in order to follow the prayer service. These skills would have been easily transferable to Yiddish.

As the century progressed, so too did formal educational opportunities for Jewish girls. Some attended *heder* with their brothers, albeit for a limited amount of time. Others received formal tutoring in religious subjects or practical skills such as letter writing or basic math. The important role played by women in the economic life of Russian Jews meant that there were very practical reasons for educating daughters. Gottlober, quoted above, also notes in his memoirs that mastery of Polish was as attractive in a young woman as beauty on the marriage market.[36]

In rabbinic families the practice of women financing their husbands' full-time devotion to Torah study had become an ideal. Although many of these men would eventually have to go to work in order to help support their families, and most families were in no position to produce a Torah scholar, this ideal influenced Jewish society. Even outside the circles of the elite *mitnagdim,* women's participation in the paid workforce was both accepted and expected.[37]

Among the wealthy sector of the community, especially those influenced by the norms of their gentile counterparts, private lessons in French, German, piano, and dance provided attractive educational options.[38] Success in salon society required not only proper deportment and attire, but also linguistic and aesthetic skills.

Such changes in educational norms came about due to interaction with the outside society and changing economic circumstances, but also due to the sustained critique of a particular group within Jewish society. The Russian Jewish *Haskalah* would have a profound influence on Jewish education.

The Maskilim *and Education*

The Russian Jewish Enlightenment, or *Haskalah,* was an outgrowth not only of the European Enlightenment and its Jewish manifestations but also of the specific social and political conditions in the Russian empire. By virtue of their common language, religion, and culture, Jews in Russia—especially those near the western borders—came into contact with ideas from the German and Galician Jewish *Haskalah.* Ideas of humanism, rationalism, faith in science, and the importance of secular knowledge and languages reached Russian Jews through business, social, and familial contacts across the western border. By the early nineteenth century some Russian Jews espoused enlightened ideas, although a coherent movement would not appear for several more decades.

The Russian *maskilim,* influenced by German Jewish models, enthusiastically embraced the study of secular knowledge and languages as a way of self-betterment. In the German Jewish context, this major platform of the *Haskalah* was part of a progression toward normalization of the community and eventual emancipation.[39] In Eastern Europe civic emancipation was a far more distant goal. The Russian *maskilim* followed their German counterparts in espousing great faith in the government and in the eventual triumph of humanistic values, but they also operated in a very different environment.

In the German lands, as well as those formerly Polish lands administered by the Habsburg monarchy, *maskilim* envisioned themselves as working together with their governments to enlighten their benighted brethren. Perhaps the best example of this is in the Jewish reaction to Joseph II's Toleranzpatent of 1782. The Edict of Tolerance, along with a series of related articles, laid out a new system whereby Jews as a nation gave up both benefits and burdens in return for the promise of privileges to be granted to Jews as individuals. Among other regulations, Jews were directed to establish for themselves modern German schools where religion would be only one subject of study.[40]

While most of the Jews in the Austrian empire viewed the emperor's reach into their autonomy and educational system as disastrous, to *maskilim* it showed his humanism and genuine desire to help the Jewish community. Naftali Herz Wessely's Hebrew work on the need for educational reform, *Divre shalom ve-emet,* was dedicated to Kaiser Joseph II. Wessely and others believed that by learning German and embracing other aspects of acculturation, Jews could become full citizens.[41]

For the early Russian *maskilim,* far more distant from their rulers in terms of both location and culture, it was not even clear which language to adopt. Seeking to take part in the greater *Haskalah*, and with little to no connection to Russian society, they produced their early works in Hebrew or German. Only later would a cadre of Russian speaking intellectuals arise. Nonetheless, they too saw the necessity of educational reform.

Isaac Baer Levinsohn published the first attempt to articulate a platform of progress for the Russian Jewish *Haskalah*. Levinsohn (1788–1860), whose father had insisted that he learn Hebrew and Russian in addition to the traditional *heder* curriculum, traveled as a young man to Galicia. There, in Brody in particular, he met and learned from the local *maskilim*. By the time he returned to Russia eight years later, Levinsohn was ready to create change in his native land.[42] *Te'udah be-Yisra'el,* published in 1828 with a subsidy from the tsarist government, explored what Jews should study and contained a critique of the current educational system.

In *Bet Yehudah,* published ten years later, Levinsohn outlined a five-point plan of improvement for the Jewish community in Russia. Although heavily influenced by the German *Haskalah*, Levinsohn's plan was tailored to the Russian situation. He advocated (1) a modern educational system for boys and girls; (2) a chief rabbi with academic advisors; (3) local preachers to teach ethical lessons rather than mysticism; (4) the establishment of agricultural colonies for Jews; and (5) giving up luxury items.[43]

As the Russian *Haskalah* developed, both its critique of the current educational system and suggestions for a better one would remain central ideologically.[44] In addition to advocating productivization, outlawing traditional garb, ending early and arranged marriages, and other changes, all *maskilim* had to tackle that most crucial institution: the *heder*.

Mordecai Aaron Guenzburg (1795–1846), in his influential autobiography *Avi'ezer,* published only in 1863, moved from a loving description of his home and the early instruction his father gave him to describing his highly mixed educational career. Although he escaped some of the worst indignities by his quick intellect and attentive parents, Guenzburg still suffered at the hands of incompetent and cruel teachers. He provides an overall impression that each *heder* was run entirely at the whim of the attendant *melamed,* with no oversight and often horrible consequences.[45] Other *maskilim* would recall their own difficult experiences in autobiographies, as well as in fiction and poetry. Their critique covered the untrained and often underpaid and cruel *melamdim,* the depressing and unhealthy physical surroundings, and the mode and content of the instruction.

Levinsohn's *Te'udah be-Yisra'el* was particularly concerned with questions of curriculum. In it he asked a series of rhetorical questions about the permissibility and value of teaching Jewish children secular subjects and foreign languages. Through his answers he presented a radically new educational program.[46]

Through education Levinsohn and the other *maskilim* hoped to create a new generation of Jewish men—educated in modern subjects and languages and ready to take up productive occupations in society. Although the *heder,* its ills and its remedies, was integral to the *maskilic* platform, the education of Jewish girls was less so. As early as 1838 Levinsohn had suggested a Jewish school system for both girls and boys:

> To establish schools to teach younger and older pupils the Torah and religion and commandments together with virtues and ethics and love for God, neighbor, and kingdom as well as for the people with whom we live. And all according to a set order. Special books will be chosen especially for this in consonance with the age of the children: the youth according to his youth and the more mature student according to his maturity. Also female children will be taught according to their abilities and the needs of women for matters of religion, ethics, and virtues. Both boys and girls will be taught a craft or trade because idleness and lack of steady income are the beginning of all sin.[47]

Most of the early *maskilim,* however, concerned themselves only with the education of Jewish boys. Women who appear in the most important autobiographical works of the first generation of *maskilim* tend to be foils to the main character: an evil mother-in-law or an ignorant young wife.[48] Thus, although a critique of the gender roles in society is inherent, men remain the focus.

This situation gradually changed in the next generations. Although women's education never became a major rallying cry of the movement, it moved from the periphery to a more central position. This change can be traced to outside influences as well as to a maturation of maskilic thinking and greater consistency and acuity. Western European bourgeois ideals of marriage influenced the Russian *maskilim.* In this milieu, girls—both Jewish and non-Jewish—were being educated to serve as proper and faithful wives and mothers.[49]

In this vein, the Russian *maskilim* envisioned the productivization of the Jews as accomplishing two goals: it would provide Jews with a useful position in society (as opposed to a "parasitic" one) and overturn the social system wherein many Jewish women provided for their families while their husbands devoted themselves to scholarly pursuits. The *maskilim* were acutely uncomfortable with this system as well as other dynamics of the Jewish family. They sought to put an end to early and arranged marriages. Ultimately, this focus on the problems within Jewish family life forced *maskilim* to confront the role of women in Jewish society.

As Shmuel Feiner has shown in his study of maskilic writing about women, many held conservative views of the role of women in the ideal Jewish society they hoped to create. Even those who espoused a more egalitarian vision had trouble imagining women with the same intellectual needs and abilities as themselves.[50] At times this ambivalence played out in overtly misogynist rhetoric. Fiction and nonfiction created by the *maskilim* offer both idealized, educated, modern Jewish women, and vapid and shrewish counterexamples.[51] In the words of Carole Balin:

> The ideological complex of the maskilim thus reveals a paradox. On the one hand, they criticized and satirized the traditional institutions of the Jewish family, undertaking measures intended to enlighten and presumably emancipate women. Yet, on the other, their reconceptualization of the Jewish family perpetuated a clear-cut gender differentiation that continued to relegate women to the roles of wife and mother. Their desire for marriages based on companionship, in which bourgeois respectability imported from the west would prevail, returned the Jewish woman ultimately to the home to act as helpmeet to her husband and enlightened exemplar to her children. Education, secular and Jewish alike, was perceived as a means to that end.[52]

Throughout the middle decades of the nineteenth century, the *maskilim* were the only really articulate progressive voices within the Jewish community, and it is sufficient to refer to all the writers in the Hebrew press, despite their varied opinions, with this term. By the 1870s Russian Jewry had produced a loosely defined group of intellectuals writing in Russian and envisioning greater acculturation into the Russian milieu. I have variously referred to these individuals as progressives, modernizers, and Russifiers. Only at the end of the century did an organized religious conservative response to these groups develop. With reference to the period prior to the emergence of a self-conscious Orthodox movement, I have used the term traditionalists for the individuals opposed to changes in the Jewish community.

Much more has been said about the ever-evolving political, intellectual, linguistic, religious, and social trends amongst nineteenth-century Russian Jewry.[53] For the purposes of this chapter, the important fact is the crystallization of the Russian Jewish *Haskalah* and its views on women's education. As the remainder of the book unfolds, we witness the parallel unfolding of these various ideologies and how they interacted with, influenced, and were influenced by the developments in the education of Jewish girls.

All these factors—the contours of the Russian Jewish encounter, the peculiar path of Russia's educational development, the traditional educational practices of Russian Jews, and their critique by a group of intellectuals growing in influence—came together to produce the conditions necessary for the emergence of modern education among the Jews. In the next chapter we see how the confluence of further factors meant that girls would be particular beneficiaries of this development.

2

UNINTENDED CONSEQUENCES
The Emergence of Private Schools for Jewish Girls

Shevel' Perel's modern private Jewish girls' school, opened in Vilna in 1831, was not the first modern educational institution for Jews in the Pale of Settlement. By that time the Jewish community of Odessa already had a successful modern school. However, the school in Odessa served only boys. Perel's innovation lay in starting a school especially for Jewish girls. This chapter investigates why Perel' and a few of his colleagues chose to open early schools for Jewish girls, and how government legislation unexpectedly swelled their ranks.

The Story of the First Private School for Jewish Girls

Shevel' Smuelovich Perel' was born at the beginning of the nineteenth century into the petty townsman, or urban, estate [*meshchanstvo*] and educated at home until he entered the Vilna Gymnasium. Attendance at a gymnasium was extremely rare for a Jew in the 1810s. The thirteen secondary schools in the Vilna province listed two Jews among their pupils in 1824.[1] Even as late as 1841 it is estimated that only fourteen Jewish boys attended general Russian educational institutions in the nearby city of Kovno.[2] The majority of these were in elementary schools rather than gymnasia. Perel' was probably the only Jew in his school and, upon his graduation, one of a small minority of Jews in Vilna who was fluent in reading and writing Russian.[3]

Documents suggest that Perel' married in his early twenties.[4] He and his wife Sara had two sons and four daughters, the oldest of whom was born in

1822.[5] After his rather unorthodox education, followed by his establishing an apparently more traditional family life, Perel' made the decision to start the first modern school for Jewish girls in Russia. Whether Perel' knew about the failed attempts at modern education in Uman and Vilna or the successful one in Odessa is unclear.[6]

Shevel' Perel' was, for his time, extremely well educated and not especially wealthy.[7] This made him an excellent candidate for the teaching profession. As a Jew, Perel' would not have been able to get a job in a Russian school, but as a gymnasium graduate who may have never attended *heder,* he was not well suited to becoming a *melamed.* Perel', as evidenced in later correspondence, was proud of his own fluency in Russian and dedicated to providing other Jews with access to Russian culture. Perhaps his decision to open a Russian-language school for Jews was perfectly natural. The only remaining question is why it was a school for girls.

In a letter requesting funds from the government in 1848, Perel' wrote the following: "It is common knowledge that the education of the female sex represents one of the most important means to the spread of enlightenment among the men; . . . consequently, if the mothers receive proper education during their maiden years, then they will raise their children with the same values."[8] It is, of course, difficult to know how much of this was constructed as a means of convincing the government that his cause was deserving, and how much represented his own point of view. But in any case, it was an oft-repeated argument among the more conservative *maskilim* and in government circles that girls were ideally suited to pass on Russian fluency to the next generation.[9] It is not hard to believe that Perel' could have taken this view seriously.

Simion Krieze, in his highly detailed study of Russian-language Jewish schools in Russia, has suggested that the particular makeup of the city of Vilna was decisive for Perel'. Vilna in the 1830s was a center for both the *mitnagdim,* the rabbinic opposition to the Hasidic movement, and the first flowering of the Russian Jewish *Haskalah.* Realizing the crucial importance of Torah study for men in the thought of the *mitnagdim,* the *maskilim,* according to Krieze, avoided a fight by opening a school for girls.[10] Krieze's notion is supported by the fact that several modern private schools for Jewish girls opened in Vilna before the first one for Jewish boys. However, this explanation suggests that Perel's plan was highly sophisticated, raising the question of why schools for girls were not opened elsewhere earlier.

It is also worth noting that Perel' did face communal opposition to his school. In January 1843 Perel' wrote to the Ministry of Education seeking to have his son released from military duty, despite the likelihood that Perel' sent his sons to Russian schools, a fact that should have been sufficient for him to be released from conscription.[11] That one of Perel's sons had been drafted suggests that the local Jewish draft board targeted the son on account of his father. If members of the Vilna Jewish community would go to these lengths to punish Perel', he undoubtedly faced other harassment as well. In a letter written to the Ministry of Education in 1861, briefly narrating the history of his school, Perel' stated, "It is not possible to describe how many were my troubles and with what obstacles I had to contend in order to earn the respect and trust of the Jewish community."[12]

Significantly, Perel' may have tried to open a school for boys first. According to several early sources, there was a short-lived private Jewish school that opened in Vilna in 1830.[13] As the sources do not mention gender, this school was likely for boys. In this scenario, Perel's initial desire to run a modern school for Jewish boys was somehow stymied, leading him to turn to educating girls. On the other hand, other early sources identify Perel's school as specifically for girls, or possibly even mixed.[14]

We may never know with certainty what thoughts and actions preceded Perel's decision to open a private school for Jewish girls in Vilna in 1831. It is certainly possible that he first had a school for boys, or even that at one point he taught both boys and girls. What is clear is that once established, the school thrived for several decades. Despite the difficulties he faced, there were also members of the Jewish community who supported Perel's work and sent their daughters to his school. The first school for Jewish girls in Russia was able to provide thousands of girls with a foundation in Russian and other subjects.[15]

Perel's school also served as a model for other educators. A private school for Jewish girls opened around the same time in Odessa.[16] In 1835 the thriving modern school for Jewish boys in Odessa added a section for girls.[17] Aron Gittels requested permission to open an additional private school for Jewish girls in Vilna in 1840.[18] By 1850 six schools for Jewish girls had opened in the Vilna educational region.[19] Raphael Lindenbraten, one of the new principals, was a brother-in-law of Perel's.[20] Meanwhile, elsewhere in the Pale other educators continued to open modern private schools for Jewish boys. To be sure, their numbers were small in contrast to the vast number of *hadarim*. Nonetheless, the new schools for Jewish boys and girls would have continued to increase in number and develop side by side were it not for the introduction of state-sponsored schools for Jewish boys.

Съ 1851 года я содержу въ г. Вилнѣ дѣвичье училище. Въ продолженіе этого времени я имѣлъ счастіе пріобрѣсти довѣріе Начальства и моихъ единовѣрцевъ. Въ 1854 году это мое училище было преобразовано въ 3-хъ классное заведеніе, въ каковомъ видѣ оно состоитъ и понынѣ. Въ концѣ прошлаго года нѣсколько дѣвицъ, окончившихъ курсъ наукъ въ моемъ училищѣ, выдержали экзаменъ въ Виленскомъ Дворянскомъ Институтѣ на домашнихъ наставницъ. Для ободренія же своихъ единовѣрцевъ къ дальнѣйшимъ успѣхамъ, честь имѣю притомъ предложить на разсмотрѣніе программу, преподаваемыхъ въ моемъ училищѣ, предметовъ:

Въ 1-мъ классѣ:

а) Русское чтеніе
б) Нѣмецкое —
в) Еврейское —
г) 4 Правила Ариѳметики и
д) Чистописаніе: Русское, Нѣмецкое и Еврейское.

Во 2-мъ классѣ:

а) Законъ Божій
б) Русская Грамматика
в) Нѣмецкая —
г) Французское чтеніе
д) Изъ Географіи: Обозрѣніе Европы
е) 4 Правила Ариѳметики (на Русскомъ языкѣ) и
ж) ... писаніе: русское, Нѣмецкое, Французское и Еврейское.

Въ 3-мъ классѣ:

а) Законъ Божій
б) Русская Грамматика
в) Нѣмецкая —
г) Французская —
д) Русская исторія
е) Ариѳметическія Задачи
ж) Упражненія письменныя на Русскомъ, Нѣмецкомъ и Французскомъ языкахъ, и
з) Географія.

○Цѣна въ годъ 10 руб. сереб. Если кому угодно будетъ брать уроки также въ рукодѣліи, танцованіи и музыкѣ, то цѣна 30 руб. сер. Со столомъ же 150 руб. сер. въ годъ.

Содержатель Училища Шевель Перель.

Утверждаю. За Директора, Инспекторъ Гимназіи Розинъ.

Печатать позволяется, Вильно, 27 Іюля, 1854 г. Ценс... А. Мухинъ. — ВИЛЬНО. Въ Типографіи Р. М. Ромма.

Broadsheet advertisement for Shevel' Perel's school for Jewish girls in Vilna, 1855. Lists tuition costs as well as course offerings in both Yiddish and Russian. (Russian State Historical Archive)

The Establishment of the Government Jewish School System

In 1844 the Russian government embarked on a bold new plan to transform the Jewish community. Instituting a state Jewish school system was yet another attempt to refashion the Jews into proper Russian subjects, but this one was based on the lengthy deliberations of a group of fairly liberal and Western-oriented government officials.

The Jewish Committee, under the leadership of Count P. D. Kiselev (1788–1872), also included Count S. S. Uvarov (1786–1855), the minister of education. Uvarov had traveled extensively in Western Europe and observed the acculturated Jews who resided there. He was especially impressed by the linguistic and cultural assimilation of the Jews in the German states. At the same time, committee members were increasingly aware of the powerful educational system of the Jews and its pervasive influence. Weaning the Jews from the Talmud and from the "fanatical superstition" of the *melamdim* became major goals.[21]

Due to his own leanings, Uvarov looked to the German-speaking lands for models.[22] The committee displayed less interest in the modern private schools closer to home, in the Kingdom of Poland, although it did make note of the number of Jews in Poland who attended general educational institutions.[23] The committee was, however, aware of similar schools in the Pale of Settlement. Between the mid-1820s and mid-1840s, private schools for Jews opened in Odessa, Kishinev, Vilna, Riga, Minsk, Mitau, and Kherson.[24] Although the schools differed in many ways, they all sought to combine some level of Jewish education with instruction in Russian and other secular subjects. Uvarov was so impressed on his visit to the school in Riga that he hired its principal to serve on his committee.

Max Lilienthal (1815–82), a German-educated Jew, came to run the modern school for Jewish boys in the relatively Germanized Jewish community of Riga in 1840. He had been on the job for only one year when Uvarov tapped him to help plan a statewide Jewish school system. At Uvarov's request, Lilienthal wrote to leaders of Western European Jewish schools and seminaries to solicit recommendations for teachers in the new schools.[25] Despite their shared idealization of the German Jewish community and its successful integration into general society, neither Lilienthal nor Uvarov was particularly knowledgeable about the Russian Jewish community or even about its more modernized and Russified segments.

For the remainder of his five years in Russia, Lilienthal toured the Pale to publicize the plans for a government school system and also served as a "learned Jew" [*uchenyi evrei*] at the first meeting of the Rabbinic Commission in 1843.[26] As Michael Stanislawski has emphasized, Lilienthal's cultural, linguistic, religious, educational, and geographic distance from the Jews of Russia did not win him many friends among the Jews. Even the *maskilim* found Lilienthal supercilious and offensive.[27] Nonetheless, Lilienthal firmly believed in his mission, at least at the beginning of his tenure in the Ministry of Education. It is also revealing that Uvarov chose a German rather than a Russian Jew to serve him in this capacity.

In all likelihood, Uvarov himself worked out the overall structure of the new school system. He then passed on his draft legislation to the Committee for the Transformation of the Jews and finally to the Imperial Commission for the Education of the Jews of Russia. The latter commission consisted of four carefully chosen representatives, including two major rabbinical figures. They were to provide a trustworthy Jewish imprimatur to the educational reforms. A reliable account of the deliberations in this commission is not yet available. Contemporary public sources differ widely in their judgments.[28] In any case, Uvarov went ahead with his plans.

The year 1844 saw the publication of the law "On Establishing Special Schools for the Education of Jewish Youth." It proposed to educate Jewish boys in special state-run Jewish elementary schools. The law further stated that Christians would direct the schools, though both foreign and local Jews were permitted to serve as teachers. The curriculum included Jewish as well as secular subjects. The subject of Jewish law was to be taught on the basis of a catechism and Moses Mendelsohn's German translation of the Bible rather than the Talmud.

In conjunction with the creation of government-sponsored Jewish schools, the government opened two modern rabbinical seminaries, and the private Jewish schools already in existence came under heavy regulation. The seminaries, essentially at the level of academic high schools, were meant to train the new Russified rabbinate. *Melamdim* in traditional *hadarim* had to register with the authorities. Anyone wishing to open a new *heder* had to pass an examination. The *talmud torah* also fell under government supervision.[29]

The government hoped the new Jewish school system would serve as a catalyst for change within the Jewish community by teaching Jewish boys secular subjects (especially Russian language and history), weaning them from the teachings of the Talmud, and encouraging them to enter "useful" professions. The government intended to supplant the *heder* system entirely, but left it in place for the present, though under closer oversight.

In actuality, the first government schools for Jewish children in the Russian empire were a number of the former private Jewish schools mentioned above.[30] Beginning in the late 1840s, when local Jewish communities did not open state schools on their own, the government proactively established additional schools in locales across the Pale. The schools were staffed by *maskilim,* who often had to travel to take up their posts, as well as by local Jews and Christians. By 1855 there is evidence of 70 schools with an estimated combined student body of 3,208.[31] That same year, the Ministry of Education counted 104 schools (including the two rabbinical seminaries) with a combined student body of 3,363.[32]

That the rate of growth of the schools and consequent decline of the *hadarim* did not satisfy the government is clear from ongoing legislation. Under Nicholas's successor Alexander II, the government tightened its regulations on Jewish schooling.[33] Nonetheless, Jewish families remained reluctant to transfer their sons from the *heder* to state institutions. To avoid censure over low enrollment, some communities allowed the poorest boys to attend the new schools. In 1862, in an apparent recognition of one source of Jewish distrust, the government for the first time allowed Jewish principals to run the state schools.[34]

Finally, in 1873 the government abandoned its grand hope of replacing all *hadarim* with state-run Jewish schools and adopted a far more modest plan. Specifically, the state authorized the retention of schools only in those areas with sufficient Jewish population, and converted the rabbinical schools into teacher-training colleges. It therefore closed all schools in areas of smaller Jewish population as well as those offering secondary education.[35] The remaining schools, mostly in the northern area of the Pale, were scaled back to offer only the most basic general studies curriculum.

The introduction, development, and eventual closure of the state Jewish schools profoundly influenced the Jewish community. Presumably their influence would have been even greater had Jewish girls taken part in this experiment.

The Government Jewish School System for Girls

Although some of the early committee plans, as well as occasional outside requests, advocated for building state schools for Jewish girls and boys, the government never actively sought to educate Jewish girls. The one and only government Jewish school for girls came into existence more by accident than by design, and was never replicated.

In 1852, as part of the process of incorporating existing private schools for Jewish boys into the new school system, the government absorbed the popular and innovative Odessa school formerly run by Betsalel Stern.[36] Stern had added a branch for girls to his school almost a decade previously. Thus, the Odessa school for Jewish girls entered the government Jewish school system. Over the next years it continued to prosper, enrolling 250 girls by 1860. An 1860 correspondent for the Russian Jewish periodical *Razsvet* also noted that articles about the girls' school had appeared in *"Odesskii Vestnik, Razsvet,* a journal for education, a journal for children, and 3 journals in the German language."[37]

With this sort of numerical success and widespread fame, why was the model not copied elsewhere? Why did the Odessa school remain the only government Jewish school for girls? In fact, long before the Odessa school merged with the government Jewish school system, the idea had been considered and even recommended. We know, for example, that Isaac Baer Levinsohn's *Bet Yehudah,* published in 1838, included a call for a modern educational system for girls and boys in the Russian empire.[38]

More specifically, Shlomo Zalkind (d. 1868), a prominent Vilna *maskil* and educator, wrote to both Uvarov and A. G. Stroganov, his counterpart at the Ministry of the Interior, with an organized plan to create government schools for Jewish girls. While it seems that Zalkind wrote in the early 1840s, before the schools for boys officially opened, he clearly knew about the planned legislation and hoped to influence the policy makers to expand their vision of Jewish education.[39] Another *maskil* published his program for educating Jewish girls and boys in a Hebrew periodical in 1844.[40]

Moreover, interest and initiative for this program came from closer to home as well. A lengthy internal MNP document from the early 1840s, which was to form the basis of the 1844 legislation, offers extensive support for providing schools for Jewish girls as well. The document opens with an eight-point plan for transforming the Jewish community. The first point is to establish special public schools for Jewish children.[41] Although gender is not specified initially, it emerges within the text of the document: "Equally necessary to men's schools is to establish also women's schools, because the Jews' rudeness and stubbornness to new ideas originate primarily from the ignorance of their women, who, due to always being at home, lack all the benefits of socialization and raise the children in the same prejudices as they are themselves full of."[42]

In 1848 the issue once again came before the Ministry of Education. In September of that year, a group of Jews from Brest-Litovsk, including the prominent banker and financier Abram Zak, wrote the minister asking that, along with the planned government school for Jewish boys, a government school for Jewish girls be opened in their city. They lauded the goals of the government and expressed their desire to fulfill them with their daughters as well as their sons.[43] However, both the director of schools for the Grodno province and his superior in Vilna opposed their request on the grounds that opening such a school would discourage Jews from enrolling their daughters in general educational institutions.[44] There is no record of the ministry's view of the proposal on its own merits.

Yet another proposal to open government schools for Jewish girls surfaced within the Ministry of Education in 1853. The idea seems to have begun with the curator of the St. Petersburg educational circuit, who wrote to the minister of education for permission to pursue a plan for opening schools for Jewish girls. Upon receiving permission, he contacted the directors of schools of the Mogilev and Vitebsk provinces, neither of which yet had any schools for Jewish girls. With their support he hired Professor Anton Osipovich Mukhlinskii (1808–77), a prominent Christian Orientalist at St. Petersburg University, to form a plan for the proposed schools. Relying on the examples provided by the government Jewish school for girls in Odessa and Perel's school in Vilna, a detailed application package was prepared.[45]

The plan called for schools to be opened in the cities of Mogilev and Vitebsk. The principals of the institutions, in contrast to those of the government schools for boys, would be Jewish men, with daily oversight administered by either Jewish or non-Jewish women. The schools would be supported mainly by the candle tax, but families would also be asked to contribute one and a half rubles per month. The eighteen-hour school week would consist of instruction in religion and European languages, as well as Russian and world history and geography.[46]

The Ministry of Education referred the application to the nascent Rabbinic Commission.[47] In its report on the subject, the commission pointed to the fact that there were at the time ten private schools for Jewish girls in seven cities educating a total of 1,072 Jewish girls. These schools, according to the commission, had the effect of both "destroying fanaticism" and creating "rapprochement between the Jews and the general population." As women were crucial in rearing the next generation, opening schools for Jewish girls was a logical way to effect further positive changes among the Jews.

While supporting active governmental involvement in educating Jewish girls, the members of the Rabbinic Commission were also concerned that "the opening of schools for girls would not agree with the understanding of the majority of Jews and thus [the establishment of such schools] would be premature." For this reason, rather than endorse the plan to open schools immediately in Mogilev and Vitebsk, they elected to decline the application until the Jewish community was prepared.[48]

To this end, the members of the commission composed a lengthy and reasonably learned treatise on the education of girls in Jewish law.[49] The document they created was meant not to weigh the issues at hand but to provide sources and interpretations favorable toward educating girls. The document would be provided to rabbis (presumably those employed by the state), and only once they had created a more favorable climate would the government begin actively to open Jewish girls' schools.[50]

In 1864 the government dispatched an official representative to assess the status of Jewish schools in the Pale of Settlement. A. F. Postel's visited numerous schools and filed a lengthy report on his return. He was quite impressed with the private schools for Jewish girls and recommended, among other things, opening government schools for Jewish girls.[51]

Although no further record of the issue of state schools for Jewish girls appears in government documents, the topic continued to appear elsewhere. In an 1860 article on the state of Jewish education, *Razsvet* correspondent H. Gornberg offered a novel justification for providing government schools for Jewish girls. He argued that since wealthy Jewish families proved increasingly able to provide their daughters with formal education in the new private boarding schools, and as mothers continued to serve as the chief socializing agents in Jewish families, government schools would meet the needs of the Jewish community as a whole.[52] Nonetheless, the education of Jewish girls was ultimately left to private initiative.

Private Initiative

The 1844 law that put into place the state Jewish school system also provided for the regulation and registration of not only all private schools but also private tutors. Through this legislation Uvarov hoped to place the entire Jewish educational system under government surveillance and eventually to transform it. As with most laws, it led to a greater degree of compliance and coherence but also to unintended consequences.

In 1844 modern Jewish private schools constituted a tiny fraction of the educational institutions available to Jewish children. The traditional Jewish school system remained firmly entrenched. A government estimate prepared in 1847 by Uvarov for Kiselev, his counterpart at the Ministry of State Domains, estimated that there were 52 *talmud torahs*, 2,702 *hadarim*, and 2,580 second-level *hadarim*. In these institutions, as well as at *yeshivot* and *bate midrash* and at home, the Ministry of Education believed that 69,464 Jewish children studied.[53] These students were overwhelmingly male, and the estimates are almost certainly low. In contrast, there were fewer than ten modern private Jewish schools, of which one was specifically for girls and another had a branch for girls.

In the decades following the 1844 legislation, most Jewish boys continued to study in the *heder*. Some boys, particularly from among the poor, attended the new state Jewish schools. A small but growing number began matriculating in Russian schools. Meanwhile, modern private schooling increased for Jewish girls. By 1881, well over one hundred private schools for Jewish girls had opened. Table 2.1 shows their dates and locations. As expected, the first schools opened in larger cities and more cosmopolitan areas, but they continued to expand into smaller and more traditional communities as well.

Table 2.1. Modern Private Schools for Jewish Girls, 1831–1881

Consecutive tenure is indicated by a semicolon; simultaneous tenure is indicated by a slash; a married couple is indicated by an ampersand between names; and a school that admitted both boys and girls is indicated by an asterisk.

Principal	City	First Record	Last Record
Vilna Educational Circuit			
Shevel' Perel'; Vul'f Kagan	Vilna	1831	1881
Aron Gittels	Vilna	1840	1850
Levin Germaize; Isaak Germaize/Wolfson	Vilna	1848	1877
Doroteia Ekert-Buchinskaia	Vilna	1848	1850
Abram Shreiber; Mariia Kaplan	Vilna	1846	1881
Raphael Lindenbraten	Vilna	1850	1850
Mendel & Rakhel Levin	Minsk	1850	1851
Markus Perel'	Novogrudok	1850	1852
Ianovik/Shlarskii/Golovchinskii	Grodno	1852	1865
Ostrogorskii; Ostrogorskaia	Grodno	1852	1881
Markus Perel'	Pinsk	1852	1874
David Ioffe	Vilna	1853	1859
Mariia Siavtsillo	Kovno	1856	1859
Movsha Kissin	Minsk	1853	1858
Khaim Funt; Mariia Funt	Minsk	1857	1879
Isaak Kisin	Minsk	1857	1859
Anna Val'ttser	Vitebsk	1857	1866
Podshkol'nik	Rossieny	1857	–
Nakhim Landshtras	Rossieny	1857	–
Nadezhda Bel'skiia	Mogilev	1857	1879
Moisei Gurvich	Brest-Litovsk	1858	–
Notel' Zaretskii	Bialystok	1858	–
Abram Markil's	Polotsk	1858	1862
Isaak Rumsh	Ponivezh	1860	1880

Table 2.1. (*continued*)

Principal	City	First Record	Last Record
Vilna Educational Circuit			
Kagan/Polonskii; Karl Kaplan	Bialystok	1861	1879
Maksimilian & Aleksandra Zel'verovich	Vilna	1861	–
Emiliia Kheifets	Dinaburg	1861	1879
Merka Vol'fsonova	Bobruisk	1862	–
Zamengof; Gvirts	Bialystok	1862	1879
Simonia Aronovicheva	Dinaburg	1863	1873
Il'ia Rakovshchik	Minsk	1864	1886
Ioffe	Oshmiany	1864	1865
Solomonov/Solomon	Brest-Litovsk	1866	1879
Gordon; Khazanovich; Rudian	Tel'she	1866	1880
Mariia Ivanova	Kovno	1866	1867
Luiza Grasman	Brest	1866	1874
Elisaveta Redelin	Vitebsk	1866	1879
B. Levinthal	Vitebsk	1868	–
Anna Lukashevich	Dinaburg	1873	1874
Izrail Voronov	Shklov	1874	1876
Tsirelson*	Borisov	1875	–
Derengovskiia	Liutsin	1875	–
Derengovskiia	Dinaburg	1876	–
Anna Tsananko	Dinaburg	1876	–
Mosiei Vol'gal*	Krynki	1876	1880
Lev Kaplan*	Minsk	1877	1879
Noi Funt	Vilna	1877	1879
S. Tsirelson*	Bobruisk	1877	1879
Shaia Kagan/M. Lifshits	Orsha	1878	1879
Pozin	Sebezh	1879	–
Emiliia Kheifets	Mogilev	1879	1880
*	Rechitsa	1879	–
Abram Katsan	Kovno	1879	1881
I.N. Esterkin	Svintsiany	1880	–
Sheindes	Svintsiany	1880	–
Mark Abramovich	Pinsk	1879	–
Berta Ritt	Kovno	1881	1895
Kiev Educational Circuit			
German Iablonski	Vasil'kov	1847	–
Vainraub	Starokonstantinov	1855	1861
Aron Frud	Berdichev	1857	1865
	Khorol	1857	–
David Shtern	Mogilev-Podol'sk	1858	1880

Table 2.1. (*continued*)

Principal	City	First Record	Last Record
Kiev Educational Circuit			
Lazar Berman	Dubno	1859	1862
Glikin	Kamenets-Podol'sk	1860	1879
Perel'shteyn/Poliak	Vinnits	1860	1861
Iakov Fistul	Poltava	1860	1861
Fidler/Veitsman	Radzivilov	1861	–
Likhtenshtein	Berdichev	1861	1880
Rashkinds	Chernigov	1862	1874
Iakov Daich	Zhitomir	1862	1865
Dobruskes	Radomysl'	1865	–
Markus Plater	Kremenchug	1867	1871
Bank	Tul'chin	1867	–
Vainraub	Zhitomir	1867	–
Matil'da Rotshteyn	Kiev	1871	–
Liuba Kenigsberg	Berdichev	1872	1874
Vel'steyn	Zhitomir	1874	–
Gofman	Chernigov	1877	1880
Stefanavskii	Skvir	1874	1880
Arona Kushnera	Nezhin	1879	1883
Skashch	Periatin	1880	–
B. Urlikht	Rovno	1880	1881
Gershengorn	Korets	1880	–
Odessa Educational Circuit			
Vol'f & Khaye Gringol'ts	Odessa	1831	1867
Markus & Anna Gurovich	Odessa	1845	1857
Abram & Maria Dubenskii; Anna Dubenskii	Kherson	1847	1850
Anna Birshenker	Ekaterinoslav	1851	–
Anna Rabinovich	Ekaterinoslav	1851	–
Iosef & Anna Khones	Kherson	1854	1865
Abram Bruk-Brezovskii	Kherson	1856	1879
Anna Rabinovich	Ekaterinoslav	1856	–
Anna Birshenker	Ekaterinoslav	1856	–
Gertz	Kherson	1856	–
Varshaver	Kherson	1856	–
Sheinfel'd/Bliumenfel'd	Kishinev	1856	1880
Abris	Kishinev	1856	–
Kleinman	Kishinev	1856	–
Skliar	Kishinev	1856	–
Chernobyl'skii	Kishinev	1856	–
Feldman	Bel'tsi	1856	–

Table 2.1. (*continued*)

Principal	City	First Record	Last Record
Odessa Educational Circuit			
Schvartsbarg	Benderi	1856	–
Perl Ortenberg	Ekaterinoslav	1856	1863
Nusan Tiutinman; Israel	Khotin	1854	1881
Mariia Mitkovitser	Balmut	1858	–
Khaim Khitrik	Kherson	1858	–
Dikker	Simferopol	1859	1860
Khorin/Vaidman	Khotin	1861	–
Anna Rabinovich	Ekaterinoslav	1861	1866
Anna Iuzefovich	Simferopol	1862	–
Brilavskiah	Bakhmut	1864	1866
Feldman	Nikolaev	1865	–
	Kerch	1865	–
Mariia Vasserberg	Odessa	1867	1880
Iakov Daich	Sorokakh	1871	1874
Lion	Kishinev	1874	–
Urovits	Simferopol	1877	1880
Beilin	Simferopol	1874	1876
Polina Nezhenskiia	Simferopol	1876	–
Anna Rabinovich	Kharkov	1877	–
A. N. Belosterkovskii	Elisavetgrad	1880	–
M. Varshaver	Nikolaev	1880	–
Zaidmana*	Elisavetgrad	1880	–
Finkel*	Elisavetgrad	1880	–
Evva Doicher	Elisavetgrad	1880	–
A. A. Segal	Odessa	1881	–
Derpt Educational Circuit			
Betti Shtern	Mitau	1848	1850
	Derpt	1859	1862
Levinson	Tukkum	1877	1880
St. Petersburg Educational Circuit			
Anna Berman	St. Petersburg	1866	1884
Sara Berman	St. Petersburg	1873	–
Total Number of Schools			130

Note: The Ministry of Education oversaw the many Jewish schools in the Pale of Settlement through the use of three main branch offices in Vilna, Kiev, and Odessa. All paperwork regarding the private schools for Jewish girls reached St. Petersburg via the curator of schools in one of these cities. The only exceptions were the Kurland province, which wrote directly to the ministry, and the schools in St. Petersburg itself. I have maintained these divisions in order to make the data more manageable.

By 1899, there were 644 registered Jewish schools in the Pale of Settlement, of which 392 were private (the remainder were primarily communal). It is estimated that 50,773 students studied in these schools, 16,546 of whom were girls.[54] Private schools were to become a major socializing agent within the Jewish community. Over the course of the second half of the nineteenth century, they grew and differentiated in ideologies within the rubric set out in this major piece of legislation.

According to the expanded version of the 1844 law found in the Ministry of Education supplement to the legal code, no Jew could teach in any institution or home without permission. Having obtained this permission, Jews had the right to apply to open private schools. The goal of a private Jewish educational institution was to provide a grounding in the Jewish religion and to help students gain entry into general educational institutions.[55] The later goal, especially relevant to upper-level schools, mandated instruction in Russian and basic mathematics.[56]

The division of private Jewish schools into lower and upper levels paralleled the state Jewish school system. In the state system, lower-level [*razriad*] schools offered instruction in European languages, mathematics, and the Jewish religion. Upper-level schools offered more hours in each of the above as well as in history (two classes) and geography (three classes).[57] In terms of private schools, the distinction between upper and lower appears to have been more subjective. Applicants to open either type of school sent their requests to local officials who then sent them on to regional and national MNP offices.[58]

Successful applicants had to convince the local officials of having received permission to teach, as well as prove the necessity for the school, the quality of its curriculum, and the stability of its funding sources. In most cases this was achieved by submitting a cover letter, a *plan,* and a *programma* for the school.[59] The cover letter stated the qualifications of the would-be principal and briefly outlined the merits of the proposed school. The contents of the *plan* and *programma* provided details on the day-to-day running of the school as well as the curriculum. By the time this information was passed on to the Ministry of Education, the original paperwork had often been replaced with a cover letter from the regional director of schools highlighting the main points and stating a recommendation.

Although school administrators existed in all major cities of the Pale, and certainly in all regional capitals, in practice paperwork for Jewish schools passed through three main branch offices—Vilna, Kiev, and Odessa. Thus, for example, educators and officials operating in the Kovno province forwarded their paperwork to Vilna rather than directly to St. Petersburg. Once a private school had permission to open, from the local, regional, or national offices of the Ministry of Education, the principal proceeded to run the school to the best of his or her abilities. Further interaction with the authorities typically came for one of two reasons. First, schools were officially under the oversight of the local school governance and regular inspections ensued. Second, principals contacted educational authorities for access to financial subsidies.

Unintended Consequences

The new regulations helped to standardize the system for opening private Jewish schools on a legal basis. At the same time, albeit unintentionally, they encouraged would-be Jewish educators to open schools for girls. Although the law did not specifically prohibit opening private schools for Jewish boys, in practice educators found themselves unable to do so. Jewish men who already ran private schools for Jewish boys were forced to integrate their schools with the new government school system. This meant ceding control not only over the curriculum, but also over the leadership of the school as well, as the law insisted on non-Jewish principals. Nor did the government look favorably on new applications for modern Jewish boys' school. These would become competition for the government schools, which were, after all, supposed to be mandatory.

Ironically, the decision to mandate state Jewish schools for boys, and the corollary choice not to do so for Jewish girls, meant that the only arena open to those who wished to open modern private Jewish schools was in educating girls. And as Table 2.1 demonstrates, the number of private schools for Jewish girls increased markedly from this point forward. The following chapter profiles who opened the new girls' schools and why.

3

ENLIGHTENED SELF-INTEREST
Teaching Jewish Girls in Tsarist Russia

In 1872, when Y. L. (Yehuda Leib) Gordon left his government Jewish school teaching job in Tel'she (Vilna province) to take up a prestigious post as secretary to the Jewish community of St. Petersburg, he also left behind the private school for Jewish girls he had opened six years previously.[1] Fortunately, he was able to leave the school in the hands of the state rabbi, Khazanovich, who, it seems, had already been teaching there.[2] Khazanovich ably ran the school for another ten years before his death in 1882.[3] At that point Lidia Rudian, a graduate of the Kovno Women's Gymnasium married to a government Jewish school administrator, took over the school and its yearly subsidy.[4] Thus, in this one private Jewish girls' school, a government Jewish school teacher, a state rabbi, and an educated Jewish woman married to an educator held consecutive leadership positions. But how typical was this situation? This chapter explores both the types of individuals who became involved in teaching Jewish girls and their motivations.

What led people to open schools for Jewish girls in the second half of the nineteenth century? Were there particular professional, educational, or social characteristics that predetermined a commitment to women's education? Was it an ideological or a pragmatic decision? How typical or atypical was the school in Tel'she? Throughout the nineteenth century, educational opportunities for male and female Russians of all estates, religions, and ethnic groups were on the rise. This in turn led to greater demand for teachers and gradually to the professionalization of what had previously been seen as a fairly low-status occupation. Both Scott Seregny and Christine Ruane have written about this transformation in the general Russian context, but little is known about how the Jewish community responded to these new opportunities.[5]

Individuals, whether responding to local demand, their own perception of the greater good for the Jewish community, economic opportunity, or some combination of all three, had to have certain knowledge and skills to open modern private schools. Here we look to both quantitative and qualitative data to find out more about these individuals. The first section of the chapter attempts to divide the educators into categories based on the available lists of schools and their principals. The remainder of the chapter examines each category in turn, looking to qualitative data to illuminate the backgrounds and motivations of the principals of private schools for Jewish girls in Russia.

Educators: Aggregate

Throughout this work I have translated the Russian term *soderzhatel'* as "principal." Although the original meaning might be closer to "manager," "director," or even "bursar," in the context of these small schools the *soderzhatel'* combined supervisory roles and financial management with regular teaching. It was the *soderzhatel'* who submitted the paperwork to open a school, gained permission to teach, and typically did most of the day-to-day instruction. In most cases there were additional teachers, full or part-time, but it was common for the *soderzhatel'* to teach some or all of the core courses.

Only a small number of the schools listed other faculty members in the records available to us, so it is not possible to examine all the educators involved. One tantalizing exception comes from Vilna in 1869, where the three private Jewish schools for girls had between sixty and seventy pupils each. Vul'f Kagan's school had six teachers on staff, five male and one female, while Abram Shreiber's and Isak Germaize's schools each employed four teachers, three male and one female.[6] While this particular document provides no further information, a separate form filed with the Vilna Rabbinical Seminary specifies that the only non-Jewish teacher in the Kagan school taught upper-level Russian. The lone female teacher there, Flora Kagan, taught French and lower-level Russian; all the Jewish men had studied at the Vilna Rabbinical Seminary.[7] However, it is unlikely that these factors can be extrapolated to other schools, as Vilna's secondary and higher educational opportunities were unmatched in most of the Pale.

Even the data on principals of Jewish girls' schools are decidedly uneven. Some names appear only on published or unpublished lists. Often the gender and ethnic background of such individuals can be safely ascertained from the name, although this is not always the case. In other situations, lengthy correspondence with the Ministry of Education and journalistic coverage of the schools offer much more information on individual principals. However, the data are too sparse for a statistical analysis. At best they offer a starting point for further exploration (see Table 3.1).

Of the 149 principals, not surprisingly, the vast majority (129) were Jewish, while only a tiny proportion (12) were non-Jews (information on the religion of the remaining 8 principals is not available). What is surprising, however, is that 11 of the 12 non-Jews were women. In fact, approximately one-third (47) of the principals were female, 35 of whom were Jewish.

As for the Jewish male principals, nearly half noted in their application materials that they were employed by the state as either teachers in the government Jewish schools (39) or as state rabbis (4). These designations would most likely have aided their applications. Thus, it is safe to assume that most, if not all, of the remaining Jewish men were not employed by the state. Little else can be inferred about them.

The data thus allow for dividing the women by confession—Jewish or non-Jewish—and men by profession—employed by the state or not. In the following section we look at individual cases and other supporting materials to shed greater light on the broad categories and in particular on what led them to open schools for Jewish girls.

Jewish Men Employed by the Russian Government in Jewish Communities

Y. L. Gordon, by far the most famous of the educators in this study, opened his first private school for Jewish girls soon after arriving in the Lithuanian

Table 3.1. Principals of Private Schools for Jewish Girls, 1831–1881

	Jews	Non-Jews	Unknown	Total
Men	94	1	3	98
Women	35	11	1	47
Unknown			4	4
Total	129	12	8	149

town of Shavli in 1861. Although he would later achieve renown as a Hebrew poet, at this point he was just beginning his literary career and serving as a teacher in the government Jewish school system. Not long after opening the girls' school, Gordon wrote to a friend of his hopes that it would improve his financial situation. His salary from the state was small and he had a growing family to support.[8] However, it is not possible to reduce Gordon's calculations to the purely financial. In prose, poetry, and journalistic pieces Gordon made abundantly clear his concern for the status of Jewish women. Undoubtedly his most enduring statement on this subject was his epic poem "Kotzo shel yud" (The tip of the Hebrew letter yud), dedicated to the Hebrew writer Miriam Markel-Mosesohn.[9]

In this dramatic and romantic poem, the main character is a good and hard-working woman abandoned by her husband and then mistreated by the rabbinate. The narrator laments both the general status of the Jewish woman and her lack of access to education. In the following stanza Gordon plays on the wording in the supposedly laudatory "Woman of Valor" (Proverbs 31:10–31), as well as making reference to the often-cited mishna in Sota (3:4), to show how women are denied education:

> And so what if you were graced with a feeling heart and beauty,
> If the Lord gave you talent and intelligence!
> For you, knowledge of Torah is a taint, beauty a detriment,
> For you, all talent is a deficiency, all knowledge a drawback.[10]

Nor did Gordon limit his advocacy for women to theoretical statements. He also encouraged women writers in his private correspondence and went to great lengths to assure his own daughters a proper education. Gordon's published letters contain numerous laments over the difficulty of finding adequate educational arrangements for his daughters. In one letter to Miriam Markel-Mosesohn, a woman writer for whom he served as a mentor, Gordon complains about his difficulties finding an appropriate teacher and asks for recommendations.[11] Gordon thus provides a telling combination of financial need and genuine dedication to women's education.

Of course, it was Gordon's latter-day fame that assured the survival of his personal letters. For the other principals, relatively little documentation remains extant. There is no way to know whether other educators wrote to friends about their financial woes, nor how they educated their own daughters. Few of the other principals published on education.[12]

Nonetheless, Gordon's case does illuminate some important issues. Gordon's position as a state school teacher gave him the credentials to open a private girls' school. The establishment of the state rabbinate in 1835 and the state Jewish school system in 1844 both led to new professional opportunities for a subset of Jewish men. Teachers and rabbis had to know Russian in order to fulfill their roles. State Jewish school teachers also had to pass examinations more than equivalent to those required for private-school teachers.

When these state teachers and rabbis later decided to open private schools for Jewish girls, their previous service to the state suggested that their schools would advance the goals of the government in seeking to transform the Jewish community. The designation of state Jewish school teacher or rabbi always immediately follows the name in correspondence with the Ministry of Education, whether initiated by the principal or by a local official.

It is equally important to note that these men, in choosing to serve as state teachers or rabbis, had already signaled their allegiances within the Jewish community. By allying themselves with the state in their employment, and their knowledge of Russian, these men had already placed themselves outside the mainstream. Traditional elements of the Jewish community would have seen them as dangerous elements. This is not to say that they were necessarily radical activists, but rather that their professional choices caused them to be viewed as progressives. Although one government Jewish school teacher who also ran a private school for Jewish girls later converted to Christianity and made a name for himself in the antisemitic press, Moisei Gurvich was not typical.[13] Most of the state rabbis and teachers remained observant Jews, although they may have adopted modern dress or other accoutrements of acculturation.

The same markers that made some members of the Jewish community suspicious of state rabbis and teachers may have led other Jews to seek out their expertise. The latter-day revolutionary Eva Broido, born in 1876 in the Lithuanian town of Sventsiani, described in her memoirs being tutored in Russian literature, along with two cousins, by a teacher in the local state Jewish school.[14] Ita Yelin's forward-looking yet rabbinic family had her tutored by a state rabbi in Jewish subjects while she attended a private Russian school in Mogilev.[15]

If enough local families looking to educate their daughters sought out teachers and rabbis, these individuals may have decided to open schools to meet the demand. Y. L. Gordon, for example, both tutored local children and taught in the local government school in Ponivezh, his first posting as a teacher. It was not until his second posting in Shavli that his tutoring blossomed into the establishment of a school for Jewish girls. He would do the same upon his arrival in Tel'she in 1865, on his third posting. Gordon may not have been the only government employee to turn a thriving tutorial business into a more formal and stable arrangement.

Other Jews affiliated with the government may have had their first exposure to teaching girls through their colleagues or other teachers. When Bentsel' Podshkol'nik, a teacher of penmanship in the Rossieny (Kovno province) government Jewish school, submitted his application to open a private girls' school, he proposed to teach religion and writing himself and to hire other teachers from the local government Jewish school for the remaining subjects.[16] Mariia Siavtsillo, a non-Jew, planned to hire the local government rabbi to teach religion in the Jewish section of her girls' school in Kovno.[17] Although there is no extant record of whom these principals eventually hired and what became of them, the transfer of authority in Tel'she may be instructive. As stated above, there is some evidence that Rabbi Khazanovich was employed in Gordon's school prior to Gordon's departure.[18] Thus Gordon hired the local state rabbi, thereby making him an ideal candidate for running the school after his own promotion.

This example also points to the fluidity between the various roles. State rabbis, teachers in government Jewish schools, and principals of private Jewish girls' schools shared, at minimum, some knowledge of Russian and some level of commitment to the modernization of the Jewish community. Which hat an individual chose to wear may have depended as much on local circumstances as on a firm professional self-consciousness. Running a private school for Jewish girls was probably the least prestigious of the options, but it fit into a rubric of jobs dedicated to transforming the Jewish community from within, and people moved back and forth between the various roles.

Markus Solomonovich Gurovich, a native of the Hapsburg empire, came to Odessa to teach in the first modern school there. As that school transitioned into the government school system, Gurovich opened his own modern private school for Jewish girls. In 1852 he was tapped to become the "learned Jew" of the New Russian and Bessarabian region.[19] Gurovich's activism in the Odessa Jewish community on behalf of modern educational endeavors made him the ideal candidate for this far more distinguished service for the state. Gurovich's career trajectory reached well beyond that of most of the girls' school principals, but his transitions between roles were more typical.

A man by the name of Bank took the necessary teacher examinations and taught for nine years in the government Jewish school in Kamenets-

Podol'sk. When the school closed, he passed an additional set of examinations to become a state rabbi. After three years in that position, and with no future, in 1867 he requested permission to open a school for Jewish girls in Tul'chin, also in the Podolia province.[20] Bank, as an educated and Russian-speaking Jew, had a number of options for employment in his community. Although teaching Jewish girls was clearly not his primary professional goal, it served his purposes.

State teachers and rabbis also shared the misfortune of low wages. According to the draft legislation for the government Jewish school system, teachers were to be paid according to the number of hours they taught and the subject. The highest paid teacher in the lower-level school could expect 200 rubles per year.[21] Such a sum, although roughly commensurate with the salaries of other low-level employees of the Russian state, was not enough to support a family.[22]

State rabbis had even less access to adequate pay. Like the Russian Orthodox clergy, state rabbis did not receive a regular salary. Rather, they were expected to work out terms of payment with their communities. These usually involved fee-for-service arrangements wherein rabbis charged local Jews to record their births, deaths, and marriages in the required metrical book.[23] In many locales, this did not add up to a means of livelihood. It was not uncommon for state rabbis to hold other full-time positions, such as in pharmacy or medicine. These individuals may have been the men with the highest level of secular education in their towns, agreeing to serve as rabbis as a service to the community. However, state rabbis without professional education had to look to other options to supplement their income.

Thus state teachers and rabbis shared financial need as well as professional and social proximity to teaching Jewish girls. In some cases we can also see how the path from tutoring or part-time teaching led to becoming a principal. What is much harder to find evidence of is their ideological motivations.

Gordon, of course, published extensively on his vision of the *Haskalah*, not only in his fiction but also in a constant stream of pieces to the Russian Jewish press. In an 1866 article for the Russian-language supplement to the Hebrew periodical *Ha-Karmel*, Gordon printed a speech he had delivered at the opening of his girls' school in Tel'she. In it he explained patiently and passionately why Russian Jews must learn Russian and how Jewish women were the key to this transformation: "Mothers play an important role in the instruction of children. Attend to my talk, my dear daughters! Do not forget—for home education you are responsible to God and to the future.

If you, for example, speak Russian in the home, not mixing jargon [i.e., Yiddish] in your pure Russian, it will be easy for your children."[24] Nonetheless, it is difficult to know how typical Gordon was. Even among convinced *maskilim* there were very real differences in the understanding of women's proper role and training.[25] Gordon was an outspoken advocate of women's rights. Although he was not the only government Jewish school teacher to submit articles on women's issues to the Jewish press of the time, he was one of a small number and was probably unusual in his commitment to educating Jewish girls.

Jewish Men Not Employed by the State

The path to opening private schools for Jewish women is less straightforward for Jewish men not employed by the state. The only obvious trait they shared is level of education. No individual who had only attended the *heder* and *yeshiva,* and sought no additional formal or informal educational avenues, would have been in a position to open a legal private girls' school. The regulations for opening a private Jewish school required certification either of graduation from a Russian educational institution or of having passed examinations to serve as a private tutor. Thus, through intensive private reading or tutoring or through a Russian education, these men had chosen to bypass or augment the traditional Jewish men's curriculum and to learn Russian.

These men were thus among the most educated and Russified members of their communities. Yet, we might ask, if they were in fact fluent in Russian and interested in teaching, why not apply for the more stable jobs of state teachers or rabbis, especially as the demand was great? One possible answer is that although these men could function in Russian at some level, they were not in a position to pass the examinations for either of those posts. Perhaps they represent those Jewish men striving toward Russification or enlightenment but hampered by their own education; men who would have liked to have attended Russian schools themselves, but not having been able to do so, strove at least to make it possible for others to reach that level. Alternately, they might have felt that private education offered them greater financial or pedagogic opportunities. For the first twenty years of their existence, the state schools required non-Jewish principals, thus cutting Jews out of leadership roles. The curriculum and salaries were also not open to negotiation. Private schools offered at least the promise of greater leeway.

The case of the Germaize family in Vilna is instructive. Levin Germaize opened a private school for Jewish boys in 1840.[26] However, the 1844 legislation led to a situation where principals of private boys schools either had to hand their schools over to the non-Jewish principals or close them down.

Germaize discovered yet another option, opting to turn his boys' school into an institution for Jewish girls.[27] He continued to run the school until passing it on to his son, Isak Germaize, in 1859.[28] The younger Germaize ran the school for girls successfully for nearly twenty years. However, in 1875 an inspector visiting the school found seventeen boys present, in addition to the properly registered girls. Germaize first claimed that he thought he had permission to teach boys as well as girls, and then later that his leg was hurting on that particular day and he found it impossible to go to the homes of all his private students. After repeated appeals and inspections, and despite Germaize's ongoing pleas, the government closed the school in 1877.[29]

What emerges from this case is that neither Levin Germaize nor his son Isak was committed exclusively to the education of Jewish girls. Levin embraced the cause for pragmatic reasons, allowing him to continue making a living when his previous school was no longer viable. Isak took over the girls' school, but he seems to have supplemented his income by teaching boys as well. The Germaizes devoted their lives to teaching Jews in a modern educational setting; however, whether it was boys or girls seems not to have been their primary concern.

The Germaize case raises another salient issue, that of family connection as a route to teaching. Isak essentially inherited the family business and continued to run it after the death of his father. The same is true of the local state rabbi of the Bessarabian town of Khoton, Israel Tiutinman, who became the principal of the private school for Jewish girls upon the death of his father, the founder, in 1865.[30]

Just as bakers' children were raised helping in the family business, teachers' children similarly received informal training in the family business. Additionally, a father who knew enough Russian to apply formally and teach in a Russian school, and who felt it was a priority to teach Jewish children Russian, undoubtedly gave his own children a formal Russian education. It was therefore no accident that both Germaize and Tiutinman had the skills to take over their fathers' schools. In fact, the younger Tiutinman's gravitation to the state rabbinate makes sense in light of his father's proclivities. Thus the sons were socialized toward teaching and the Russian language and were able to fill their fathers' roles. As we see in the next section, not only sons were in a position to replace their fathers.

Family connections, therefore, provided one route toward teaching girls for educated Jews. Indeed, for the Jewish man with some knowledge of Russian and some commitment to changing the Jewish community, education was among the best professional options. Such men could not, however, obtain employment in non-Jewish schools, and the government-sponsored Jewish schools were not for everyone. Teaching Jewish girls may not have been the first choice for these men but it did advance their goals. In the end it is not possible to ascertain the degree to which ideology played a role in their decisions, but social proximity to modern causes and education, especially through family connections, could play a causal role.

Jewish Women

Of the thirty-three Jewish women listed as principals, seven were co-principals with their husbands. Although each of the couples filed a joint application to open a private girls' school, only the certifications and qualifications of the husband accompanied the documentation. The school plan of the Levin family in Minsk, for example, twice referred to Mendel Levin's status as a teacher of Russian in the local government Jewish school, and also stated that he would teach all academic subjects. Mendel's wife, Rakhel, although listed as co-principal, had no stated qualifications or role in the school.[31]

For these wives and co-principals it is simply not possible to ascertain any information about educational background or motivations. Some may have been deeply devoted to the cause of women's education and may have married men who would help them achieve their goals. Theofaniia Ostrogorskaia, for example, seems to have shared her husband's educational training and commitment to teaching. Both Meer, her husband, and Theofaniia had passed the examination to serve as tutors for Jewish students, and although she was not listed as a co-principal, she became principal of his school for Jewish girls in Grodno, presumably after his death.[32]

On the other hand, some of the wives listed may simply have served as figureheads, obviating the potential improprieties of a man running a school for girls. Many of the male principals who did not list a wife as co-principal made sure to show that their schools would nonetheless include the perceived benefits of the feminine presence. Bentsel Podshkol'nik's plan for his school in Rossiene (Vilna province) in 1857 stated, "A special governess, with appropriate permission, will be [employed] for the ongoing supervision of the orderliness and morality of the pupils."[33]

However, the majority (twenty-eight) of the Jewish women who opened schools for Jewish girls did so entirely on their own merits. For these women an unusually high educational level was a necessity. They had either to provide certification of their graduation from a gymnasium or to pass an examination. Unfortunately in most cases little to no information appears in their files on how they obtained their educational level. A few letters contain more information, such as when the curator of the Vilna educational circuit informed the MNP offices in St. Petersburg that the girls' school originally opened by Y. L. Gordon and later passed on to Rabbi Khazanovich would now, following Khazanovich's death, be placed in the able hands of Lidia Rudian, a graduate of the Kovno Women's Gymnasium.[34] Most of the paperwork, however, simply states that the principals had the "proper certifications."

Simion Krieze, based on data collected by the Jewish Colonization Association from a slightly later period, has suggested that Jewish women who worked in modern educational institutions were more likely than their male counterparts to have themselves received a modern formal education, whereas Jewish men were more likely to have had a traditional Jewish education.[35] In her recent monograph on Jewish women and literacy in Eastern Europe, Iris Parush comes to a similar conclusion based primarily on literary sources.[36] The data available on these educators offers a mixed picture. Some Jewish women, like Anna Berman and Matil'da Rotshtein, hired Jewish men to teach religion in their schools and themselves taught general subjects, suggesting that their secular educational backgrounds outweighed their Jewish knowledge.[37] Other women, like Mariia Mitkovitser and Anna Birshenker, taught religion themselves in their private schools for Jewish girls.[38]

So what led these and other educated Jewish daughters to open schools for their coreligionists? As we saw with men, sometimes family connections were an important catalyst toward a career in education. Khaim Funt passed his school in Minsk on to his daughter Mariia.[39] We can see a similar dynamic at work in the known cases of educators who were following in their parents' footsteps while not inheriting their actual schools. Sara Berman applied for and received permission to open a private school for Jewish girls in St. Petersburg in 1873[40] that joined the twin private schools for poor Jewish boys and girls run by her parents, Lazar and Anna Berman.[41] Before coming to the capital, Lazar had taught in a government Jewish school in Dubno (Kiev province) and run a private school for Jewish girls there.[42] Liuba Kenigsberg, who established a school for Jewish girls in Berdichev in 1872, was the daughter of a government Jewish school teacher.[43] According to the memoirist Judah Loeb Benjamin Kazenelson, the daughter of Iakov Daich, who taught in a government Jewish schools and ran private girls' schools in two cities, later opened a private school for Jewish girls in the city of Khotin.[44]

Another reason Jewish women opened schools for Jewish girls was that they had so few other viable opportunities. Teaching and tutoring were the only professional options open to female high school graduates in the Russian empire without further study. At various times, depending on the vagaries of officialdom, careers in medicine, midwifery, pharmacy, and dentistry were open to female professionals, but even when the legal climate was favorable, pursuing higher education required funding and, often, travel outside the Pale of Settlement.[45]

To be sure, Jewish women did actively pursue higher education and were in fact overrepresented in the women's courses outside, and especially inside, the Pale of Settlement.[46] Nonetheless, the actual numbers remained fairly small. Professional education required not only money for tuition but also often a move to another location and thus added living expenses. Residency restrictions also severely limited the opportunities for study outside the Pale. For most Jewish women, even those with a good secondary education, higher education was simply out of reach.

Although slightly outside the parameters of this study in terms of both geography and chronology, Puah Rakowski (1865–1955) offers one example of a woman's difficult educational career. After separating from her husband, she sought to support herself and her children as a midwife. However, neither her husband nor her father approved, which meant that she had neither a valid passport nor funds. In the end she was able to garner support for a second plan. Rakowski was to reside with her grandfather while she completed the necessary reading and tutorials to pass examinations to become a teacher. The process took seven months of intense work. In her memoirs Rakowski describes all the subjects she studied as well as the grueling oral examination and model classroom teaching. Rakowski gained permission to open her first school for Jewish girls in Lomzhe and later opened a popular Zionist school in Warsaw.[47]

Rakowski exemplifies both financial need and passionate commitment. She needed a way to support herself and her children, but it is also clear from her writings that Rakowski considered her school a holy mission. Both as a feminist and a Zionist she was committed to providing the best possible education to her pupils. In the following passage Rakowski explained what was at stake:

> "Who says a girl should be allowed to learn Hebrew! Why, that is certainly heresy [*apikorsos*], because one who teaches his daughter Torah it is as if he taught her licentiousness [*tiflus*]." Our people paid dearly for this archaic attitude. If our grandfathers and fathers and rabbis, as spiritual leaders, had not held this to be true, but the opposite, that Torah education should know no gender differentiation, such that Jewish daughters, ex-

actly like the sons, had to be brought up on our Torah, and our culture and doctrines, unknown thousands of Jewish mothers would have been saved from assimilation, from apostasy, and through them also their sons, whom we have lost due to the attitudes they inherited from their assimilated mothers.[48]

Like Y. L. Gordon above, Rakowski combined conviction and commitment with genuine need. Also like Gordon, Rakowski, as a memoirist and active Zionist, was unusual among her contemporaries. Most left no record of their hopes and dreams. Mathil'da Rotshtein applied to open a school for girls in Kiev in 1871. Her application highlighted her difficult financial situation, with her husband unable to work for health reasons and three children in the home. She also stated that she herself would be able to teach German, Russian, and crafts and that she had graduated from a school, although she was no longer in possession of the documents and did not offer specifics.[49]

It seems clear that Rotshtein would not have turned to teaching at that particular moment in her life had it not been for her husband's illness. Here, then, is a case where a Jewish woman turned to educating other Jewish women for purely utilitarian reasons. On the other hand, Rakowski's story began in a similar way. She, too, needed money for her family and turned to teaching only reluctantly. Yet she went on to embrace the possibilities of educating her sisters. No such records exist for Rotshtein. She was granted permission to open a school but there is no way of knowing whether the school served primarily as a source of income or whether she also actively used it to broaden the horizons of her coreligionists.

Fortunately, the words of one female principal were recorded by a visiting journalist. The journalist, who in all likelihood signed *his* name with only initials, attended the public examination of Simonia Aronovicheva's school in Dinaburg in 1863. He was favorably impressed by the ceremonial as well as the educational components of the event and sent a report, including Aronovicheva's speech, to the Russian language supplement of the Hebrew periodical *Ha-Karmel:* "The education of Jewish girls must go together with the education of Jewish boys; because an educated fellow seeks in a wife not simply a woman and a worker, but a good wife and mother for his children. Nowadays, thanks to the attention of the government, the majority of the young Jewish generation of boys receives proper education, and, consequently, it has become necessary for girls, not only within the rich class, solely for etiquette (as it was previously), but in all others as well."[50] It is worth noting that although Aronovicheva certainly justified her school at least in part based on gendered expectations, these were different from those of the *maskilim* mentioned in chapter 1. Whereas they viewed women chiefly as conduits of education for the next generation, Aronovicheva articulated the need for a more balanced marriage. Her speech, mediated by a reporter, represents the only published writing of a female principal of a private school for Jewish girls during this period.

Women in the tsar's empire had limited educational and professional opportunities. Nonetheless, as we saw in chapter 1, these increased dramatically over the course of the nineteenth century. Jewish women took an active part in the newly available programs and possibilities; however, they also faced particular obstacles, including residence restrictions and discrimination in hiring. Teaching other Jewish girls was in many cases the only available professional path for an educated Jewish woman. At the same time, it could also serve as an opportunity to fulfill a cherished mission.

Non-Jews

Twelve non-Jews opened and oversaw their own private schools for Jewish girls. All but one of them were women, and all resided in the northern regions of the Pale. An examination of the case of Doroteia Ekert, later Buchinskaia, helps to illuminate some of the questions and commonalities regarding these educators.

In June 1848 the Kurland native Doroteia Ekert requested permission to open a private school for Jewish girls in Vilna. Her application materials included a letter of support signed by several prominent members of the Vilna Jewish community. Ekert had the educational qualifications to teach Russian and other secular subjects and stated in her school's academic plan that "for the teaching of religion and literacy in the Judeo-German language, we shall invite learned Jews, as per the pupils' parents' choosing and with the permission of the government."[51] Her school soon received approval and opened its doors. But what led this educated Christian woman to turn her talents and background to the education of Jewish girls?

The evidence suggests that rather than Ekert coming to the Jews, the Jews came to Ekert. From 1845 until 1848 Ekert had run a private women's school in Vilna, but she was forced to close it for lack of students. The fact that a few months later Ekert had the support of local Jewish dignitaries to open a Jewish school suggests that she had some previous connection with them. It seems most likely that some Jewish girls had attended her general women's institution. When that school closed, Ekert realized that a group of Jews desired to educate their daughters in a modern, Russian, upper-class setting. She was thus able to count upon the support and attendance of local Jews in her new school.

Ekert's materials do not speak of motivations or goals. As a single woman, it would seem that she turned to teaching at least in part to make a living. That she taught girls was a given; that she taught Jews may well have developed out of the particular circumstances in Vilna at the time. Was she, as an educated woman, convinced of the great societal or individual import of teaching women? It is difficult to know. Perhaps the only hint that she enjoyed what she was doing and considered it important was that she continued running the school after she married.[52]

In 1856 the principal of a boarding school for upper-class girls in Kovno, Maria Siavtsillo, requested permission to open a section of her school to Jewish girls. The Jewish pupils would be taught in a separate room and receive religious instruction from the local government rabbi.[53] Although Siavtsillo does not say as much, her case appears to mirror Ekert's. Siavtsillo became aware that her school could expand by accepting Jewish girls. Perhaps local Jews had even approached her. Unlike Ekert, she chose to allow her original school to remain open but to add a separate section for Jews.

For a single, well-educated Russian woman in need of making a living, education was a good option. It was moderately respectable and the field of girls' elementary education was growing. For many women in this position there was undoubtedly a personal interest in seeing that girls had opportunities for self-improvement and self-fulfillment. But it would surely have been far more natural for these women to educate others of their own faith, since culturally and linguistically Jews were very different from their neighbors.

It would thus appear that the demands of the market were crucial in leading non-Jewish women into Jewish schools. It is interesting to note that all eleven of the non-Jewish women who ran schools for Jewish girls did so in the northern provinces of the Pale of Settlement. In fact, this was where the most private schools for Jewish girls opened and where Jewish families first sought out a modern and formal education for their daughters, an endeavor they pursued more steadfastly than did those in other regions. And it was also here, significantly, that a particularly well-educated group of non-Jewish women lived.

From the time of the annexation of the Baltic lands well into the nineteenth century, Baltic Germans held a privileged position in tsarist Russia. The usefulness of an educated native elite for the purpose of administration, as well as dynastic ties, guaranteed their status. The Lutheran Church in Russia thus maintained and oversaw high-level educational institutions.[54] Among the various ethnicities listed in the 1897 census, the Baltic Germans, male and female, surpassed all others by several percentage points in terms of formal education beyond elementary school.[55] Some of the women who came through the Lutheran educational system in the Baltic provinces later turned to educating their Jewish neighbors. No parallel population group existed in other regions of the Pale of Settlement, nor did any non-Jews open schools for Jewish girls elsewhere.

To my knowledge, no personal writings of these women survive. Their correspondence with the Ministry of Education, of course, conforms to the styles and expectations of such writing. In requesting additional funds for her school for Jewish girls in 1878, Nadezhda Bel'skiia wrote plaintively of the difficulty of obtaining the best teachers on limited funds and of the importance of helping these girls to complete their education. However, there is nothing unusual about a request for funding resorting to hyperbole as well as making the case for the importance of the endeavor.

It is thus difficult to find motivations beyond opportunism in understanding how and why non-Jewish women opened schools for Jewish girls. Certainly non-Jewish Russian women in the late nineteenth century did not set out to become teachers of Jewish girls. No matter how they came to be teachers, they turned to teaching Jewish girls in particular because Jewish families wanted to educate their daughters and were willing to use non-Jewish teachers and principals. What we cannot know is how this relationship affected both sides. Did it lead to greater understanding between the two communities? Did the non-Jewish women see for themselves some sort of mission in Russifying the Jews? We cannot as yet answer these questions.

The one non-Jewish man who opened a private school for Jewish girls did so with his daughter and by request, at least according to his own account. Maksimilian Zel'verovich, a former teacher and current titular official, wrote to the local school authorities in Vilna in 1861 stating that a local Jewish merchant had approached him and asked him to open a school for Jewish girls. Although he does not say so explicitly, the letter suggests that his school would be designed for the daughters of the wealthy.[56] This view is corroborated in a funding request from Shevel' Perel', who pointed out that the daughters of the rich attended the Zel'verovich school, and thus he, Perel', needed more support for his own students.[57]

On the whole, non-Jewish men did not open schools for Jewish girls. To be sure, many non-Jewish men taught in such schools on a part-time basis, but in most cases these men were employed in other local schools and merely supplemented their incomes by teaching Russian or other subjects to Jewish girls. Indeed, non-Jewish men had by far the most professional opportunities of the groups we have surveyed. Zel'verovich, who had previously taught

French, according to Perel', is the only known exception, and it is important to note that he felt it worthwhile to open the school in his own name as well as in that of his daughter Alexandra. Perel' also states explicitly what was implicit in the materials on many of the schools run by non-Jews—that they were aimed at the monied elite of the Jewish community. The attraction of wealthy Jews to the perceived superiority of the training of upper-class non-Jews made private schools for Jewish girls a viable professional opportunity for a small number of non-Jews in a limited geographic area.

Conclusion

Part of what makes these educators intriguing is that they were both products of the changes filtering into the Russian Jewish community and agents of its spread. The expansion of Jewish women's education during the second half of the nineteenth century was the result of many interrelated factors, including a growing interest in women's education in educated Russian society, the influx of *Haskalah* ideas from the west, Russification in the Jewish community, and a grass-roots recognition of the benefits of modern formal education for girls and for boys.

These forces joined to create a new professional opportunity for the Jews of Russia and for a selection of their neighbors as well. Over the course of the second half of the nineteenth century these one hundred and fifty or so educators succeeded in providing thousands of Jewish girls across the Pale of Settlement with access to basic literacy in Russian and new conceptions of the Jewish religion. The men and women and Jews and non-Jews who took upon themselves the task of educating the next generation of Jewish girls did not do so solely out of a conscious concern to change the face of the Jewish community. It appears, in fact, that some of these individuals turned to teaching Jewish girls for purely pragmatic reasons, because that was the best job they could get. Others wrote passionately of their commitment and concerns. Of course, the norm lies somewhere in the middle. Most of those who opened private schools for Jewish girls did so out of a combination of enlightened concerns and pure self-interest.

Examining the available information about these educators helps us to understand not only their motivations, but also the paths that led to teaching Jewish girls. With the exception of Y. L. Gordon, none of these individuals was a major writer or political figure.[58] Six of the principals merited entries in the comprehensive *Evreiskaia entsiklopediia,* published between 1906 and 1913. Again, beyond Gordon, these entries are short.[59] The principals of private schools for Jewish girls were not the leaders of their generation.

On the other hand, their influence on the next generation may have been even greater than that of better-known individuals. In evaluating the legacy of Isaak Rumsh, a minor Hebrew writer and *maskil* who also taught in a government Jewish school and ran a private school for Jewish girls, Mordechai Zalkin points out that it was precisely the "peripheral" individuals like Rumsh who ensured that the ideas and writings of the leading intellectuals of the time reached the youth.[60] In describing his own childhood, Eliezer Ben-Yehuda, who is credited with reviving Hebrew as a spoken tongue, counts his encounter with Rumsh's Hebrew translation of Defoe's *Robinson Crusoe* as a major step on his path to enlightenment.[61] Rumsh's most popular publication led Ben-Yehuda, and doubtless others, to pursue further secular Hebrew reading and expand their horizons.

In a similar vein, Rumsh's teaching would allow Jewish girls far greater opportunities to interact with Russian culture and language. Despite their lack of status, and the sometimes circuitous routes that led them to teaching girls, these educators would go on to provide thousands of Jewish girls with a modern formal education. In the next chapter we see how these enterprising educators reacted to the difficulties of procuring funding for their schools.

4

FOR WISDOM IS BETTER THAN PEARLS
Financing Jewish Girls' Education

Although many educators opened private schools for Jewish girls for financial reasons, running a private school turned out to be less lucrative than many of the principals had hoped. Whereas the government-sponsored Jewish boys' schools had a dedicated funding source, the *talmud torah* was supported by the Jewish community, and *hadarim,* with their extremely low overhead, had the weight of tradition obligating parental support. Girls' schools, however, could count on no such bounty. The same would-be principals who confidently guaranteed that their schools would run entirely on the income from tuition soon found that many parents could not, or would not, meet their tuition responsibilities. This left the principal in a difficult situation.

As Table 4.1 illustrates, running a modern private school required substantial resources. For Aron Frud in Berdichev, as well as other principals, salaries were the majority of the school budget. Rent, materials, furniture, and seasonal heating costs could also not be avoided. Although not all schools had as large a student body or faculty as Frud's, all shared similar responsibilities and many had difficulty meeting their financial obligations.

Table 2.1 shows all the private schools for Jewish girls on record between 1831 and 1881, and the first and last years of their recorded activity. This list is based upon correspondence, applications, published articles, and local almanacs,[1] and many schools appear only once in the available records. This could mean there are gaps in the documentation, leaving open the possibility that schools actually stayed open for longer but left no written trace. It is more likely, however, that many of these schools simply closed within their

Table 4.1. Annual Expenses for School of Aron Frud in Berdichev, 1859

Instructors by subject	Hours/week	Salary/ lesson (Kopeks)	Total annual cost to school (Rubles)
Russian	20	50	400
Hebrew	18	50	360
German	20	50	400
French	18	50	360
Arithmetic	14	50	280
Penmanship	20	25	200
Geography	12	50	240
History	12	50	240
Catechism	4	50	80
Teaching assistants			700
Other Expenses			
Desks			300
Rent			1,200
Maintenance			500
Total			5,260

Source: RGIA, f. 733, op. 98, d. 427, l. 6.

first years. Given the dire letters the MNP received from many Jewish educators, making ends meet with a girls' school was almost impossible.

Despite closures and financial troubles, other schools managed to stay open for years, even decades. The principals of these schools discovered methods of covering their expenses. This chapter traces the major funding sources exploited by private school principals over the second half of the nineteenth century. The gradual evolution of funding sources mirrors changes in the schools and student body, as well as in Russian Jewish society as a whole.

How to Fund a Private School?

The private school principals who opened the new schools and hoped to maintain them began their search for additional funding close to home. Local communal organizations, philanthropies, and wealthy individuals proved the most obvious sources for subsidies. However, the principals employed these resources in ways that were often far from predictable.

Tuition

The primary source of income for all private schools was tuition. In fact, the original principals hoped to finance their schools with generous tuition payments from wealthy families. The first private schools for Jewish girls in Russia may have used textbooks from German Jewish schools, but their educational models were far closer to home. Perel's school in Vilna, and those opened in Odessa in the 1830s by Betsalel Shtern and Vol'f and Khaia Gringol'ts, were designed on the model of local private schools for the Russian elite.

Institutes and boarding schools for wealthy Russian girls had begun to replace home tutoring in urban areas of the empire by the first decades of the nineteenth century.[2] Educators recognized that such an option appealed to the Jewish upper classes as well and sought to fill that gap. They would provide Jewish girls from wealthy and upwardly mobile families with the requisite linguistic and aesthetic training in return for generous payment.

Reality did not match the expectations of these entrepreneurial educators. On the one hand, there were not enough daughters among the wealthy families to fill their classrooms and coffers. On the other hand, plenty of other Jewish girls did want to attend their new schools. Large enrollment was a plus for applying for government subsidies and filing periodic reports on their schools. However, this new group of students proved less able to meet the original tuition demands.

It would be overly simplistic to speak of a rising middle class in this context. Simple class distinctions do not convey the complexity of Russian Jewish society in the changing conditions of the mid-nineteenth century. However, at the same time as Tsar Alexander II's Great Reforms made it possible for the first guild merchants to leave the Pale for the capitals, they also helped to create the conditions for economic and professional progress for other sectors of the populace. The educational and professional opportunities on offer, combined with the influence of the *Haskalah*, encouraged the growth of a more self-confident and open-minded mood that valued education for women as well as men.

The combination of broader societal interest in the schools but less sure tuition payments would lead to new paradigms for assigning tuition payments. The first private schools for Jewish girls had fixed tuition amounts. When Markus and Anna Gurovich first opened their boarding school in Odessa in 1845, they set the yearly tuition at 142 rubles for full-boarders, 100 rubles for half-boarders, and 52 rubles for local pupils. Additional fees of 20 rubles for music classes and 14 for school materials were also charged.[3] Such tuition and fees were well outside the budgets of most Odessa Jews. The

Guroviches clearly expected a wealthy clientele. In practice, however, the Guroviches also accepted some pupils who could not pay the full amount.[4]

Over time this situation became normative. Schools opened to serve the wealthy had to respond to the reality of mixed student bodies. New schools no longer advertised fixed fees. When Abram Bruk-Brezovskii opened his school in Kherson in 1856, he explicitly included sliding-scale tuition based on family income in his application materials.[5] Isaak Kisin made the same calculation in Minsk in 1857.[6]

Even boarding schools, so clearly modeled on the institutes available to the Russian nobility, had to respond to the realities of Jewish society. The school of Aron Frud in Berdichev offered four tuition options. Students who stayed at the *pansion* were charged 180 rubles per year. Half-pansioners paid 125 rubles and non-resident students paid between 20 and 50 rubles per year, depending on the family's resources.[7] In addition, there were ten slots available at no cost to students from poor families.

In effect, Frud allowed wealthy families to experience the full boarding school élan while at the same time subsidizing the education of those less fortunate. He was able to offer scholarships to deserving girls without funds by overcharging the rich families. And he was not the only principal to use tuition in a savvy manner.

Several of the schools offered supplementary courses in such subjects as music, dance, and French, targeted in particular to the wealthy, who sought to train their daughters to fit into salon society. For these subjects, principals charged fees that reflected a knowledge of their constituencies. The teacher Bentsel Podshkol'nik in Rossiene (Kovno province), for example, required a yearly tuition of between 50 and 120 rubles, with a disproportionate optional fee for music and dance of 100 rubles.[8] Shevel' Perel' managed another clever manipulation of tuition and fees. As of 1854 the tuition was a modest 10 rubles per year. However, students wishing to study drawing, music, and dance paid 30 rubles for the privilege, and those who took their meals at the schools paid 150 rubles.[9]

Although such wide variations in payment for different services may have increased rather than decreased class distinctions with the schools, they also made it possible for girls from less wealthy families to attend. The principals of the schools knew that families that could afford to would pay dearly for the prestige that came from a daughter who took dance or drawing lessons weekly. By charging a premium for these supplementary services, the principals could afford to keep the standard tuition relatively low and welcome a broad spectrum of students.

Communal Charity

In addition to tuition, the principals continually explored other funding options. Budgetary shortfalls were a constant problem for even the most successful schools. Even the government school for Jewish girls in Odessa, supported almost entirely by tax monies, ran into financial difficulties. In an 1862 letter to the editor of the Russian language Jewish periodical *Sion*, Bernard Bertenzon, the school's honorary guardian, complained bitterly of discrimination against his school. He claimed that the local government school for Jewish boys, as well as the local *talmud torahs* for poor Jewish boys, had all their needs met by the Jewish community, whereas the girls' school received no communal aid. Rather, it was forced to survive on the measly tuition of one to one and a half rubles per year per student and an undisclosed candle tax payment. He added that of the 240 pupils in the school, most were so poor that when winter descended, the classes emptied out due to lack of proper outdoor clothing.

In order to combat this enormous problem, Bertenzon himself turned to the local Jewish and non-Jewish communities for financial and material aid. He reported that in the course of one and a half months of assiduous work he collected 200 rubles and a goodly collection of winter articles of clothing.[10] Bertenzon was obviously pleased with his success and optimistic for the future. However, it is clear from the appended list of donors and donations that individuals gave very small sums and that Bertenzon was forced to approach a great many people for help.

In 1867 Bertenzon was once again involved in supporting girls' schools. He wrote to a Jewish philanthropy in St. Petersburg regarding the private school for Jewish girls in Vitebsk. According to Bertenzon, the wife of the local governor had taken the school under her wing. Although her generosity had made an important difference for the school, he requested further help.[11] Undoubtedly other principals also found local benefactors, Jewish and non-Jewish, but few records survive.

The school receiving the most generous funding from local sources was that of the Bermans in St. Petersburg. Unlike most of the schools under discussion here, which were founded by individuals or small groups of educators, the private schools for Jewish boys and girls in St. Petersburg were founded by the local Jewish oligarchy. Responding to the needs of the Jewish poor of the capital, the elite set about collecting funds and hiring principals to educate underprivileged youth. It was thus that the wealthy Jews remained involved with the schools and their funding.

Lazar Berman's school for poor Jewish boys, opened in 1865, and Anna

Berman's school for poor Jewish girls, opened in 1866, were to receive a total of 3,600 rubles from local Jewish sources in the year 1867. The banker Ginsburg had promised 1,600 and the Jewish community of St. Petersburg was to contribute an additional 2,000. Thirty-six hundred rubles would have been a significant amount. However, the community found itself unable to gather the necessary funds, and the Bermans were left with only 1,600 rubles to run their two schools.[12] They applied for, and eventually received, a government subsidy. Over the next two decades the Bermans' schools would continue to grow while their communal subsidy would not keep pace. They repeatedly requested increases in funding to meet their growing needs.

If even these two privileged institutions, under the auspices of either governmental or communal largesse, had such difficulty making ends meet, the situation was even more challenging for the remainder of the schools. Fortunately, private school principals managed to create two more reliable sources of income.

The Candle Tax

Sliding-scale tuition charges and local charity could only go so far. Over time the principals were, however, able to find a way to receive government subsidies. But how did the Russian government, after repeatedly avoiding the creation of a school system for Jewish girls, find itself in the business of funding private Jewish girls' schools?

An internal Ministry of Education document on the proposed school system for Jewish boys from the early 1840s reached the conclusion that some 211,300 silver rubles would be required per annum at maximum capacity. The figure was based on the number of educational districts within each province of the Pale of Settlement, population figures for Jews, and the assumption that, in toto, thirty second-level schools and one hundred and sixteen first-level schools would meet the needs of this population. Each individual lower-division school was expected to cost 1,025 rubles yearly and each upper-division school 3,080 per year.[13] These figures in turn were based upon a fixed curriculum requiring a set number of teachers and some additional funding for such expenses as rent and heating costs.[14]

To my knowledge there was no discussion of having the Jews pay directly for sending their sons to the new government Jewish schools. Although all but the poorest Jewish families expected to pay for their sons to attend *heder,* sometimes at great family sacrifice, the Ministry of Education officials recognized that Jews would not be as eager to send their sons to government-sponsored schools. Thus the need for the candle tax.

Sumptuary taxes levied on Jewish ritual requirements were not new. Jewish communities in the Polish lands had often obligated themselves to such measures in order to pay off communal debt. The tsarist government, inheriting the *kahal* system, had benefited from these sorts of taxes. However, as of 1839, they had decreed taxes on cultic objects, "incongruous with the goals of the government," and abrogated their usage.[15] Nonetheless, when funding was needed for the new Jewish school system, a tax on Sabbath candles was reinstated.

The original 1844 Statute on the Education of the Jews did not specifically refer to funding for the new schools. The legal basis, definition, and collection system appear in law as of 1 September 1845. Each married couple or individual (if that person resided alone) was liable for the candle tax, but the amount varied based on social rank. The most impoverished Jews were excused. Jewish tax collectors gathered the monies from the various groups within Jewish society and then passed it on to the municipal authorities, who sent it to the Ministry of Education.[16]

In practice this system led to a number of problems. The newly created tax collectors and their contacts with the municipal authorities created two new levels of bureaucracy needlessly and wastefully. Not only were these Jewish and non-Jewish officials each keeping a percentage of the money, but they reproduced work already in place for other Jewish taxes. The redundancy and waste was particularly disturbing during the cholera epidemic of 1846–47.[17]

In recognition of these issues the Ministries of Education and the Interior jointly issued recommendations for its restructure that were adopted into law on 31 December 1851. This latter statute took the collection of the tax from the jurisdiction of the Ministry of Education to that of the Ministry of the Interior, already charged with collecting the *korobka* tax, the major tax within the Jewish community, and therefore in possession of the necessary bureaucracy and know-how.[18] The amount to be collected was 230,000 silver rubles per year. Each year, based on *korobka* tax returns, the Ministry of the Interior would provide each Jewish community with a tally of the required sum. The community then had to use whatever means it chose to collect the given amount.[19]

The candle tax was established to support a major school system. Uvarov imagined the entire school-age male Jewish population eventually attending the new schools. But starting such a system is a major undertaking, even when there are enough qualified teachers and willing students. As of 1847, the only schools signed on were a few private schools that had existed before the 1844 Statute.[20] In 1855, even accepting the Ministry of Education's optimistic numbers, there were 104 schools. This number included the two rabbinical seminaries as well as 13 second-division and 88 first-division schools.[21] Although the first decade had witnessed impressive growth, the program had still not reached its fiscal capacity.

In these same years, private schools for Jewish girls had begun to spread across the Pale of Settlement. It seems that the chief obstacle to the success of the schools was financial. Shevel' Perel', who opened the first private school for Jewish girls in Vilna in 1831, was also the first to tap into the candle tax largesse. In 1842, based on Max Lilienthal's positive evaluation of his school, he began receiving a yearly sum of 700 rubles from the *korobka* funds.[22] Over time the source of this yearly stipend was gradually transferred from the *korobka* to the candle tax funds. By 1846 Perel's school was funded via candle tax monies. In 1850 Perel' sought to expand his school to three classes and requested additional funding from the candle taxes.[23] At this time there was no other private school for Jewish girls receiving a candle tax subsidy.[24]

Yet others shortly followed in Perel's footsteps. Already in 1848 a group of Jews from Brest-Litovsk had specifically requested candle tax funds to open a school for Jewish girls.[25] Meanwhile in Perel's native Vilna, word of his good fortune had clearly spread. Between 1848 and 1851, two additional schools applied for candle tax monies. Aron Gittels, who ran a second school for Jewish girls, applied for a candle tax subsidy and had good reason to expect success. However, when it was revealed that he was under court investigation, his application was held up and he died before the matter was decided. Levin Germaize applied for candle tax money for the private school he ran for Jewish boys. The MNP denied his application as his school competed with the local government-sponsored school for Jewish boys. Germaize duly responded by opening a school for Jewish girls and received the subsidy.[26]

Although it is unclear how word of this funding source spread, soon the idea had reached far beyond the Lithuanian and Byelorussian areas of the Pale. Jews from every province applied for candle tax funds to aid their private schools for girls. In 1856 the curator of the Odessa educational circuit wrote to the Ministry of Education outlining the educational options for Jewish girls in the Odessa educational circuit and recommending candle tax funding for those schools he considered particularly important. Of the eleven schools for Jewish girls under his jurisdiction, the curator chose three to receive the financial support of the government.[27] In 1863 the editors of the Yiddish weekly *Kol Mevaser*, advising a community to open a private school for its daughters, mentioned the promise of candle tax monies.[28] The following year the Society for the Promotion of Enlightenment among the Jews of Russia refused to subsidize a needy school, suggesting instead that the school seek help from the candle tax fund.[29]

By the 1860s the Ministry of Education began requesting information from regional school directors in order to compile data on how and to whom this money was disbursed. The 1867 list shows twenty-six private schools for Jewish girls receiving a total of 10,600 rubles from the candle tax fund (see Table 4.2).[30] In 1879, eighteen private Jewish girls' schools received a total of 7,200 rubles per year (see Table 4.3).[31] The two charts show a surprisingly uneven distribution. The amount allocated was not based on the size of student body, proven need, or some other obvious factor. Rather, it seems that one of the consequences of the unplanned nature of this subsidization of private schools for Jewish girls was an arbitrary quality. Certain principals and institutions were favored for larger sums, others for smaller ones. A comparison of the two charts suggests that the amount of the subsidy remained relatively stable. Over the course of twelve years most of the schools that retained funding kept it at the same level. A few merited increases.

In 1863, most likely in recognition of the excess of funds and the scope of possible uses, the MNP reformed the candle tax disbursement. In responding to the reality that the candle tax monies could best serve the educational goals of the ministry regarding the Jews with more flexibility, candle tax funds could now go even to non-Jewish institutions.[32] Educators responded quickly. In 1864 the curator of the Odessa educational circuit contacted the minister of education for permission to set aside a sum of candle tax money for help to fund a successful series of afternoon courses for poor girls in the city of Kerch (Tavrida province). He explained that there was no other educational institution for daughters of the poor and that the school, with its mix of thirty-nine Russians, thirty-six Greeks, thirty-eight Jews, seven Armenians, and one French girl, served the ministry's goal of integrating the Jews.[33] This request was one of several granted to non-Jewish institutions.[34] By the late 1860s the candle tax began to fund teachers of the Jewish religion in Russian gymnasia.[35]

The Ministry of Education, beyond sporadic requests for information and a readiness to grant subsidies, never officially recognized or sought to regularize the process for funding private schools for Jewish girls. Local officials of the ministry consistently advocated for Jewish girls' schools but also made no effort to create a special fund or application process. Nevertheless, there can be no question that these officials were aware of the import of the excess candle tax funds for Jewish girls' schools.

The collection and disbursement of candle tax funds remained a major issue for the Ministry of Education. The offices of the ministry were flooded with requests from individual wealthy Jews to be excused from the requirement, from towns and regions that felt they were being charged dispropor-

Table 4.2. 1867 Candle Tax Disbursement to Private Schools for Jewish Girls

City	Principal	Rubles
Vilna Educational Circuit		
Vilna	Shevel' Perel'	700
Vilna	Germaize	300
Vilna	Shreiber	300
Minsk	Funt	300
Minsk	Rakavshchik, Schur	200
Minsk	Perel'	200
Grodno	Golovchinskii	500
Bialystok	Kagan, Plakhad	200
Kovno		600
Ponevezh	Rumsh	200
Tel'she	Gordon	150
Vitebsk	Redelin	600
Dinaburg	Kheifets	250
Dinaburg	Aranovicheva	250
Mogilev		600
	Total	5,350
Kiev Educational Circuit		
Berdichev	Likhtenshtein	400
Chernigov	Rashkind	200
Zhitomir	Daich	350
Kaments-Podol'sk	Glikin	600
Moghilev-Podol'sk	Shtern	600
	Total	2,150
Odessa Educational Circuit		
Vinnits	Perel'shteyn	600
Odessa	Gurovich	600
Odessa	Gringol'ts	300
Kherson	Bruk	600
Kishinev	Sheinfel'd, Bliumenfel'd	600
Khotin	Tiutinman	500
	Total	3,200
Total: 26 schools		10,600

Source: RGIA, f. 733, op. 189, d. 170, l. 3-3 ob.

Table 4.3. 1879 Candle Tax Disbursement to Private Schools for Jewish Girls

City	Principal	Rubles
Vilna Educational Circuit		
Vilna	Vul'f Kagan	700
Vilna	N. Funt	300
Minsk	Khaim Funt	300
Minsk	Eli Rakavshchik	300
Grodno	Ms. Ostrogorskaia	500
Bialystok	Gvirts	300
Vitebsk	Redelen	600
Sebezh	Pozin	300
Brest-Litovsk	Salomonov	300
Ponivezh	Rumsh	200
Tel'she	Khazanovich	350
	Total	4,150
Kiev Educational Circuit		
Berdichev	Ms. Likhtenshtein	400
Skvir	Stefanavskii	150
Kamenets-Podol'sk	Glikin	600
Mogilev-Podol'sk	Shtern	600
Chernigov	Ms. Gofman	200
	Total	1,950
Odessa Educational Circuit		
Kishinev	Sheinfel'd	600
Khotin	Tiutinman	500
	Total	1,100
Total: 18 schools		7,200

Source: RGIA, f. 733, op. 189, d. 581, l. 26-26 ob.

tionately, and from various groups wishing to benefit from the funds. Jewish and non-Jewish educators seeking to fund their educational institutions for Jewish girls were heavily represented among those petitioning for funds. In some ways they were the ideal recipients. Unlike private schools for Jewish boys, girls' schools could uphold the goals of the government without competing with governmental institutions. Indeed, regional officials supporting funding for schools for Jewish girls often pointed to the importance of educating Jewish girls along with their brothers.

Between 1850 and 1881 dozens of private schools for Jewish girls received government funding. Although the combined total of grants given never exceeded five percent of the candle tax funds, the individual stipends were fairly generous, ranging from 200 to 900 rubles per year. These funds not only kept individual schools functioning but encouraged the growth and development of private schools for Jewish girls as a whole. Knowing that a supplemental funding source was available emboldened educators to open private schools.

With the closure of the majority of state schools for Jewish boys in 1873, many Jewish communities finally achieved their desire of jettisoning the candle tax. The many individuals and communities burdened by an additional tax and eager to lower their payments may not have known that the same tax that funded the hated government schools also enabled private education for Jewish girls. Faced with the imminent cessation of candle tax funds in 1879, the curator of schools for the Vilna educational circuit articulated what educators knew:

> Private women's educational institutions for Jews in the North-Western Region [of the Russian empire] are primarily attended by children from poor families and serve as their sole preparatory institutions for Russian language instruction. Up until this time, subsidies from the Ministry of Education have kept tuition costs within reach of poorer families. . . . With the end of payments, the principals of private women's schools will be forced to increase tuition, thus causing these unfortunate families to stop sending their daughters to schools. Thus, the cessation of payments to private women's schools would equate to their closure, and therefore would have a negative effect on the spread of the Russian language and literacy among Jewish women.[36]

Fortunately, the same set of enterprising educators who seized on the concept of education for Jewish girls and discovered the candle tax bounty continued to respond creatively to the circumstances around them.

The Society for the Spread of Enlightenment among the Jews of Russia

The changes in the Russian political scene, and in internal Jewish politics, are clearly reflected in the gradual development of Russian Jewry's most prominent philanthropic society. When the Society for the Spread of Enlightenment among the Jews of Russia (*Obshchestvo dlia rasprostraneniia prosveshche-niia mezhdu evreiami v Rossii,* OPE) was founded in 1863, reforming Jewish education was among its highest priorities. However, for its first thirty years of existence this effort was chiefly reactive and lacked a coherent direction. Over time the OPE would gradually become a far more important actor and director of Jewish educational endeavors and serve to sustain many schools for Jewish girls.

The founding members of the society, mainly wealthy St. Petersburg Jews, gave generously of their own funds to establish the OPE. Most prominent among their inspirational, if fairly vague, goals was the betterment of Jewish society through education.[37] But despite lofty goals, the OPE had neither the funds nor the power to effect radical change. In fact, the St. Petersburg magnates were cut off from the people they wanted to change by both geography and lifestyle.

These factors have led historians to take a generally negative view of the import of the OPE. Of late, several scholars have offered a more nuanced view of the society.[38] But whatever the views of later academics, progressive Jews at the time quickly embraced the possibilities of the new society. Jews committed to modernizing Jewish life and involved in a vast array of projects aimed at bringing about this change began to send petitions to the OPE immediately after its inauguration. Among these were principals of private schools for Jewish girls.

In the early years the society's monthly meetings were primarily concerned with discussing the latest batch of requests. Jews from the Pale hoped to open free libraries, publish textbooks and translations, attend Russian educational institutions, and support their own fledgling schools with the OPE's funds. With so many worthy causes but with limited monies, the OPE tended to reward many deserving applicants with small subsidies.

Over time the OPE leaders reached a certain consensus on how best to distribute their funds and influence. Although there was still an arbitrary quality to their funding decisions, patterns began to emerge. For example, the OPE made a real effort to enable Jews to pursue secondary and higher education by providing them with monthly stipends. Between 1864 and 1888 the OPE distributed 286,000 rubles to individual students.[39] During these same years, however, far less was granted to Jewish schools. By the time of the founding of the OPE, the state Jewish school system had already been in place for twenty years. There was thus no need to fund private schools for Jewish boys. As the OPE was committed to Jewish children learning Russian and being exposed to modern intellectual and educational trends, funding traditional Jewish education was also out of the question.

One might expect that the OPE would turn to supporting modern pri-vate schools for Jewish girls, and, in fact, the problem of educating Jewish daughters was raised periodically at meetings. In 1865 the board voted unan-imously to support better schooling for girls. This meeting also included a discussion of the lack of educational options for Jewish girls in St. Peters-burg, which would eventually lead to the OPE support for Anna Berman's school.[40] Despite this one case, funding for private schools remained entirely reactive until the Russian government changed its own policies.

In 1874, after the Russian government closed the government state Jew-ish school system, the OPE met to decide on its own plan going forward and formally committed itself to proactive support of modern Jewish schools for the first time.[41] According to the published minutes of the meeting, the initial sum to be set aside for this purpose would be 3,000 rubles. In order to qualify, the schools had to function legally, offer some slots tuition-free, teach Russian, and submit to yearly inspections. Crucial to our story, the committee also specified that the schools could serve either boys or girls.[42]

This step proved advantageous for the private schools for Jewish girls, as they sought a new source of subsidization with the diminution of the candle tax. In 1880, a woman by the name of Hofman (*Gofman*) wrote specifically to say that the government would be canceling the 200-ruble candle tax subsidy that her school for girls in Chernigov had been receiving. The OPE granted her 100 rubles.[43] Of course, the change in law also signaled the pos-sibility of legitimately opening private schools for Jewish boys once again, and the OPE would spread its funding to support schools for both sexes.

Although in 1874 the OPE moved toward educational reform, there remained no system of accountability and oversight. Wherever possible, the OPE sought independent confirmation of the quality of the schools. In Minsk, for example, they corresponded with the local member and philan-thropist Afanasii Wengeroff and relied upon his recommendations.[44] Often, however, no references were available and the OPE had only the principals' own judgment. In 1894, as a response to the still reactive nature of its ef-forts, the OPE founded the School Education Commission to form a coher-ent policy on schools.[45] Finally in 1899, the OPE effectively solved its two major problems in regard to educational reform: insufficient funds and lack of oversight. It was at this time that the OPE formed an official relationship with the Jewish Colonization Association (ICA).[46]

Although it was not always smooth, the subvention with the ICA pro-vided the OPE with a great deal more funding and a system of oversight. Beginning in 1900 an official inspectorate made periodic visits to all the schools supported by the OPE. There was also more paperwork and a clearer set of standards.[47] In the next decade the OPE would publish two important and useful books, sponsor a host of conferences, establish an educational journal, and introduce a teacher-training course. Teachers and inspectors became increasingly professionalized. Meanwhile, although the OPE continued to support Jewish attendance at secondary and higher educational institutions, the percentages began to shift. Whereas in 1881 the society spent over 10,000 rubles on university students and only 2,000 on schools, by 1905 the students' 31,310 rubles in subsidies had been surpassed by the schools' 47,000.[48]

By its very nature, as a large philanthropic society based outside the Pale of Settlement and with members representing a variety of interests, the OPE could never have become a single-issue institution. Nonetheless, over the decades, it moved increasingly into education and gradually established methods to make a difference. Like the Russian government, the OPE realized that it had neither the resources nor the influence to utterly transform Jewish education. Unlike the government, it persevered and became increasingly successful. Although the OPE never fully dedicated itself to girls' education, it consistently made funds available to worthy girls' schools.

Both the evolution of the OPE over the final decades of the nineteenth century and its relationship to girls' schooling reveal important facets of the Russian Jewish community during those same years. At its origins, a group of wealthy St. Petersburg Jews wanted to help their benighted brethren in the Pale to escape their poverty and isolation. Not knowing precisely how to go about achieving this, they had to rely upon petitions and requests from *maskilim,* state rabbis, school principals, aspiring students, and others from the Pale to guide their efforts. Over time, as their ties to members and informants in the provinces strengthened, and as they grew to rely on aid from western philanthropies, they were finally able to act in a more directed and effective manner. The tribulations of the post-1881 period helped to draw Jews together, and also helped to place education at the center of debate.

Throughout this period, the education of Jewish girls, despite coming to the fore occasionally for debate or study, remained essentially marginal. But in this new modern organization marginality meant lack of attention, but not exclusion. From its inception and throughout the period of study, the OPE sent subsidies to private schools for Jewish girls. Although educational questions still fundamentally concerned boys, girls and their schools were at times able to insert their own needs.

Conclusion

This chapter demonstrates not only the clever tactics employed by Jewish educators to fund their private girls' schools but also how these evolved over time and reflected on their changing environment. The principals of the first private schools for Jewish girls expected that their schools would attract daughters of the wealthy Russifying elite. Yet, as Mordechai Zalkin has written, Jewish schooling did not follow Russian patterns in its socioeconomic divisions.[49] Instead, Jewish families from across the socioeconomic spectrum saw the advantages of educating their daughters. The principals responded by savvy use of tuition scales, looking to local philanthropy and forging relationships with national funding sources.

Like the government Jewish school system as a whole, the candle tax existed to transform the Jews through education. With promises to conduct their lessons in Russian, assign approved textbooks, and conform to other expectations for the state schools, principals of private Jewish girls' schools were able to convince local authorities that their institutions merited the same access to funding. Arguably, although receiving far less assistance, the private schools were more successful in employing the candle tax in the service of transformation.

In view of the growth in Jewish attendance at Russian schools, and the continuing unpopularity of the state Jewish schools, the government began to close the schools and scale back the candle tax. This in turn led the principals to seek other funding sources. They came to rely increasingly on the OPE during the same years that it moved more confidently into educational reform. This shift from outside reliance and common cause with the government toward a more internal Jewish communal or even national solidarity highlights the general trend, even before 1881. In a commensurate manner, the OPE's more strenuous efforts at educational reform would have consequences for Jewish education, and for private schools for Jewish girls in the later years of the century.

Principals of private schools for Jewish girls had to combine teaching skills with fundraising acumen in order to stay afloat. It is very clear from the speed of the spread of both curricular and financial innovations that many of them were, if not in direct contact, at least aware of one another. As soon as one principal carved out a new funding source, others were quick to follow. The next chapter traces how educational trends and innovations similarly spread throughout the schools and evolved over time.

5

EDUCATING JEWISH DAUGHTERS

See for yourselves, the anomaly of the *Russian* Jews speaking *German*. Must we not, as Jews, speak in Hebrew, or speak, as the Russians do, in Russian? . . . I know this is a difficult challenge. Changing language is the reeducation of an entire nation. But before adversity we must not waver. This sort of change occurred many times in our four-thousand-year history. . . . Russification does not interfere with us retaining the Jewish religion, just as Judaism does not at all preclude us from becoming Russian.[1] —Y. L. GORDON

While each of the private schools for Jewish girls that opened between 1831 and 1881 has its own history and unique character, based on the personality of the founding principal, the location, its time of establishment, and the makeup of the surrounding community, all the schools shared certain fundamentals. In a speech delivered at the opening of his school for Jewish girls in Tel'she in 1866, Y. L. Gordon emphasized the importance of the Russian language while also touching upon Hebrew and religion. In most cases, Russian and religion made up the bulk of the curricula. Other subjects usually included other languages, basic mathematics, penmanship, and crafts. Hebrew, while not offered in the early schools, was frequently taught in later ones. This chapter focuses on the common elements of the schools. It also traces how these developed over time.

Numbers and Location

Despite the fact that both the Ministry of Education and Shevel' Perel' pointed to his school as the first private educational institution for Jewish girls in the Pale of Settlement, other Jewish educators also claimed the same distinction. According to an 1867 request for funds, Vol'f and Khaia Gringol'ts had been running their school in Odessa since 1831. They claimed to have provided 2,500 Jewish girls with primary education in the course of thirty-six years.[2] The school received high praise from the local Odessa branch of the MNP in 1854 as part of an evaluation of Jewish education in the city.[3] No information is available on the educational background of the couple. Despite the impressive record of the Gringol'ts, it is the girl's division of the Odessa private school for Jewish boys, opened in 1835, that is always mentioned in secondary sources as the first school for Jewish girls in Odessa.[4]

This scenario nicely illustrates the difficulty in obtaining accurate data on the private schools for Jewish girls and in determining how to work with the available data. No one in or outside the government was keeping track of the private schools for Jewish girls. These schools operated to a large degree beyond the realm of official oversight. The government did collect applications and send out subsidies and even occasional inspectors, but the private schools were not their main concern, and the already stretched bureaucracy was simply not able to keep tabs on yet another school system.

At the same time, whether or not Perel' managed to open his school before the Gringol'ts, the location of the two schools is not coincidental. Vilna and Odessa were, although very different in character, two of the most cosmopolitan and enlightened cities in the empire. Both cities had mixed populations and strong ties to Western and Central Europe. Vilna, a center of rabbinic learning and opposition to Hasidism, would also develop as a center of the Russian Jewish *Haskalah*. Odessa, a frontier city far from rabbinic or tsarist authority, developed a mercantile and urban culture all its own.[5]

These two cities were uniquely able to provide both educators to teach in modern schools and families willing to send their children to such schools. Thus, although extant records may not be able to provide accurate data on the opening and closure of all the schools, they can still help us to paint a picture of general and emerging trends.

Thus far my research in archival sources, published primary and secondary documents, and journalistic sources has revealed 130 schools for Jewish girls that opened between 1831 and 1881 (see Table 2.1). While some of these institutions are amply documented, others appear on only one list. Significantly, but alas inconclusively, every mention of a school suggests the existence of other similar institutions for which no records remain. The school of Veitsman and Fidler in Radzvilov (Volhynia province) profiled in an 1861 article in *Sion,* for example, is not mentioned in any other source.[6] We may never know how many schools history has concealed.

Nevertheless, we can rely on Table 2.1 to tell us, for example, that few private schools for Jewish girls opened in the 1830s or 1840s. Even after the 1844 legislative clarification, schools opened slowly, primarily in larger cities. The 1850s and 1860s saw a major expansion of schooling for Jewish girls. Moreover, the schools gradually spread from regional urban centers to smaller and less acculturated towns and cities. Although many of these schools would remain open in the following years, fewer new schools were established during the 1870s, and a number of them sought to serve both boys and girls.

This same basic arc is confirmed by the occasional, and decidedly incomplete, lists compiled by the government. In 1850, the Ministry of Education knew of six private schools for Jewish girls.[7] By the 1854–55 school year, it was providing support for ten such schools. A total of twenty-six private schools for Jewish girls received candle tax subsidies in 1867.[8] However, by 1879 the number was down to eighteen.[9] While these latter figures include only those schools receiving government funding, they still illustrate the expansion and then contraction of private schools for Jewish girls over the second half of the nineteenth century. The reasons for the eventual decline in numbers are discussed in chapter 8.

Nomenclature and Level

Most of the forms and letters regarding private schools for Jewish girls use the Russian term *uchilishche* for school. However, quite a few favored the Polish *shkola.* Less frequent, but still numerous, were the boarding schools referred to by the French term *pansion.* On the whole, both the principals themselves and the Ministry of Education officials with whom they dealt used various terms for schools almost interchangeably; for example, a *heder* could be a traditional religious school or simply a school for Jews, and the terms *shkola, pansion,* and *uchilishche* were often applied to the same institution.[10]

Thus, the title of an institution did not announce its academic pretensions. In many cases, neither did the division (*razriad*). David Shtern's 1858 school plan created a school in Mogilev on par with a first-division government school. Specifically, the program of study was two years in length with six hours of instruction per day.[11] Khaim Khitrik, in Kherson, also called his school first division, but offered a four-year course of study with six hours of instruction per day.[12] In fact, many of the new private schools explicitly compared themselves to the government Jewish schools. Such a reference, it would appear, did not mean the exact same courses or hours but that the school would meet regularly and expect the students to master the subjects at hand.

Only a few schools compared themselves to the more demanding second-division public schools. Relatively more called themselves *pansions* and offered a less rigorous program of study. But even that division is unstable, as other schools adopted the name *pansion* with reference to serving as boarding schools rather than offering a particular curriculum.

Hours of instruction in the institutions, although not predictable by the name given to the school, did vary significantly. Table 5.1 shows a chart of the distribution of hours per school. Based on the schools for which this information was available, the average number of hours of instruction per week was twenty-five. For the sake of comparison, the government Jewish schools for boys had twenty-five and thirty-eight hours per week of instruction in the lower- and upper-division schools, respectively.[13]

The schools for girls advertised themselves as having between one and four classes. In practice many also had a preparatory class and thus really

Table 5.1. Hours of Instruction per Week in Private Girls' Schools

School	Principal	Judaic Studies[1]	Russian[2]	Total hours of instruction
Kherson	Bruk	4.5	4.5	40.5
Kishinev	Shenfel'd, Bliumenfel'd	6	5	33
Mitau		6	4	30
Mitau	Shtern	2	3	24
Vitebsk	Val'tser	7.5	6	24
St. Petersburg	Berman	7	5	23
Mogilev	Shtern	9	5	18
Berdichev		6	3	15
Vilna	Ioffe	1	3.5	15

Note: In schools where hours of instruction varied by year in the program, I have used the numbers from the first class.

1. Included in Judaic Studies is both religion and Hebrew but not Hebrew penmanship.
2. Russian language instruction excluding Russian penmanship.

contained two to five classes. Generally the students were divided into classes based on educational background rather than age.

Academic Content

The more than one hundred private schools for Jewish girls were opened by men and women, Jews and non-Jews, from a variety of educational backgrounds, in different locales, and over the course of several decades. Each principal sought to create an educational institution that would draw on his or her own strengths and convictions, but that would also meet the needs and expectations of the local Jewish community. That the schools they created reflected their own personalities and local conditions and differed from one another should hardly be surprising.

More remarkable is the amount the schools had in common. Some of this can be explained in terms of their shared legal and societal limitations. No school, for example, could hope to open legally without devoting significant time to the study of the Russian language. In founding the state Jewish school system, in demanding that all *hadarim* introduce Russian instruction, and in requiring teachers to pass examinations in Russian, the government had clearly signaled that linguistic Russification of the Jewish population was one of its major goals. Religion, in nineteenth-century Russia, as in Europe as a whole, was considered an integral part of the educational process. Neither the Jewish community nor the Russian government would have accepted a school without instruction in religion.

Beyond legal and societal imperatives, however, it is clear that the principals learned from one another. Early on some of the principals actually referred to Perel's school as a model for their own.[14] More often, however, in place of attribution, there was only emulation. Whether they learned about one another's successes and failures from the many articles about individual schools in the periodical press, or from correspondence and personal contact not available to the historical eye, information about curriculum clearly spread. We will see how, despite the retention of certain unique characteristics, schools across the Pale could adopt particular educational innovations with remarkable speed and ease.

In addition to religion and Russian, regular subjects included European languages, arithmetic, penmanship, and crafts. Table 5.1 provides a breakdown of course hours. Many schools also offered drawing, music, and dance, sometimes as electives. A small minority of schools offered a more demanding and advanced academic curriculum, including such subjects as history, geography, and science. We begin with the Judaic curriculum.

Religion

The data from Table 5.1 show that whereas all schools offered Jewish religion classes, the number of hours of instruction varied considerably. The average number of hours was slightly over five per week, but in some ways this number is less useful than a comparison to Russian instruction or a percentage of the total number of school hours. David Ioffe's seemingly paltry one hour per week makes more sense in the context of a school that met for a mere fifteen hours weekly.

A few of the schools offered a more rigorous Jewish studies curriculum. These were often the same schools whose general studies curriculum was also broad. In his close analysis of published sources on Russian-language schools for Jews, Simion Krieze established a three-tier hierarchy of Jewish coursework based on hours of instruction. Private Jewish schools that offered ten to fifteen hours of instruction in Jewish studies per week were extremely rare before 1881. Those offering between five and eight hours were the most common for boys. For girls, two to four hours per week was standard.[15] Krieze explains that the discrepancy was due to a general lack of interest in women's education and a growing focus on Russification.[16] It is also worth noting that schools for boys tended to offer more hours of instruction overall than those for girls.

Krieze's data are based primarily on newspaper reports on the schools. My own data, based upon unpublished documents, suggest that Krieze underestimates the level of Jewish education offered to girls in private schools. Of the nine schools whose hours of instruction were clearly broken out, combining religion and Hebrew but excluding instruction in Hebrew calligraphy, three schools offered between two and four hours of Judaic instruction per week, five schools offered between five and eight hours, and one—David Shtern's school in Mogilev—offered more than nine hours.[17]

Although there could be no question that a school for Jews must include religious instruction, what and how to teach Jewish girls was less obvious. Beyond the generally upheld injunction that Jewish girls ought to know those religious duties incumbent upon them, there was no set traditional curriculum for girls. In designing religion courses, educators drew upon societal norms, texts, and ideas from the German lands, and their own vision of what Jewish girls in the modern world should know.

Prayer served as the common denominator of religion courses. In and of itself, this shows the entrenchment of traditionalism. Either because educators did not want to offend the traditionalists within their communities or because even they were unable to escape the dominant paradigm of what women should know, the major focus of religious education was on prayer. Just as Jewish girls tutored by family members or by paid tutors were most likely to learn the rudiments of Hebrew reading and prayers appropriate to a woman's life, so the situation remained in the new schools.

The principal of a proposed Jewish girls' school in Berdichev in 1854, for example, explicitly equated religion with prayer.[18] His two-year course of study began with learning prayers for the Sabbath and the new moon and progressed in the second year to studying the prayers associated with holidays and women. However, whereas in the home setting a girl would learn to read prayers aloud directly from the prayer book and perhaps have access to a Yiddish translation, in the Berdichev school all prayers were studied in German translation using the text *Yesode ha-da'at* by the Polish *maskil* Judah Leib Ben Ze'ev.[19]

Most of the other schools for which detailed documentation exists also taught prayer during their religion classes. However, some teachers did express their modern leanings in the supplemental subjects offered. Abram Bruk-Brezovskii expected his first-year students to master Hebrew reading and to memorize the Ten Commandments in addition to their prayers. Focusing attention on the Decalogue, for example, allowed the educator to highlight Judaism's universalistic and ethical teachings as opposed to the more particularistic aspects that offended modern sentiment. By the second year, an element of sacred history was added to the curriculum.[20] The teaching of Jewish history rather than simply the Torah represented a great paradigm shift and allowed an unprecedented degree of interpretation and even mild biblical criticism. In the school of Vol'f and Khaia Gringol'ts in Odessa, the study of prayer was to be supplemented by reading short, edited, didactic biblical stories in the text of Peter Beer, which was a far cry from the traditional method of reading through the entire text.[21] David Shtern in Mogilev taught a catechism in addition to prayer.[22] Of course, the catechism was a method of teaching adopted from Christianity and favored in modern Jewish schools in Germany. In fact, all these innovations were based upon modern pedagogic ideas from Western Europe and many of the texts involved, as discussed below, came from there as well.

Listing of names and grades in Levin Germaize's school for Jewish girls, 1873. Each student has a mark of between one and five in subjects ranging from Russian to religion. (YIVO Institute for Jewish Research)

Judaic Textbooks

In most cases, the academic plans deal with textbooks only so far as to state that all books in use have the approval of the Ministry of Education. Only a few schools specifically listed the texts used. At times these texts correspond to those used in the government Jewish school system. They include Hebrew, German, and Russian language works.

Both the Hebrew and German language texts in use in Russian Jewish schools had been written for the use of Jewish students in German-speaking countries. As modern Jewish education had evolved far earlier in these countries, many of these books had been written in the previous century. One example is Peter Beer's *Toldot Yisra'el,* first published in Prague in 1796. As the title suggests, Beer's text is devoted primarily to providing a summary of ancient Jewish history. Although it follows the chronology presented in the Bible, large non-narrative and prescriptive sections of the Bible are omitted. The work includes a Hebrew text, a German translation, and a German commentary. As in Moses Mendelssohn's famous German translation of the Torah, the German sections are rendered in Hebrew letters.[23]

Beer included a preface that illuminates his goals in writing the book. As a *maskil* he was deeply committed to improving Jewish education in numerous spheres. His book would serve to elevate the level of both German and Hebrew taught to Jewish boys. In German footnotes Beer also gave teachers advice on how to draw moral examples out of the stories. In short, he sought to reform Jewish education from within, providing the traditional *melamed* with a textbook that reflected the pedagogic and linguistic agenda of the *maskilim.*

Initially, Beer's work was found too moderate for the new modern schools and too radical for the *hadarim.* However, in the course of time, as both movements spread and influenced one another, a growing number of teachers in the German and Habsburg lands adopted *Toldot Yisra'el.* It was reprinted numerous times, with minor changes, and in 1870 was translated into Russian.[24]

Both the German and Russian versions were used in Jewish schools in Russia. Vol'f and Khaia Gringol'ts were already using the German text in their school in Odessa in 1856.[25] Lazar Berman, a principal as well as author of a book about the first fifteen years of the private Jewish schools for boys and girls in St. Petersburg, wrote that although biblical history had been taught originally using Peter Beer in German and Hebrew, a variety of texts, including Beer in Russian translation, came into use as the schools moved toward teaching Jewish subjects in Russian.[26] Beer's text is also mentioned in the carefully prepared applications for government Jewish schools for girls in Vitebsk and Mogilev.[27]

Beer's *Toldot Yisra'el* was only one of several books written by German or Austrian *maskilim* that came to be used in Russian Jewish schools. Another popular text was Judah Leib Ben Ze'ev's *Yesode ha-da'at.*[28] Ben Ze'ev (1764–1811), a Polish *maskil* and grammarian, also wrote his work in the late eighteenth century for use in schools in German-speaking lands. Unlike

Advertisement for Russian translation of Peter Beer's textbook published in Russian Jewish periodical *Razsvet*, 1879. (Hebrew Union College Library)

Beer's *Toldot Israel,* it was a religion text, and it does not seem to have been translated.

The religion teacher in Anna Val'tser's school in Vitebsk used *Imre shefer* by the well-known *maskil* Naftali Herz Homberg (1749–1841) in religion classes.[29] In a classic article on religion texts produced by German-speaking Jews, Jakob Petuchowski, using both *Imre shefer* and *Yesode ha-da'at* as examples, showed how the production of such works was part of a process of redefining Judaism in a new era.[30] These early attempts to distill the Jewish religion also met the needs of the first generation of Jewish teachers in Russia.

As time passed, and Russian-language schools for Jews proliferated, Russian Jewish educators also produced their own religion texts. Leon Mandel'shtam (1819–89), the learned Jew at the Ministry of Education appointed to replace Max Lilienthal, took it upon himself to write several Russian and Hebrew texts for the state-run Jewish schools. None of his books receives mention in the curricula for the girls' schools. Additionally, some of the teachers themselves produced textbooks.

Lazar Berman (1830–93), as mentioned previously, was a teacher in a government Jewish school as well as the principal of a private school for Jewish girls in his native Kurland before the Jewish community of St. Petersburg brought him to the capital to run a school for poor Jewish boys. In 1874 he applied his considerable experience in Jewish education to writing a textbook. *Osnovyi Moiseeva zakona* (Foundations of the Mosaic Faith) was popular enough to be printed again in 1880.[31] As of 1884 it was the religion text in the school for Jewish girls in St. Petersburg run by Berman's wife, Anna.[32] It is also one of the religion texts recommended in a 1901 guidebook for Jewish educators.[33]

There was considerable crossover of textbooks between the private schools for Jewish girls and the government Jewish schools. Books written to provide Jewish boys with a modern outlook on religion were often deemed appropriate for girls as well, but this did not hold true for religious treatises. Whereas all *hadarim,* the government Jewish school system, and even many of the modern private schools for Jewish boys also made use of traditional Jewish texts, girls' schools did not. When girls were taught biblical history, it was out of works like Peter Beer's synopsis. When girls studied Jewish law, it was out of works like Lazar Berman's treatise on Jewish law. The use of Talmud, or even Bible, in the girls' classroom was extremely rare.

The only exception I have located is Nusin Tiutinman's school in Khotin. As per his 1857 academic plan, Tiutinman planned to introduce his students to the study of the Jewish religion with the use of the Talmud and

ОСНОВЫ МОИСЕЕВА ЗАКОНА.

РУКОВОДСТВО

къ

ЗАКОНОУЧЕНІЮ

для

ЕВРЕЙСКАГО ЮНОШЕСТВА

обоего пола.

СОСТАВИЛЪ

Л. БЕРМАНЪ,

Законоучитель С.-Петербургскихъ Коломенской и Маріинской женскихъ
гимназій и содержатель С-.Петербургск. еврейскихъ училищъ.

«Путь *вѣры* избралъ я,
Законы Твои поставилъ
предъ собою».
(Пс. CXIX, 30).

С.-ПЕТЕРБУРГЪ.
Типографія и Литографія Л. Бермана, Измайловскій проспектъ, д. № 7.
1874.

Russian title page of Lazar Berman's *Osnovyi Moiseeva zakona* [Foundations of the Mosaic Faith], St. Petersburg, 1874. (Jewish National and University Library)

ספר

מוסדי דת־משה

להורת לבני ישראל

דרך אמונה

מאת

אליעזר בן יעקב בעהרמאן

מורה דת־משה בשני בתי ספר (גימנאזיען) לנערות ומחזיק בתי ספר העברים
לנערים ולנערות בס״ט-ספעטערבורג.

דֶּרֶךְ אֱמוּנָה בָחָרְתִּי
מִשְׁפָּטֶיךָ שִׁוִּיתִי.
(תהלים קי״ט ל׳):

ס״ט פטרבורג

בדפוס המחבר אליעזר בעהרמאן.

ה׳תרל״ד.

Hebrew title page of Lazar Berman's *Sefer mosde dat Moshe* [Foundations of the Mosaic Faith], St. Petersburg, 1874. (Jewish National and University Library) the *Hayei Adam,* a law digest.[34] In state Jewish schools the Talmud had been replaced by the *Hayei Adam,* a far more limited legal compendium. Tiutin-man's students may have been among a small number of Jewish girls with direct access to either text.

Hebrew Language Instruction

Although studying prayers in German translation was quite common, Hebrew reading was also offered in many of the schools.[35] In fact, Shevel' Perel' was quite unusual in offering instruction in Yiddish rather than Hebrew. This can be explained largely by the fact that his school was the first of its kind. Teaching Hebrew in a systematic fashion to anyone, let alone girls, was still new in 1831.[36] In the traditional *heder* boys learned to translate the biblical text into Yiddish, but there was no instruction in grammar, syntax, or even writing.

When the Dubinskiis opened their school for girls in Kherson in 1847, Hebrew reading appeared on the curriculum. But it is important to note that although the academic plan included the four languages of Hebrew, Russian, German, and French, it explicitly proposed to teach the grammar of only the last three.[37]

Most of the schools opened during the 1850s appear to have taught Hebrew reading. Yiddish just about disappeared from the curricula. Only later do we find schools where not only decoding but also grammar was taught. David Shtern's school, opened in 1859, taught Hebrew using the text *Lashon 'ever.*[38] Y. L. Gordon also offered Hebrew language instruction in his school in Tel'she from 1861.[39]

It is possible that the growth in teaching Hebrew language to girls coincided not only with greater societal acceptance but also with the expansion of the government school system for Jewish boys. These schools offered Hebrew instruction, and many of the instructors, including David Shtern and Y. L. Gordon, taught in them as well.[40] However, whereas the government schools had to work with a set curriculum and texts, the private schools could far more easily respond to changing needs and circumstances.[41]

These examples show the development of Hebrew instruction for Jewish girls. When Perel' first opened his school, teaching girls even to read Hebrew was unheard of, and yet over the next decade it became normative to offer Hebrew reading instruction in schools for girls. By the 1860s some schools for Jewish girls had begun to teach Hebrew as a language. The progression was not entirely linear, with other new schools continuing to teach only reading skills, but over time more and more Jewish girls' schools taught Hebrew along with other languages.

In both the use of textbooks and the teaching of Jewish subjects, certain factors obtain across the schools. Religion, a key subject in all the schools, was taught with a combination of traditional practices and new innovations. Maskilic textbooks and modern approaches to the Jewish religion existed side by side with instruction in prayer. Additionally, both the textbooks in use and instruction in Hebrew changed over the course of the century. By the end of the period of study not only were there books prepared by Russian Jews to meet the needs of their own community, but Jewish girls could also study the Hebrew language.

Russian

In addition to religion, every private school for Jewish girls in the tsarist empire required extensive instruction in the Russian language. In many cases, this was the course with the most hours, clearly reflecting the central goal of the principal in Jewish education. If the Jews were ever to become a part of Russian society, speaking the language fluently was a necessity, as articulated by Y. L. Gordon at the opening of this chapter. Indeed, principals and writers often restated this point, and inspectors and dignitaries visiting the schools were always sure to comment upon progress in Russian.

It is, of course, difficult to know exactly how the Russian language was taught in each of these schools. The academic plans suggest that immersion was a key tool employed by educators. It was not uncommon for all general studies subjects to be taught in Russian. This closely paralleled the government Jewish school system where religion was taught in German and all other subjects in Russian. Other academic plans state that all subjects would be taught in Russian, without excluding religion.

In addition, Russian was taught in a more frontal manner. Teaching methods at the time relied heavily on both dictation and recitation. Abram Bruk-Brezovskii described his method in an article in *Sion:* "Russian Language: reading with translation into German, taking dictation, learning by heart certain articles of prose and poetry, of moral and historical content, and grammar. Special attention will be paid to practical learning."[42] Aron Frud in Berdichev described a spiraling grammar-based program, which sounds quite contemporary. In the preparatory class his students covered reading in Russian and the parts of speech. By the first class they were working on word combinations and by the second on composition. In the third class, word composition, agreement, and case work allowed for more sophisticated composition. Finally, in the fourth class the students focused on subordinate clauses, accents, and review.[43]

A number of Jews wrote Russian language textbooks specifically for Jewish pupils. Leon Mandel'shtam produced numerous textbooks in his time at the Ministry of Education. The noted *maskil* and educator Abraham Paperna (1840–1919) published *Lehrbukh der Russishen shprakhe nakh Alendorfs metode* in 1876.[44] This text moves from Yiddish to Russian with a series of well-organized lessons and exercises. Although there is no record of either Mandelshtam or Paperna's works being employed in private school for Jewish girls, it is likely that either these or similar works were used.

In addition to religion and Russian, almost all Jewish girls' schools offered penmanship, arithmetic, and languages. This focus on languages reflected affinity to Russian girls' schools rather than either to the state Jewish schools or Russian gymnasia. German was a required course in most of the schools. French was sometimes required and sometimes supplementary, along with music and dance. Only a handful of schools offered Polish, and these only in the northern reaches of the Pale and only before the second Polish Uprising in 1863.[45] Geography, history, and science were all rare.

Crafts

What most strongly differentiated the girls' schools from schools for Jewish boys was instruction in handicrafts. In the early years of the private schools for Jewish girls, handicrafts, sometimes called "Womanly Crafts" (*zhenskiia rukodeliia*), was often offered as a supplemental course, once a week or in the late afternoons. That it was marginal to the curriculum can be seen in the fact that some schools even asked families to pay extra for training in crafts.[46] Such training was outside the academic curriculum but remained ubiquitous even as Jewish boys in *heder* and government Jewish schools had no access to handiwork.[47] In describing a private Jewish girls' school in Kishinev, the *maskil* Abraham Baer Gottlober (1810–99) explicitly stated that, with the exception of crafts and music, all the subjects were similar to general educational institutions.[48]

Over time, crafts became a more important part of the education of Jewish girls. I have not found any school plan calling for extra payment for crafts after 1857. On the contrary, there is a gradual increase in hours devoted to hands-on education. Already in 1850 there was a school with two hours of religion per week, three of Russian and four of crafts.[49] A school opened in 1857 offering six hours of Hebrew, five of Russian, and ten of crafts.[50]

The reasons for this expansion, as well as its further trajectory, are discussed further in chapter 8. For the present discussion, the important point is that almost all Jewish girls received training in crafts. Unlike music and dance, which were offered selectively and especially for the daughters of the wealthy, instruction in crafts became nearly ubiquitous. Apparently girls across the socioeconomic span were expected to be able to work with their hands.

Conclusion

Private schools for Jewish girls expanded over the course of the second half of the nineteenth century not only in terms of numbers, but also in terms of curriculum. While recognizing that each school had its own particular culture and practices, the material in this chapter clearly demonstrates that the private schools responded to one another and introduced and followed new educational trends. Most noteworthy among these was the enhanced rigor of instruction in both Hebrew and crafts over time.

However, it was not only these two subjects. On the whole, as the century wore on, the schools expanded from somewhat tentative institutions offering limited hours of instruction and subjects of study to far more rigorous and academically challenging schools. Shevel' Perel's school, as we have seen, began by offering two classes and Yiddish instead of Hebrew. He would over time expand to three classes, add more subjects of study, and switch to Hebrew. Of course, some schools continued to offer the same classes, but overall the trend was toward experimentation and expansion.

In *Reading Jewish Women* Iris Parush has provocatively argued that, as individuals, Jewish women had more educational freedom that their brothers. Parush termed this phenomenon "the benefits of marginality." The information in this chapter could suggest expanding this theory to the collective level. While Jewish boys remained in unchanging *hadarim* or attended the rigid new state schools, Jewish girls took part in a dynamic educational experiment. Marginality meant that Jewish girls' schools had significantly more room to maneuver and to innovate.

Parush's construct is attractive partly because of her novel perspective. Marginality, generally viewed in a negative light, is reinterpreted to have beneficial aspects. In this case Jewish girls' schools, largely outside either communal or governmental purview, could succeed partly as a result of that relative disinterest. At a time when educational institutions for Jewish boys were strictly controlled, private schools for Jewish girls had the scope to experiment and expand.

On an individual level, as the next chapter discusses, assessing the effect of education is far more difficult. In a recent article about textbook consumption in Israel, Dan Porat shows the multiple, sophisticated, and even contradictory ways in which a small sample of readers interprets a short historical excerpt. Their alternative readings are conditioned by politics, language, and prior information, among other factors.[51] Textbooks and curricula cannot even adequately illuminate the classroom experience, much less the interior construction of meaning of each student. And yet, as Benjamin Jacobs points out, curriculum is not only culture, but also a historical agent.[52] The evolution of subjects and hours over the decades demonstrates the evolution of Russian Jewish life. It also suggests the influence of a new generation of educated Jewish daughters.

PART II

TRANSFORMATION

6

THE WISDOM OF WOMEN BUILDS HER HOUSE
Jewish School Girls

And it came to pass after all had been done according to plan and the teacher began to test them on their learning, and asked them to recite from memory excerpts in Russian and German, and all of those in attendance were astounded by the accents of the girls because they were pleasant to the ear, and they had answers for all questions in math and geography. And for the Jews there was light and happiness and joy and dignity to see these daughters of Israel performing valiantly and to see that the Lord gave them knowledge and enlightenment in all areas of inquiry.

—SHOLEM YANKEV ABRAMOVICH

Here, Sholem Yankev Abramovich (better known as the Hebrew and Yiddish writer Mendele Mocher Sforim) expresses his awe at the public examinations held at a private school for Jewish girls in his home city of Berdichev in 1859.[1] So great was Abramovich's rapture in seeing Jewish school girls excel in secular subjects that he explicitly called upon the language of the Book of Esther to capture his experience. But who were the girls who so impressed Abramovich and the other attendees? And perhaps more important, as well as more elusively, what did they do with their newfound knowledge?

This question is strengthened by the noted preponderance of Jewish women in political and educational endeavors in the Russian empire at the dawn of the twentieth century. Jewish women were active in the Zionist movement, remarkably active in the Jewish Labor Bund, consistently over-represented in the sporadic higher educational opportunities for women,

Studio portrait of Roza, Odessa, 1902. (YIVO Institute for Jewish Research)

and well known in revolutionary circles. Did the graduates of the modern private schools go on to apply their newfound knowledge and skills to activism on behalf of the major ideological movements of the day? Did they flock to secondary and even higher educational institutions, becoming professionals? And even if no direct link can be established, surely these capable and literate young women must have influenced their society. This chapter is an attempt to gauge the effects of education on the young women themselves and on their communities.

Numbers

Given the difficulty of ascertaining the precise number of schools open at any time or how long each of them stayed open, it is obviously not possible to say with any precision how many girls attended private Jewish schools. Nonetheless, there can be no question that it was a significant figure.

Relying on the lowest enrollment year on record based on inspections and periodic data gathered by regional offices of the Ministry of Education, the average number of pupils per school was sixty (see Table 6.1). Thus, if each of the schools had stayed open for only one year, more than 7,000 Jewish girls would have received at least the rudiments of an education over the course of the century. Of course, many schools were open for far longer than one year. Isaak Moiseevich Rumsh operated his school in Ponevich from 1860 to at least 1880.[2] In 1879 he had forty-six pupils in attendance.[3] Rumsh alone may have taught as many as one thousand students. Granting each school two years of activity would yield close to 15,000 girls, but even this is undoubtedly too low an estimate.

Another approach would be to add up the number of years each school can be shown to have operated and multiply that by the average number of pupils. Assuming that each of the schools for which only one date is known was open for only one year, the result is nearly 40,000 girls. Averaging the number of years each school was open at six yields roughly the same figure.[4]

It will never be possible to ascertain the exact number of Jewish girls who passed through the private schools established for them during the mid- to late nineteenth century. These attempts, however, demonstrate that even the most conservative estimates yield a significant number of girls. There can be no question that thousands, and most likely tens of thousands, of Jewish girls passed through the network of private Jewish schools by the latter decades of the nineteenth century. This fact alone necessitates further examination of the girls and their influence.

Table 6.1. Enrollment in Private Schools for Jewish Girls

City	Principal	Enrollment	Year
Vilna	Kagan	116	1879
Kishinev	Shenfel'd	107	1879
Odessa	Gringol'ts	103	1867
Minsk	Funt	102	1867
St. Petersburg	Berman	94	1880
Minsk	Rakavshik	92	1864
Vilna	Funt	82	1879
Kremenchug	Plater	80	1871
Vilna	Perel'	77	1861
Mogilev-Podol'sk	Shtern	75	1880
Sorokakh	Daich	65	1874
Berdichev	Likhtenshtein	58	1880
Khotin	Tiutinman	53	1880
Nezhin	Kushner	50	1881
Berdishev	Frud	50	1859
Nezhin	Kushner	50	1881
Vitebsk	Redelin	48	1866
Berdichev	Kenigsberg	46	1873
Zhitomir	Daich	40	1864
Chernigov	Gofman	40	1880
Tukkum	Levinson	39	1878
Kamenets-Podol'sk	Glikin	37	1880
Brest-Litovsk	Solomonov	26	1870
Ekaterinoslav	Rabinovich	25	1861
Chernigov	Rashkinds	24	1865
Skvir	Stefanovskii	20	1880

Note: All the enrollment figures given here are taken from either requests for funds for schools already in operation or from inspection reports. Where different figures were available for different years, I have taken the highest enrollment number available.

Characteristics

Correspondence between educators in the Pale and the various offices of the Ministry of Education focused primarily on the academic content and financial standing of the schools. But despite the fact that students were not the subject of conversation, it is possible to glean some information about them from these applications and requests.

In their applications to open private schools, most principals included the proposed ages of students to be taught. Girls were usually admitted at the age of six or seven and could remain in school until either eleven or twelve years of age. Enrollment data suggest that the lower classes were significantly more full than the upper ones. In 1880 the school of David Shtern in Mogilev-Podol'sk had fifty pupils in the preparatory class, sixteen in the first class and nine in the second and highest class.[5] These numbers were not unusual. I would suggest that there were two major reasons for this imbalance, both relating to the goals of the parents. Jewish families were able to use the schools to either limit or expand their daughters' educational opportunities.

In his epic work on schools for the peasants in Russia, Ben Eklof showed convincingly that peasant families, often considered fairly unsophisticated consumers, actually used the schools at their disposal for their own purposes, thereby subverting the goals of the various stakeholders who established and ran the schools. Whereas the church and government sought to inculcate religious and political quiescence via the schools, and the teachers may have wanted to empower the students through literacy, the peasants themselves were able to use the schools to reach their desired level of functional literacy and then leave.[6]

We can see a similar dynamic at work within the Jewish community. The educators who opened and ran private schools for Jewish girls were themselves from among the more Russified parts of the Jewish community and often sought to further Jewish acculturation through their teaching. However, in taking their daughters out of the schools after a relatively short period of time, Jewish families may well have been opting for concrete skills over lofty goals.

Shoshana Lishansky, in describing her childhood in the Lithuanian town of Malin, provides testimony of this sort of decision making. Lishansky narrates the arrival of a teacher of Russian in their town. He rented a house and arranged to hold classes for boys in the mornings and girls in the afternoons. When Lishansky and her sister wanted to join the classes, their Hasidic grandfather agreed to allow them to attend for two terms. Just enough, in his words, "to learn to read and sign a contract."[7] Thus, whereas the teacher might have hoped to create a generation of Jewish girls fully conversant in Russian language and Russian literature, Lishansky's grandfather was able to use his school to meet far more practical and limited goals.

On the other hand, there were other families who used the schools as stepping stones to a higher level of education. For these parents, the private Jewish schools offered the introductory Russian education that was needed to enter into the more prestigious Russian schools. They, therefore, kept their daughters in the Jewish schools only long enough for them to pass entrance examinations into Russian schools. Thus, for example, in 1869, Vul'f

Kagan's school in Vilna could boast no graduates, but eight of his students had passed entrance examinations to local gymnasia.[8]

The documents also support the findings suggested by the tuition scales, namely that the schools drew from a large cross-section of the Jewish community. In Khaim Funt's school in Minsk in 1867, thirty-three merchant daughters studied with sixty-nine daughters of the urban estate.[9] In 1870 the combined student bodies of the three private Jewish girls' schools in Vilna had nearly twice as many town dwellers as merchant daughters enrolled, although the percentages in the individual schools varied.[10] Although estate was not always an accurate indicator of wealth, it is certainly clear that these schools relied heavily on families outside the financial elite of the merchantry.

Even a look at the names of pupils supports the conclusion that the student body was diverse. Where such information is available, Yettas and Rakhels attended classes with Mariias and Terezas.[11] In other words, the schools were not composed entirely of the wealthy or the Russified elements of the Jewish community, who might have chosen to give their children Russian names, but instead drew on a far wider selection of families, including those who relied on traditional Yiddish and biblical names. The families, in turn, had a variety of motivations for sending their daughters to school.

Case Study: The Berman School

Due to its location in the administrative capital of the empire, Anna Berman's private school for Jewish girls in St. Petersburg is more fully documented than any of the other schools in this study. In addition, Berman's husband, Lazar, wrote a book to commemorate the first fifteen years of his own school for Jewish boys in the capital as well as Anna's for Jewish girls.[12] These two factors make Berman's school ideal for an in-depth case study of the students.

However, whereas the school's location and the advocacy of its founders are advantageous from the perspective of documentation, precisely these factors also make it far from representative. Located in St. Petersburg, where the vast majority of Jews were unable to take up legal residence, the schools drew from an unusual population. Anna Berman describes her pupils as chiefly from among the poor, especially the daughters of soldiers and servants.[13]

First Guild merchants and survivors of Tsar Nicholas's brutal twenty-five-year military service held the highly cherished right of permanent settlement outside the Pale of Settlement. The merchants, who could bring a limited number of Jewish servants with them, sent their children to elite Russian schools in the capital. However, the soldiers and servants were not in a position to do so, and, unlike in the Pale, there was not the option of numerous *hadarim*. This led the Jewish community of St. Petersburg to establish the two schools specifically to serve the children of the Jewish poor.

In nearly all the other cases, educators chose to open their private girls'

Advertisement for schools of Lazar and Anna Berman in St. Petersburg, *Ha-Karmel*, 1866. (Hebrew Union College Library) schools with no guarantee of financial backing or student enrollment. Moreover, whereas the Bermans' schools were in St. Petersburg, where Jewish residence was limited by law, in all other cases the schools were opened in towns or cities within the borders of the Jewish Pale of Settlement, where Jews often made up the majority of urban dwellers. And of course the student body in the Berman schools was disproportionately from the lower classes, whereas other schools were likely to be more mixed or even to favor the wealthy. Nonetheless, documentation from Anna Berman's school is of great interest in and of itself and can be used to help illuminate issues that other schools faced as well.

In 1868 the Bermans prepared a chart showing the enrollment in their schools between 1866 and 1868 (see Table 6.2). Of the 112 pupils who enrolled between April 1866 and July 1868, 53 remained at the school and 59 left.[14] Among the most prominent reasons for leaving appear to have been other educational opportunities, relocation, and poverty. Of the 59 who left school between 1866 and 1868, 22 were known to have been accepted into other educational institutions. In only one of the cases was the new school Jewish. Some of the schools were, like Berman's, equivalent to elementary schools, while others were secondary institutions.

Table 6.2. Educational Careers of Students in Anna Berman's
Private School for Jewish Girls, 1866–1868

Family Name	Date Started	Age	Date Left	Reason for Leaving
Markuson	4/1/66	11		
Khost I	4/1/66	12	8/22/67	Dressmaking
Gal'prin	4/1/66	10	3/20/67	Poverty
Kolodina I	4/1/66	10	4/1/67	Managing household
Briliant I	4/1/66	10	3/20/67	General school
Goberman	4/1/66	10	3/20/67	Russian pansion
Pogulevich	4/1/66	14	8/12/66	Managing household
Segal' I	4/1/66	11	8/22/67	Left the country
Miuller	4/1/66	11	4/9/67	Dressmaking
Shlezinger	4/1/66	11	4/1/67	Went home
Nikhamova	4/1/66	9	5/20/67	Russian pansion
Dalkin	4/1/66	8	8/22/67	Gymnasium
Valershtein	4/1/66	9		
Valershtein	4/1/66	8	6/1/66	(Uncertain) Died
Bonder	4/1/66	8	4/9/68	Russian pansion
Kolodina II	4/1/66	8	4/1/67	Russian pansion
Girshkovich	4/1/66	7	5/2/67	Gymnasium

Table 6.2. (*continued*)

Family Name	Date Started	Age	Date Left	Reason for Leaving
Segal' II	4/1/66	8	8/22/66	Left the country
Malkin	4/1/66	10	8/22/66	Went home
Gal'prin I	4/1/66	8	3/20/67	Poverty
Kamen'er	4/1/66	10		
Berman	5/1/66	7		
Khoke	7/5/66	8	8/22/66	Unknown
Iakobson I	10/1/66	12	8/15/67	Russian pansion
Iakobson II	10/1/66	7	8/15/67	Russian pansion
Revich	10/1/66	6		
Borishanskoiia I	10/1/66	9		
Borishanskoiia II	10/1/66	6		
Maltakova	10/1/66	10		
Kuznetskaiia	10/1/66	9	11/66	Managing household
Bukhgal'ter	10/1/66	14	12/12/66	Married
Gamburger	10/9/66	12	4/30/67	Managing household
Ol'shtein	10/9/66	13	7/1/67	Managing household
Khaimovich	10/11/66	14	4/30/67	Managing household
Amikova	10/12/66	7	8/22/67	Russian pansion
Gossel'	11/14/66	7		
Kolbodkina	11/17/66	11	11/19/66	General school
Satsinskiia	11/29/66	8	7/19/67	Unknown
Galant I	12/12/66	9	3/2/67	Went home
Galand II	12/12/66	7	3/2/67	Went home
Grimin	12/12/66	7		
Margoles	12/13/66	12	2/1/67	Managing household
Medalos	12/13/66	9	4/9/68	Heder
Kruchinskaia	12/13/66	12	7/1/68	Dressmaking
Gobernan	1/15/67	10	3/20/67	Russian pansion
Falk I	1/15/67	12	3/20/67	School
Falk II	1/15/67	10	3/20/67	School
Notik	1/15/67	10	8/22/67	Death of mother
Rachkoskiia	1/15/67	8	3/20/67	Unknown
Movshovich	1/15/67	7	3/20/67	Russian pansion
Vainberg	2/5/67	11	8/22/67	Went home
Zhemaites	4/20/67	7		
Geller	4/20/67	10		
Kissel'man	4/20/67	12	8/22/67	Managing household
Savvin	4/20/67	10	12/9/67	Russian pansion
Kaplun	4/20/67	10		
Glikman	4/20/67	7		
Kats I	4/20/67	7	6/1/67	General school
Kret	4/20/67	9		
Al'terman I	4/20/67	9	4/9/68	Unknown
Al'terman II	4/20/67	7	4/9/68	Unknown

Table 6.2. (*continued*)

Family Name	Date Started	Age	Date Left	Reason for Leaving
Shafir	4/20/67	10		
Kamras I	4/20/67	12		
Kamras II	4/20/67	8		
Abramson	4/20/67	7	6/1/67	Left school, displeased
Gurdin	4/20/67	10		
Khost II	4/20/67	10		
Sameonova	4/20/67	11	10/15/67	Fanaticism
Ravich	4/20/67	11	4/9/68	Poverty
Zemenskaia	4/20/67	9	7/31/67	Lost residence permit
Gissin	4/20/67	12		
Geskin I	4/20/67	10	10/13/67	Russian pansion
Geskin II	4/20/67	8	10/13/67	Honor school
Briliant II	4/20/67	8	4/9/68	Honor school
Zelenskaia	6/4/67	10	7/31/68	Expelled for morals
Levias	6/4/67	8	10/15/67	General school
Eliasova	6/4/67	8		
Rachkovskaia	6/4/67	8	7/9/68	Unknown
Nachulina	10/13/67	7	4/9/68	Unknown
Shapiro	10/13/67	6		
Pozin	10/13/67	7	6/9/68	Unknown
Vital'	10/13/67	9	4/9/68	Unknown
Levinson	10/13/67	9		
Nalodina I	10/13/67	9		
Vital' II	10/13/67	12		
Tsvet	10/13/67	10	11/1/67	Managing household
Khost	10/13/67	7		
Salamonova	10/13/67	14	4/9/67	Managing household
Iafet I	12/?/67	12		
Iafet II	12/?/67	10		
Levin	2/1/68	9		
Azgut I	2/1/68	9		
Azgut II	2/1/68	7		
Akhun	2/1/68	7		
Brishch	2/1/68	12		
Veinshtein I	2/1/68	13		
Veinshtein II	2/1/68	11		
Gol'den	2/1/68	11		
Kats II	2/1/68	12		
Lotker	2/1/68	9		
Poliakova	2/1/68	10		
Pakhot	2/1/68	12		
Rozeneak	2/1/68	8		
Mendelovich	2/1/68	7		
Keileberg	4/9/68	10		

Table 6.2. (*continued*)

Family Name	Date Started	Age	Date Left	Reason for Leaving
Nadvorneniia	4/9/68	12		
Krepiva	4/9/68	9		
Gel'man	4/9/68	10	7/1/68	Expelled for bad behavior
Fridliander	7/1/68	9		
Bdelman	7/1/68	6		
Fish	7/1/68	9		
Baranova	7/14/68	8		

Source: RGIA, f. 733, op. 189, d. 170, ll. 36 ob.-39 [Chart prepared by Anna Berman in 1868].

Certain factors of life in the capital city made student retention more of a problem for Anna Berman than for her colleagues in the provinces. School choice was only a reality in the larger cities of the Pale, and the availability of high-quality, prestigious schools for girls in St. Petersburg was unparalleled in the western regions. Where Russian schools for girls existed, they would still be attractive to the wealthy and Russified elite but less so to the more traditional masses. Of the 102 students in his school in Minsk in 1867, Khaim Funt was able to send nine girls on to non-Jewish *pansions* and twelve to local gymnasia.[15] Even Funt's numbers, far lower than Anna Berman's, were still probably higher than those for many schools in the Pale. His was a rather academic school and located in a city.

Berman's chart allows us to monitor families as well as individuals. The Iakobson sisters, for example, both entered the school in October 1866. By the next school year, in August 1867, both had transferred to a Russian *pansion*. The Falk sisters, according to the chart, spent less than three months at Berman's school before moving on to another school. This evidence would seem to support the use of Jewish schools as stepping stones to entry into Russian schools.

Although such data are mostly lacking for schools in the Pale, certainly turnover was a major issue for private girls' schools overall. Abram Schreiber in Vilna began 1869 with 59 pupils, of whom 30 left over the course of the year, but another 41 arrived. He thus started 1870 with 70 pupils.[16] While some of his students may have pursued other educational opportunities, it is likely that more of them left when their families relocated or could no longer afford the tuition.

In St. Petersburg, families could lose their right of residence or simply face such normal issues as rent increases, job losses, or family separation. Among Anna Berman's students, only Zemenskaia explicitly left due to a loss of permission to reside in the capital, but five other girls are said to have gone home. It may well be that at least some of these girls had been residing illegally with relatives before returning to their homes within the Pale. The one family that told the school they were leaving the country, the Segals, may also be but one of a larger number who left via step-migration, although 1867 was too early for mass emigration.

Mobility was a reality in the Pale as well. Families near the borders or in rural areas faced expulsion, but the vast majority of Jews barely survived, and it was quite common to move in order to avoid problems or seek new opportunities. Throughout the nineteenth century, what had been major Jewish population centers in the northern Pale gradually lost numbers to the growing metropolises in the southern Pale.[17] Emigration would soon surpass migration as advances in transportation and the intensity of push factors led well over one million Russian Jews to leave the country before the onset of the First World War.[18]

Whereas some Jewish girls used Berman's school to climb the social ladder, others clearly fell down. While only three girls listed poverty as their primary reason for withdrawal, other factors, such as entering apprenticeships, moving residence, assuming managerial responsibilities within the household, marriage, and even expulsion for bad morals may have been consequences of impoverishment. Overcrowding and lack of economic opportunities in the Pale made economic survival a trial for Jews there. The legal and social quotas that increased against Jews in education and in the professions following the assassination of Alexander II only worsened conditions.

Thus the detailed information on Anna Berman's school both reinforces and provides a corrective to the theory of family choice advanced above. Although many students left the school to pursue other educational opportunities, many others were forced to leave school to enter apprenticeships. Some of these students may have preferred to continue their educations, but their families could not afford this. Still others left when their families moved. Mobility was a very real factor in Russian Jewish life as the century wore on, and its consequences may have been more severe for girls. Whereas Jewish boys were likely to find commensurate educational institutions wherever they went, relocation may have meant the end of formal schooling for many girls.

Life Paths

It is tempting to suggest that these girls, educated in private Jewish schools during the 1850s, 1860s, and 1870s, were the vanguard of the new generation, that it was these pupils who grew up to become doctors, revolutionaries, Zionists, or other leaders among the Jewish people. Unfortunately, such a direct link has proved elusive. The many biographical dictionaries and encyclopedias of important figures from this period include the names of numerous Jewish women, but they do not include information on primary education. *Entsiklopediyah le-haluze ha-Yishuv u-vonav* provides only very brief biographical sketches of Zionist leaders.[19] The membership of the Jewish Labor Bund was one-third female, but even in works such as *Doyres bundistn,* which offers longer entries, including attendance at secondary school and higher education courses, primary schooling is excluded.[20]

Patti Kremer, born Matle Srednitski in 1867, for example, attended the Vilna Gymnasium before earning her certification as a dentist in St. Petersburg. Her family was wealthy and it is difficult to know whether they sent her to one of the several local private schools for Jewish girls or brought tutors into their home. We do know that Kremer herself, even before encountering Socialist thought in the capital, began her path toward activism by offering to tutor the daughters of a poor acquaintance when she found out that the family could not afford to educate them.[21] Later she would join the Bund. Historians have noted the prominence of Jewish women in these

Studio portrait of young men and women, members of the Jewish Labor Bund, Grodno, 1905. (YIVO Institute for Jewish Research)

and other revolutionary movements, but it is not possible to demonstrate a direct link to primary education.[22]

What is easier to show is that graduates of private girls' schools often went on to further their education. In his fifteenth anniversary volume, Lazar Berman charted the achievements of students from both his and his wife's schools. Of the six hundred graduates by this time, Anna Berman had information for 161. Of these, 87 were listed simply as having pursued further education. An additional 12 finished gymnasia. Three attended the women's courses at the university, two were in the musical conservatory, two in theater schools, and one was studying outside the country. On top of these quite a few others were practicing professions that would have required further schooling, such as midwifery, medicine, feldshering, and teaching.[23] The numbers are truly impressive. The many educational opportunities in the capital city made it possible to pursue professional schooling in a way that was beyond the reach of most residents of the Pale.

Nonetheless, Jewish women were disproportionately likely to receive a secondary and higher education in the late Imperial period throughout the Pale. In 1886, Jewish women represented 8.11 percent of the girls attending Russian high schools.[24] At the time of the 1897 census, the only group of women with higher educational achievements were the Lutherans, who had their own highly developed school system in the Baltic regions of the empire.[25] Jews also figured prominently in the various experiments with higher education for women. Jews were the single largest minority group taking part in the women's higher courses and going abroad to study as well.[26] In 1879, Jewish women made up 33 percent of the student body in women's medical courses.[27] Almost 17 percent of the women enrolled in the St. Petersburg higher courses in 1885–86 were Jews.[28] Of the one hundred Russian women granted degrees outside of Russia, twenty were Jews.[29]

According to a rather hagiographic article written in 1880, shortly after her untimely death, Anna Gertsenshtein was the first Russian-Jewish woman to attend university abroad. The author, Nikolai Rubinshtein, states that before leaving Kherson in 1869 to attend university, Gertsenshtein was graduated from a Russian women's boarding school. Apparently her first formal schooling, however, had come at a private school for Jewish girls in Kherson.[30]

As of 1856, there were four private schools for Jewish girls in the New Russian city of Kherson.[31] Gertsenshtein might have attended any one of them given the solid foundation she received in the Russian language as well as instruction in her own religion. This primary education then allowed her to enter a Russian women's school and complete her secondary education before traveling to Europe for a university degree. Gertsenshtein may have been the first to take this path, but she was certainly not the last.

An easier path, and one that undoubtedly many more Jewish girls pursued, was to become educators themselves. Tsilia Shikman took the examination to become a teacher in a Jewish school after graduating from Shevel' Perel's school for Jewish girls in Vilna. As of 1869 she was teaching Russian and penmanship in a Jewish grammar school in Vilna.[32] Perel's daughter Flora, who also attended his school, later became a teacher of French and Russian there. After finishing the school's educational program, she went on to study at an elite Russian secondary institution in the same city.[33] One member of the 1861 graduating class of Khaim Funt's private Jewish girls' school in Minsk stayed on at the school to teach crafts.[34] Funt's daughter Maria attended the Minsk Women's Gymnasia after graduating from her father's school. In 1879 she replaced her father as the school's principal.[35]

Thus a small number of individuals who attended private Jewish girls' schools can be shown to have used their education to achieve even higher levels of education and a larger number to have devoted themselves to educating others. But while it is exciting to trace the links between the schools and famous and influential people, this can only be part of the story. Of the thousands of girls who spent time in private Jewish schools, most did not make names for themselves in politics or academics. Nonetheless, each went home to her parents and siblings, and later her husband and children, with her education.

Research in the field of anthropology over the past few decades has revealed some significant effects of schooling on human society that are difficult to quantify. Schools are institutions of acculturation. In the case of populations that are distant from the dominant culture due to geography or ethnicity, education also leads to interculturality. That is, children are in the position of navigating the juncture between their homes and the official state language and culture.[36] Concomitantly, literacy itself is a concrete step toward greater participation in the society at large.[37]

On the other hand, scholars have also stressed the importance of conceiving of multiple literacies. In a useful overview of this literature, Tamar El-Or points out that Enlightenment thinkers assumed that exposure to books would automatically lead all people to the same set of conclusions. In fact, the apprehension of literacy can neither be controlled nor predetermined.[38] This is noticeably true for groups new to the formal secular educational arena, such as women and Jews, and Jewish women in particular. David Vincent highlights this new heterogeneity by referring to new readers from the lower classes as "lifelong poachers."[39]

Phyllis Stock, in her history of women's education, has pointed out that one can tell a good deal about a society by how it educates its women. "With reference to women, it is necessary to discover the type of woman postulated as ideal in a particular period, in order to understand the education provided for her."[40] The opposite, however, is not true. The education that women or girls receive, and what they do with that education, does not necessarily reflect the goals of any particular authority structure. In reality, the distance between the regulations laid out by the government, the day-to-day practice within classrooms, and the knowledge and socialization absorbed by students can be enormous.

In essence, exposure to education provided these young women with a greater array of options. Although it is not possible to trace the life paths of the many thousands of students in private schools for Jewish girls, it is nonetheless clear that these young women experienced the effects of their education vis-à-vis their families and communities and Russian society as a whole. Their increased Russian literacy opened up the possibilities for greater participation in Russian culture and at the same time for changing Jewish society. This in turn led to some anxiety among other Russian Jews.

7

WHO CAN FIND A WOMAN OF VALOR?
Jewish Women's Education in Public Discourse

The wife, brought up in infernal terror, so to speak, sees in every more or less free act of the husband—a great transgression, from which will imminently follow horrible consequences. . . . This hostile attitude of the father toward the mother and of the husband toward the wife has a pernicious influence on the raising of children. The father, with all his might trying to give to the children some amount of decent instruction, must often give in to the tears and entreaties of his fanatical wife and her tribe, and in catering to their old-fashioned understanding must sacrifice the happiness of his children. —D. LAZAREV

As more Jewish men received a western education and became enlightened, the consequences of women's lack of access to these same opportunities became increasingly troubling. Here D. Lazarev used vibrant language to paint a picture of the Jewish family in chaos.[1] The Jewish woman, with only the rudiments of a practical religious education, is utterly unable to understand the moderately modern improvements made by her husband. She reacts by retreating into her faith and family, thereby harming her children and her marriage.

And Lazarev was not the only Jewish man to focus his criticism of the traditional system of education on its effects on the institution of marriage. M. G. Gershfel'd, writing for *Russkii evrei* in 1880, pointed out that women, much more than men, had "maintained an entire series of absurd prejudices and superstitions."[2] He went so far as to blame the high divorce rate among Jews on this particular imbalance.

In addition to decrying the outmoded educational status quo, writers for the progressive Jewish press in the final decades of the nineteenth century also noted some of the changes going on in Jewish communities and provided their visions for further improvements. This chapter traces the reception of the new private schools for Jewish girls among the liberal Jewish intelligentsia as well as among the increasingly vocal traditionalists.

Announcing the Schools

While writers argued over the nature of the educational ills perpetrated on Jewish women and how best to heal the resultant societal wounds, enterprising educators across the Pale of Settlement were actively changing the status quo by opening private schools for Jewish girls. As the new schools spread, writers for the Jewish press could hardly fail to notice them. Indeed, in local reports, the press celebrated the new schools.

A common feature of many of the Hebrew- and Russian-language Jewish periodicals of this era was a section providing news from around the Jewish world. In some cases correspondents living in St. Petersburg, Berlin, Paris, or other major Jewish communities provided regular updates. Other papers simply printed letters from individuals reporting from far and near. Reports from abroad included major international news, as well as news from within particular Jewish communities. Given the tenor of the papers, local reports often focused on the status of the *Haskalah* in a given community. It was in these letters that many new schools for Jewish girls were announced.

A thematically typical yet idiosyncratically written example came from Grodno to the Hebrew journal *Ha-Karmel* in 1866. The author opened with a somewhat messianic portrayal of the coming of the *Haskalah*:

> Through all the generations which have come and gone, and the innumerable ages through which the eternal people have passed, from generation to generation knowledge grows, from day to day wisdom [*haskel*] is multiplied, and at the passing of the generation the wisdom [*haskalah*] goes on, there will arise a new generation which will also invigorate and add strength, because there is no end of understanding, and no limits to knowledge. . . . How pleasant for the soul and sweet to see the light of the *Haskalah* arriving. And how dear to pronounce that it dawns also in the windows of our city.[3]

After describing the general improvement, the author went on to catalogue specific changes to support his claim, including the school for Jewish girls, in its eleventh year of existence. The author marveled at its success: "Who would not rejoice to see his young daughter of seven or eight years standing for exams in the Russian language, and would not express wonder when young girls would show their knowledge in other languages?"[4]

Likewise, a more straightforward report appeared in the Russian paper *Razsvet* from the city of Kaments-Podol'sk in 1860. The author, who signed himself simply with the Russian letter 'Ia,' devoted his letter to advances in education [*prosveshchenie*] in his place of residence. Accordingly, not only was the government Jewish school growing, but a new private school for Jewish girls had just opened. The school was off to such a good start that the curator of the Kiev educational circuit, N. I. Pirogov, had already visited and was very favorably impressed.[5]

These and other announcements for Jewish girls' schools in regional reports appear throughout the Hebrew- and Russian-language Jewish press, particularly during the 1860s and 1870s. The reports included a few details about the school—number of pupils, subjects of study, name of principal—and were almost always entirely positive. Even when local reports addressed faults with the schools, the blame was usually placed at the feet of larger societal concerns. A report filed from Ponevich in 1880 candidly stated that its school for Jewish girls was not on the highest level educationally. Nonetheless, the author praised the principal roundly for his efforts and decried the chronic poverty of the Jewish community, leading to its difficulties.[6] Likewise, a report from Berdichev rated local Jewish schools highly while blaming slow progress on local Hasidim.[7]

This generally optimistic view of Jewish women's education prevails in articles about specific schools as well. In the same vein as the local reports, writers would sometimes submit brief articles about specific institutions worthy of note for one reason or another. A few such pieces describe local private schools for Jewish girls. In 1860, nearly one year after a Mr. Dikker opened his private school for Jewish girls in Simferopol, I. Likub wrote in *Razsvet* about the successes of the school in that brief period. Likub expounded enthusiastically about the teachers and subjects and described significant local support. The only problem, according to him, was financial.[8]

After attending the public examination at Aron Frud's school in Berdichev in 1860, an author who signed himself "D.M." was left with an overall favorable impression, but with certain concerns. Chief among these was the power wielded by wealthy families. According to D.M., the school's financial situation was unstable enough to require the principal to cater to the vanity of the donor families at the expense of academic integrity: "Mr. Frid [*sic*] knows only too well the local so-called civilized society, not to perceive that the deprivation of a mediocre female pupil of her undeserved award threatens his passion with the loss of that pupil and the mortal animosity of her parents."[9] In the author's view, the result was that awards were given to almost every pupil and therefore lost their value. Even worse, the overall educational level had to be limited, so that even mediocre pupils could succeed. Nonetheless, D.M. praised the school's curriculum and the tireless efforts of Mr. Frud.

In local reports, whether devoted to all aspects of progress or to a particular school, the new private schools for girls provided evidence of the progress of the *Haskalah* in Russia. The schools were the antidote to the superstition and ignorance of the past. But at the same time that the new schools merited praise in these short and largely descriptive pieces, longer articles in the very same journals demonstrated an entirely different attitude toward private schools for Jewish girls.

Discussing the Schools

In a speech delivered at the twelfth anniversary celebration of his own school for Jewish girls, and later printed in *Sion*, Abram Bruk-Brezovskii attacked the other educational institutions for Jewish girls:

> In recent times *heders* and schools have begun to open also for girls, where they have been primarily taught elementary Hebrew reading and writing and occasionally also Russian grammar as well as some arithmetic. The principals of these schools lack all knowledge, except good Hebrew handwriting. These *melamdim,* or teachers, did not pay any attention to the development of the intellectual abilities of the female pupils, nor to their morality, nor to the teaching of the native country's language; there was no trace of teaching crafts. Calligraphy received all of the effort.[10]

By referring to the other schools and teachers with the traditional Hebrew terms *heder* and *melamed,* Bruk-Brezovskii meant to belittle their claim to reform and suggest that they were no better than the traditional schools. Yet, in mentioning their typical curricula, clearly far broader than a traditional *heder,* he betrays the modern aspirations of the schools, though he dismisses them as only concerned with penmanship.

L. Dreizen, a seminary-educated man serving as a private tutor in the city of Minsk, wrote to the Russian-language supplement in the Hebrew periodical *Ha-Karmel* about an incident he experienced. One of his private students in Russian and German asked why they were not studying the German Romantic writer Johann Christoph Schiller. She had recently left the third class of a local Jewish girls' school and was surprised not to be continuing with her reading of the works of Schiller. The thrust of his article was that educators should be paying more attention to teaching basics and appropriate works to Jewish girls. He was outraged that Schiller was being taught to girls who lacked both the linguistic skills and maturity to understand the work.[11]

Dreizen was not the only writer to express concern specifically about Jewish girls reading Schiller. Khaim Funt dismissed the popularity of Schiller's works as follows: "Previously only the rich educated their daughters, restricting, however, their education to the reading of Schiller and Goethe and a few elegant French phrases."[12] Lazarev also complained about the contrast between Jewish girls' enthusiasm over Schiller and their "utter ignorance."[13] The anxiety of these writers seems to have stemmed from a concern that the women were enjoying the romantic tales without grasping their deeper messages.

Another common complaint leveled at both schools and wealthy families who hired tutors for their daughters was the "useless" content of the education, in particular the effort devoted to learning French, as opposed to Russian or Hebrew. A. Zeidler went so far as to question whether such study was in fact educational training: "A girl, in order to gain for herself an advantageous match—her parents imagine—must speak French and play the pianoforte, just as she needs a luxurious wardrobe, diamonds, and so on. They draw this conclusion when the matchmaker comes to them with offers of marriage. And so, at fifteen, their daughters begin their education. But could education have a positive effect on a stubbornly ignorant heart, which only breathes with the passions of crude materialism?"[14] B. Ts-n, writing for *Razsvet* in 1860, blamed this misdirection of educational efforts on the mothers. They were so proud, in his view, to have their lovely French-speaking "mamselle" that they neglected to teach their daughters to be good mothers and housewives.[15]

A St. Petersburg correspondent for *Russkii evrei* ridiculed the results of the gendered expectations for education among wealthy religious Jews: "And these two systems coexisted in complete peace within the same family, sister dressed in the latest fashion, speaking several languages and playing piano, and brother in a long garment, with longer *payes,* not knowing how to write in even one language, not even ancient Hebrew."[16]

These writers were not contesting the existence of new educational initiatives for Jewish girls, but rather their worthiness. Was the ignorant and superstitious Jewish woman of the past to be replaced with the shallow and arrogant Jewish woman of the new era?

The Schools and Their Detractors

While some of the articles reflect a certain misogyny, or at least skepticism about the possibility of enlightened women, there are also the normal pangs of a community in flux. Education was changing all around. The *heder*, once the only educational option and vilified by the *maskilim*, was now one among a number of choices. Men and women, boys and girls had to find their way through a maze of educational options. Those who supported these changes wanted to see them occur more systematically, more completely. Instead there were fits and starts, successes and failures, steps forward and back.

Thus it was not only girls' schools that came under suspicion and reprimand in the progressive press. In St. Petersburg, outside the Pale of Settlement and thus outside the reach of the government Jewish school system, Lazar and Anna Berman's schools were attacked in the Russian-Jewish paper *Den'* in 1869. The correspondent, who signed himself M.S., claimed that the schools accepted major communal subsidies without the requisite communal oversight. In particular he was concerned that poor children were being turned away and that the level of education was low. He went so far as to call Lazar Berman's school "a gigantic *heder*."[17]

As the article goes on, however, it becomes clear that the author's complaints go beyond the particulars of the Berman schools to all Jewish schools. In fact, the author eventually states that all Jewish children should be in Russian schools, which prompts the editor to cut in with a strong caveat.

In the end, it would seem, attacking the Berman schools was a cover for a more radical critique of the practice of educating Jewish children. Although both Lazar Berman and a group of his students' parents would write into *Den'* supporting his schools and refuting his detractor,[18] Berman's schools could never have satisfied M.S. The fact that Berman accepted fifty students free of charge and that the school curricula and teaching methods were exemplary would not have changed his mind on the more fundamental issues of disagreement.

For many of the writers for the Jewish press, the new modern schools represented all the frustrations inherent in the process of social transformation. The schools were new and modern, but how could they possibly be new and modern enough? The writers wanted to create a whole new reality, but the schools around them were in no position to do that. Intellectuals and thinkers can work in the abstract and imagine ideal solutions. Educators have to work with present realities. This refers not only to the limitations of texts and teachers, but more fundamentally to the confines of the Jewish community. Communal norms required some conformity. A school that paid no respect to old forms, that sought to overthrow five thousand years of history overnight, would never survive.

In point of fact, the criticisms leveled against the new schools were often justified. The private schools for Jewish girls occupied a precarious position. On the one hand, their principals were well educated and committed to the modernization and Russification of the Jewish community. On the other hand, the schools operated within largely traditional communities and could not hope to survive if they antagonized their constituents.

As we have seen, not only did the schools rely on the good will of the community at large, but they counted on direct support from a variety of diverse groups. Private schools for Jewish girls throughout the Pale of Settlement could not hope to fill their enrollment and tuition needs exclusively from daughters of the wealthy and enlightened members of their communities. They had to appeal to a broader market of families who sought literacy in Russian and a Jewish education for their daughters, without the trappings of modernity. Both the moderate nature of the Judaic studies curricula and the sliding-scale tuition options provide evidence of this need to attract students broadly. Serving the needs of the daughters of the poor as well as the wealthy, the progressive as well as the traditional, required careful compromise.

That such schools would not entirely satisfy the most progressive elements of the Russian Jewish community is hardly surprising. Between their chronic lack of funds and the unique role these schools served in their communities, radical educational experiments were out of the question. What is surprising is the emotional and exaggerated rhetoric of many of the schools' detractors. Even if the new schools were not overly ambitious ideologically, surely they were a great improvement over the past and worthy of some praise.

Indeed, they did receive praise in the local reports and announcements. For the writers and readers of the Jewish press in Russia, new modern educational institutions were manifestations of the improvements taking place. Each new school was a step forward. Yet the level of disdain evinced for the new schools in the articles about women's education shows more complex sentiment. The schools were bringing change, but it was not progressing fast enough, and many of the authors expressed concern about what the future would look like.

Who Can Find a Woman of Valor?

As the educational norms and options for Jewish girls continued to expand, the anxiety over the status of Jewish women spread to the traditional community as well. Whereas at the beginning of this chapter we saw progressive men concerned that they would not be able to find appropriate wives, by the turn of the century it was the traditionalists who bemoaned the lack of proper helpmates.

In a 1901 work dedicated to preserving the memory of East European Jewish religious life in the face of changing circumstances, Tsevi Hirsh Lifshits contrasted the Jewish woman of old and her modesty with contemporary Jewish women and their focus on appearance. He suggested that even in Orthodox families more attention had to be given to training modest daughters and wives.[19]

At about this time, Rabbi Isaac Reines, a Russian rabbi deeply committed to preserving the traditional way of life in changed circumstances, was working to create a new kind of *yeshiva*. Rabbi Reines planned, and eventually succeeded in opening, a *yeshiva* where Russian, Hebrew, and other secular subjects would be taught along with the Talmud. The major purpose of offering secular subjects was to give traditionally trained rabbis the academic skills to supplant state rabbis, thereby doing away with the pernicious dual-rabbinate.[20] A secondary reason was to save the institution of marriage. Rabbi Reines recognized that Jewish women trained in European languages and manners would not want to marry Jewish men trained only in Talmud.[21] Similar concerns would later help to motivate the Bais Yaakov movement in Independent Poland.[22]

By the end of the nineteenth century, both traditionalists and progressives recognized the changed circumstances in Jewish women's education. Modern, formal, and Russian education was rapidly becoming the norm for Jewish women, and Jewish men of a variety of ideological stripes had to come to terms with the new reality.

8

NEW BIRDS, NEW WINGS
Educational Developments in the Jewish Community

Writing after the cataclysm of the Second World War, in an effort to memorialize the recent past, a native of Horodets (Grodno province) chose to describe girls' education in his city of origin not as static traditionalism, but as a dynamic process. Girls, he said, had once learned only to read Yiddish and to pray, but times had changed: "Apparently, the above-mentioned curriculum didn't satisfy the younger generation. *New birds, new wings.* When the demand that girls be taught how to write addresses in Russian became widespread, a man who was a bit more modern and knew a little Russian was needed." Soon, however, even this was not enough: "Yet the march of progress continued; new winds began to blow, and they found their way to Horodets as well. No longer were the girls satisfied with just an address in Russian and the Yiddish alphabet; they wanted to be able to read books in Russian, and some of them wanted to learn the holy tongue as well."[1]

Indeed, just as new developments inside and outside the Jewish community led to the creation and spread of private schools for Jewish girls, further transformation would lead to the schools changing over time, and eventually giving way to other educational institutions. This chapter traces some of these changes and shows that the private schools for Jewish girls held a unique niche in the Jewish community and that they actively contributed to developments around them.

In particular, the private Jewish girls' schools provided a forum for educational experimentation that enabled later developments in educating the poor, reforming the *heder,* and expanding educational opportunities for Jewish children. The turn-of-the-century schools that employed these innovations have often been viewed as radical and representing a break with the past. This chapter shows that they sprouted from the fertile soil provided by their predecessors.

Educating the Poor

The first private schools for Jewish girls were designed for daughters of the wealthy and middle classes. Yet, as it became clear that Jews from across the socioeconomic spectrum wished to educate their daughters, principals adapted in both practical and pedagogical ways. Practically speaking, some schools increased fees for services demanded by the wealthy while decreasing fees for standard educational services. Others simply accepted a set number of students free of charge. In pedagogic terms, educators expanded their curricula to include more academic offerings. Obviously principals of private schools needed robust enrollment as evidence of success for both the community and the authorities, and many highlighted their rising enrollment figures when corresponding with the MNP regarding yearly stipends. Encouraging poorer students was not only a matter of financial self-interest, however, and many educators devoted themselves to teaching out of a combination of practical and ideological goals. Some of the founding principals wrote with great passion of their commitment to raising the level of enlightenment in the Jewish population. For such individuals, economic standing was immaterial.

In addition to the self-serving and ideological reasons for encouraging broader enrollment, there were altruistic motivations. In Russia as a whole, the era of the Great Reforms opened up the public discussion of societal problems. Whereas the education of the peasantry had been largely ignored under previous administrations, Tsar Alexander II's 1864 statutes on education and the *zemstra* local self-government led to direct results in the countryside.[2] The necessity and content of education for the masses became issues of public discourse. For Jews also, there was a growing awareness of the plight of the poor. Educators like Iosef and Anna Khones, who opened a private school for Jewish girls in Kherson in 1854, were proud to state that six of their thirty-six slots were to be set aside for those unable to pay tuition.[3] An 1856 letter submitted in support of Markus and Anna Gurovich's school for Jewish girls in Odessa made specific mention of their generosity in accepting poor pupils.[4]

In some locales, what began as inclusion of poor girls in the educational process led to schools specifically for needy Jewish girls. David Shtern opened his school for poor Jewish girls in Mogilev (Podolin province) in 1858.[5] In the case of the Bermans in St. Petersburg, it was the local magnates who brought in Lazar to open and oversee a school for poor Jewish boys in 1865. It would seem that these communal-minded and wealthy individuals were not satisfied that the education poor Jewish boys could get in a *heder* in the capital would prepare them for the future. Because the government Jewish school system did not operate in St. Petersburg, they recruited a successful government Jewish school teacher to create a school where students would receive instruction both in the Russian language and in a modern approach to Judaism. In 1866 Anna Berman convinced them to support a similar school for the underclass Jewish girls of the city.[6]

Impoverished Jewish boys had viable options for schooling, whereas educational opportunities for their sisters were severely limited. Most Jewish communities sponsored at least one *talmud torah*. The *talmud torah* offered a free religious education to orphans and other needy boys. In addition, in those locales where state Jewish schools existed, tuition was free and the children of the poor were often encouraged to attend. In fact, it has been suggested that many communities filled their attendance quotas by forcing poor families to enroll their sons.[7]

The author of an 1860 article in *Razsvet* proposed opening government Jewish schools to meet the needs of girls from poor families.[8] Writing the following year in *Sion,* Abram Bruk-Brezovskii lamented the reality that some people believed education was wasted on poor girls.[9] In 1862 the overseer of the Odessa government school for Jewish girls, as we saw above, became so irate about the funding disparities between boys and girls that he himself went out and raised private funds to purchase winter clothes for his students.[10]

By the 1860s many of the educators involved in teaching Jewish girls had recognized both the importance and the potential of integrating girls from impoverished families, and by that time almost all the plans for new schools for Jewish girls included provisions for the poor. Yet a discussion of the particular educational needs of those students was slow in coming.

As we saw in chapter 5, modern private Jewish schools for girls began to focus more on crafts, and the reasons were at least partly in response to the new face of the student body. While the purpose of the schools shifted from serving the wealthy to serving the community-at-large, educators began to envision training in crafts less as decoration and more as marketable skills. This should also be understood in the context of both the ongoing maskilic ideal of the "productivization" of the Jews as well as the growing interest in vocational education in Russia and abroad.

The effects of the Industrial Revolution in Europe, most notably urbanization, as well as both mass immigration and the end of slavery in America, led to new conceptions of the purpose of education in many Western countries. That the discussions of professional and trade schools often had racial and class-based biases cannot be denied; nonetheless, very real economic and practical concerns were also involved. Both progressive social reformers and governments made efforts to steer the poor, new immigrant groups, and racial minorities into educational programs that would provide them with steady and stable work at what was considered to be their proper societal position.[11] Russia, with its rapidly expanding educational programs and enormous pool of newly emancipated unskilled laborers, also took an active role in these discussions and experiments.

In addition to questions of audience, educational reformers in Russia and abroad also discussed both what should be taught and by what methods. At the 1876 World Fair in Philadelphia, Russia unveiled what would become known as the "Russian System," an innovative and experiential method of teaching practical skills in the school setting.[12] Thus both the growing popularity of handicrafts and the development of trade schools within the Russian Jewish community were part of a larger phenomenon.

Around 1869 several prominent Odessa Jewish women began to petition the local authorities for permission to establish a society to promote professional and elementary education among poor Jewish girls. Although they did not receive official permission until 1872, they had already begun to disseminate their ideas and work toward their goal.[13] In 1871 the Russian-language Jewish periodical *Den'* printed the text of a speech delivered by a Ms. Saker, at a conference sponsored by the as yet unofficial society. The Saker quoted is undoubtedly Maria Saker, a participant in the Odessa Jewish literary circle and a writer in her own right.[14]

In her speech Saker proceeded, with both logic and passion, to point out that Jewish men had always had the advantage in all spheres of education. Even though women had been active in the marketplace, they had not received the requisite education. Even though poverty knows no gender, only poor Jewish boys were provided with educational opportunities: "Therefore it is upon us women ourselves, knowing the helpless position of our fellows, and with the responsibility to help them get out of this sad situation, in which they are held ignorant and destitute. . . . We must with great strength assist in giving intellectual and moral standards to the destitute classes by means of proper education of future mothers." The society aimed to create free schools for poor Jewish girls to study both basic general education and useful trades.[15]

The first school to emerge from this effort was that of the woman A. A. Segal in 1881. With the help of funding from dedicated donors and some volunteer teachers, the school had 168 pupils, 108 of them attending free of charge, by 1896. The curriculum included Russian, mathematics, history, geography, Jewish religion, and Hebrew, in addition to general handicrafts and advanced study in the needle trades.[16] Three more professional schools for Jewish girls opened in Odessa in 1887, 1891, and 1893. Although their funding came from different sources, they all received significant support from various sectors of the Jewish community. Other needs were filled with tax monies, the tuition of a few of the more well-off pupils, and the proceeds from selling the students' wares.[17]

Already at the end of the 1860s in Odessa—a community with many more modern Jewish schools than almost any other, and with a more materially focused and materially successful Jewish populace—a group of comfortably situated Jewish women realized the need to provide Jewish girls of the lower classes with not only literacy but also access to trades. The school they opened in 1881 quickly led to the formation of other schools under similar auspices. By the end of the 1890s more than 500 girls studied in four communally funded professional schools for Jewish girls in Odessa.[18] Other Jewish communities responded more slowly to the same set of needs.

Saker was probably not aware of a similar initiative in the Lithuanian city of Kovno, where a society of Jewish women had taken it upon themselves to care for their less well-off sisters. The Society for the Union of Women provided poor Jewish girls with stipends to attend educational institutions. According to an article in the Hebrew journal *Ha-Magid,* as of 1872 eighteen Jewish women were taking advantage of the largesse of the society. The author of the article, Avraham Tsukerman, was pleased that thirteen of them were studying crafts; however, he was quite disturbed that the five others were being supported to study in gymnasia, thus placing them outside their accustomed class and place in society.[19]

An 1880 correspondent to *Russkii evrei* mentioned the same society in a brief piece on educational opportunities for Jewish girls in Kovno. According to this author, the society had been founded by wealthy women seven or eight years previously, and its membership, financial holdings, and influence had continued to grow.[20]

And it was not only these two groups of wealthy benefactors in Kovno and Odessa who believed that impoverished Jewish girls had special needs. An anonymous correspondent to *Russkii evrei* in 1884 supported the cause of providing Jewish girls with professional training on purely economic grounds: Jewish women often serve as the breadwinners in their family, and thus the Jewish community should support teaching them marketable skills.[21]

Another *Russkii evrei* correspondent presented a longer and more complex argument in 1880. In the past no Jewish women had been educated, according to the author. Then the wealthy began to provide their daughters with a somewhat weak but nonetheless useful education. Now only the poor women are left behind, and it is up to the better off to start philanthropic societies to support them in gaining a rudimentary education.[22]

And indeed such schools were opened, albeit not in a systematic fashion. Bit by bit across the lands of Jewish settlement, trade schools for Jewish girls came into existence, often with communal funding. By the time the OPE's guidebook for Jewish educators was published in 1901, there were fourteen such institutions in eleven Jewish communities.[23] Table 8.1 shows the courses offered in the school in Simferopol. As is clear from the number of hours, the highest-level class was truly akin to an apprenticeship offering intensive vocational training.

Parallel to the trade schools, new organizations emerged to support them financially and otherwise. Certainly the OPE made available subsidies to support trade schools as well as other Jewish schools. In 1904 the group even held a conference to highlight the topic of professional education for Jews.[24] Although the OPE continued to fund a wide variety of educational endeavors for Jews, the conference suggests the degree to which an awareness of the import of teaching trades to Jews was growing. Organizations committed specifically to this goal also emerged in this period.

In 1880 a number of St. Petersburg Jews associated with the OPE founded a provisional committee that would eventually become the Society for Trade and Agricultural Labor among the Jews of Russia (*Obshchestvo remeslennago i zemledel'cheskago truda sredi evreev v Rossii*, ORT). In addition to working to have a greater number of Jewish craftsmen admitted to

Table 8.1. Courses Offered in A. M. Kagan's
Free Professional School for Jewish Girls in Simferopol

Subject	I	II	III	IV	Master
Russian	12	8	8	10	4
Hebrew	6	6	6	6	3
Handicrafts and Sewing	5	5	10	18	36
Practicum	–	2	2	2	2
Jewish history	–	2	2	2	1

Source: Spravochnaia kniga, 383.

the interior Russian provinces, the new society raised funds to support related educational endeavors.[25] In its first decade of existence ORT disbursed over 30,000 rubles to vocational schools, programs, and students.[26] In 1910 the society, already well established, sent out two fact-finding missions, one to examine the trade education being offered to Jewish boys in elementary schools and the other to examine craft education for Jewish girls in elementary schools. In that same year, out of a budget of over 10,000 rubles for trade schools and courses, 789.50 rubles went to girls' schools.[27]

In Odessa, the society mentioned above joined *Trud* or labor, which had similar goals for the Jewish population as a whole.[28] By the turn of the century, professional education was a major topic of discussion in the Jewish community. Articles about the import of providing youth from the lower classes with concrete skills appeared in all the periodicals and in particular in the new journal *Evreiskaia shkola,* devoted to the topic of Jewish education. In 1905 *Evreiskaia shkola* included a beautifully rendered and calligraphed pullout map of the Pale of Settlement, showing all professional schools for Jews.[29] The Jewish Colonization Association (ICA) made teaching the trades one of its main forms of activity in tsarist Russia.[30] There can be no question that Jewish education for the poor had been transformed.

In the following excerpt, Pauline Wengeroff depicts the pride and joy experienced by wealthy donors in helping their less well-off coreligionists. Both Wengeroff and her husband reconnected with their Judaism through philanthropy. Here she describes a public examination in the trade school for Jewish girls that she helped to found in Minsk:

> This was another beautiful day in my life. The girls, who just a short time ago had been poor, miserable, wild children, stood in the festively decorated exhibit room. They were clean and healthy, and surrounded by the leaders of the city, who examined and praised their work.
>
> Our school gave the poor and neglected the possibility to earn their bread in an honorable and efficient way and gave them health, freshness of youth and, above all, human rights. Maybe some time soon the day will come again when Jewish *bal meloches* [working people] will stand on the same rung of society as the learned. In talmudic times many of the *tana'im* and *amora'im*, like Rabbi Yochanan the bootmaker or Rabbi Hillel the woodcutter, delivered lectures even though they worked with their hands. With tears in my eyes I watched our Jewish

children. A quiet joy filled me, for I knew at that moment that
God had blessed our effort.[31]

But to what degree was this a gendered phenomenon? Most of the journalistic work at the turn of the century dealt with the need to provide all Jews
from the poor classes with viable skills and trades. In terms of literary output,
it was recognized that the need encompassed both boys and girls. In reality,
of course, boys and girls were treated differentially. Outside the relatively
small organizations that had been formed expressly to serve poor Jewish girls,
most of the funding agencies and individuals favored boys.

Nonetheless, certain circumstances led to a greater focus on the needs of
girls than might be expected. Jewish communities already had educational
institutions serving boys from poor families, the ubiquitous *talmud torah*.
However, the spread of Jewish educational institutions for girls, let alone
those specifically for the lower class, was far slower. On the ground, poor
Jewish boys had some opportunities, whereas poor Jewish girls, despite the
slow and steady spread of private schools for Jewish girls, quite often had no
viable educational options.

As a result, local educators and philanthropies had to decide how best to
apportion their monies based on gendered expectations and needs. For example, in Orsha (Mogilev province) the local *talmud torah* added a women's
branch, devoted to teaching Jewish girls literacy, religion, and sewing. It does
not appear that the boys' section offered instruction in trades. The girls,
however, had one hour per day of handiwork, and after 1902, at the request
of the ICA (which provided funding for the school), even more.[32] In this
case the need to provide poor Jewish girls with an education in the trades
was greater than the need to spread professional education evenly among
the population. That this was not an isolated phenomenon finds support in
1904 statistics published by the ICA. At that time, there were in the Pale of
Settlement forty-five schools for Jewish girls devoted either primarily to the
trades or with a section for this purpose. There were forty such schools for
boys.[33]

An additional, if muted, goal in educating poor Jewish girls in the trades
may have been to help them avoid other less savory professional avenues.
By the end of the nineteenth century the ills of prostitution had become a
topic of public concern in Russia. Although prostitution had always existed,
the combined factors of mass urbanization, poverty, and limited economic
opportunities for women had greatly increased the number and visibility of
prostitutes. Efforts to address this growing problem became one outlet for
socially active upper-class Russian women.[34] It would not be surprising if

the potential dangers of prostitution also served to motivate Jewish men and women to provide Jewish girls with safe and secure professions.[35]

The desire to teach Jewish children, male or female, a useful trade emerged both from an assessment of the very real needs of the Jewish poor and from the influential maskilic critique of the Jewish community. One of the central tenets of the maskilic philosophy had been a "normalization" of the Jews. In order for Jews to gain parity with the surrounding societies, they would have to transform themselves. Leaving so-called "parasitic" professions and adopting productive ones was to be part of this greater transformation. The *maskilim* wanted to replace the many scholars and traders with farmers and craftsmen, thereby creating a Jewish polity more closely resembling Russian society, if not the needs of the new era.

Despite the fact that the later Jewish ideologies rejected much of the maskilic project, they were also very much its intellectual heirs. Thus, although the unquestioning faith in the secular state was discredited, later thinkers were very much concerned with changing the Jewish occupational structure. The Jewish Labor Bund, despite its intellectual roots, saw itself as a movement of the workers and was deeply committed to creating a broad Jewish working proletariat. A good deal of its efforts were devoted, on the one hand, to training Jews to hold productive positions and, on the other, to providing workers with continuing educational opportunities. The Zionists were similarly devoted to creating a vanguard of Jews ready to build and feed the new Jewish settlements in the Land of Israel. Both groups would come to embrace and sponsor practical educational endeavors among the Jews. Although the schools they created differed in language of instruction and ideological content, they agreed on providing poor Jewish boys and girls with trades.

What began as a desire to include the daughters of the poor in the Jewish educational system became, over the course of the second half of the nineteenth century, an active and at times politicized movement for trade schools for Jewish children. No doubt many poor girls benefited both personally and professionally from the years of primary education they received for free in private Jewish girls' schools. But a growing awareness of the plight of the poor, coupled with the development of new institutions committed to modern solutions to Jewish communal problems, meant a growing recognition that this was not enough. Gradually, beginning in the late 1850s and early 1860s, schools were developed that catered specifically to the needs of poor Jewish girls. These schools combined basic literacy and numeracy with skills in a variety of trades. By the 1890s both the trade schools for girls themselves and the ongoing need for others were frequent topics of debate in the Russian Jewish community. After the turn of the century, groups committed to a political solution to the Jewish situation increasingly opened and adapted such schools.

Although as many as two Jewish trade schools may have existed before the 1844 statute on Jewish schools, once the new government-sponsored schools were in place, the time for expanding vocational education for Jewish boys had passed.[36] For the next several decades Jewish boys attended either *hadarim* or state Jewish schools and had no access to school-based professional training. During these same years, however, both the function and amount of training in crafts changed dramatically within the private schools for Jewish girls. The experience garnered in teaching trades in the school setting would undoubtedly benefit the growing number of educators interested in this area after 1873. Thus the advancement of trade schools in the Jewish community, certainly influenced by general societal trends, was enabled by the private schools for Jewish girls.

Reforming the Heder

In addition to vocational education, one of the major educational advances at the turn of the century among Russian Jewry was the *heder metukan*. The *heder metukan*, or improved or reformed *heder*, was an outgrowth of the early Russian Zionists, who embraced using Hebrew. In seeking to create educational institutions where Hebrew could be taught according to new pedagogic theory and as a living language, they hit upon a novel idea. Local competition made it difficult to open and maintain a *heder*, but teaching jobs at the *talmud torahs* for poor Jewish boys were low enough in status to be widely available. By taking up teaching positions in *talmud torahs*, these lovers of Zion were able to gain a foothold in communities across the Pale.

Beginning in the 1880s, and growing in popularity in the following decades, such institutions spread throughout the areas of Jewish settlement. In addition to a focus on the Hebrew language, the *heder metukan* offered a serious course in Jewish history, often centered around the Land of Israel, and some general subjects. The new schools were also committed to hygiene, especially airy spaces, new methods of classroom management, new conceptions of child development, and often co-education. Because of both their modern ideas about education and their interest in spreading their Zionist message as widely as possible, teachers in the *heder metukan* tried to open their schools to girls as well as boys.[37]

As with vocational schools, these new schools developed out of a complex series of circumstances. Much about these institutions was entirely innovative and catered to the exigencies of the day. However, at the same time a great deal of the new structure was built on earlier foundations. Here again, some of the necessary factors grew out of the experience of private schools for Jewish girls.

First among these was certainly the advancement in Hebrew teaching techniques. Whereas the state Jewish schools had set curricula and textbooks, and *hadarim* did not teach Hebrew as a language, private girls' schools offered the ideal laboratory for Hebrew instruction. As we saw in chapter 5, in the early years some of the schools did not offer Hebrew, preferring to focus on ethical components of Judaism or even Yiddish. By the 1850s most Jewish girls' schools included Hebrew in their curricula, but only a minority taught comprehension as opposed to only decoding skills.

Within the next decade most of the private Jewish girls' schools would embrace instruction in Hebrew as a language. In order to do so they had to experiment with textbooks and techniques. After the end of the state Jewish school system in the mid-1870s, private schools for Jewish boys could draw on this experience in formulating their own educational programs. And when the precursors of the modern political Zionist movement began to move into education, they in turn could draw upon the combined experience of several decades of teaching Hebrew in Russian Jewish schools.

In addition to their contribution in the realm of Hebrew instruction, the experience of private schools for Jewish girls in the Jewish community also helped to bring about increased comfort with co-educational settings. Based on the memoir literature, the phenomenon of girls attending a traditional boys' *heder* was not unknown in the latter half of the nineteenth century.[38] However, it appears that such situations were circumstantial rather than designed. *Hadarim* were essentially for boys, but on occasion, due to the request of a particular family, girls attended. To quote the memoir of Sheyna Korngold, for example, the *melamed* to whom she was sent taught "boys and also three or four girls."[39] Additionally, several of the girls who went to *heder* with boys specifically mention a point at which they were no longer welcome. Whether formally or informally decided and enforced, girls were usually not allowed in second-level *hadarim,* those where Mishna was taught. Nonetheless, it emerges that the Jewish community did not enforce a strict ban on mixed educational settings, although the norm was certainly to separate the sexes.

This norm existed in both the state and private educational spheres. Thus when the government Jewish school system was created, the question was whether a parallel system for girls should also be opened, not whether girls would be pupils in the schools. Inspection records of the private girls' school also offer evidence that girls and boys were to be kept separate.[40] When a group of Jewish educators wished to open a school in Grodno in 1852, they highlighted the importance of having a school for Jewish girls and sought the appropriate permissions. They also noted that some local boys might be attracted to the curriculum and that they would be interested in teaching boys as well. However, the application made it entirely clear that boys would be taught separately, if at all.[41]

It is evident from chapter 3 that many of the educators who opened private schools for Jewish girls did so in response to legal and social circumstances rather than out of deeply held conviction. State rabbis and Jewish school teachers responded to demand for their services as tutors by establishing formal schools. Some Jewish men only turned to teaching girls when their paths to teaching boys had been blocked. But whatever their initial motivations, along the way these educators learned that Jewish boys and girls had the same abilities and appetites. They became accustomed to the import of educating girls as well as boys. They, as well as the girls themselves, also helped to spread these ideas into Russian Jewish society.

Once the 1873 ruling had reopened the possibility of private schools for Jewish boys, quite a few educators opted for co-education instead. In 1879 such a mixed school opened in the town of Vishtynets (Kovno province).[42] Although the author of the article announcing the new school did not specify reasons for the school's co-educational status, it clearly fit into his or her view of the enlightenment of the Jews:

Students and teachers in front of *heder metukan,* Virbalis, 1900. (YIVO Institute for Jewish Research)

> The spirit of the *Haskalah* blows across the land, dispelling the smoke. Every man who loves knowledge and awe will rejoice as all the land is filled with knowledge. Boys and girls go together like in the dance in the camp to schools in every large and small hamlet of Jews in our homeland. Their parents rejoice and sing finding general knowledge [*torat ha-adam*] in their hearts. In these days the sun rises also on small cities distant from men of the city.

For this author, at least, equal opportunity for boys and girls was part of the *Haskalah* vision.

The private schools for Jewish girls offered educators both a forum for experimenting with Hebrew education and an educational setting in which to interact with girls. As other historical circumstances combined to usher in the *heder metukan,* a new generation of educators would build on several of the innovations developed in part or entirely within the older girls' schools.

Expanding Opportunities

One of the stated goals of both the Russian *Haskalah* and the Russian government was the gradual merging of the Russian and Jewish peoples. The path to achieving this goal was far more contested. As early as 1804, Jews were granted admission to Russian educational institutions. The 1844 legislation was a recognition that permission was not sufficient. Jews had to be coerced into learning Russian and interacting with the larger community. Linguistic acculturation would be the first step, and the legislation required Russian to be taught not only in the new schools but in the vast network of *hadarim* as well.

Nonetheless, it is noteworthy that the new schools did not offer Jewish boys an opportunity to interact with their non-Jewish peers. Although some portion of the faculty was Christian, and there was certainly a desire that the students would use their new skills and knowledge to attend more advanced educational institutions, the schools themselves were entirely within the Jewish sphere. How, then, was the much vaunted merging to take place? In fact, I would suggest that as with many aspects of the proposed transformation of the Jews, there was profound ambivalence on both sides and the details were left entirely to chance.

The result was that the mingling of Jewish and non-Jewish students developed over time and without either planning or oversight. Private schools for Jewish girls were important in a number of aspects to this gradual merging. First of all, like the government schools for Jewish boys, they offered Jewish children literacy and fluency in the Russian language. This facilitated the increase in Jewish attendance at non-Jewish institutions in the latter decades of the nineteenth century. Additionally, as in the cases above, private Jewish girls' schools offered a unique setting for experimentation when there was no parallel setting for Jewish boys.

The organic development of mixed-religion schools is well illustrated by the situation in Kovno. In 1856 the local girls' school offered a separate room for educating Jewish girls apart from non-Jews. Reflecting perhaps some discomfort with educating their daughters under the auspices of gentiles but not with intermingling among them, in 1860 some local Jews sought permission to open and run a mixed-religion school. Their request was rejected on the grounds that it was preferable to have Jews educated by Christians. By 1866 the Jews of Kovno were so ready to acquiesce to educating their daughters in non-Jewish institutions that the mixed school was more than 80 percent Jewish.[43] Both the local Jewish and Christian population, as well as even the school governance apparatus, seem to have come a long way over the course of almost a decade of modern education.

In 1865, after running a school for Jewish girls in Kherson for more than ten years—during most of which his institution was in competition with another local school for Jewish girls—Iosef Khones, the former government Jewish school teacher, closed his school and immediately opened a mixed-religion school for girls. Soon after getting it started, he wrote the Ministry of Education requesting that his former yearly subsidy of 600 rubles from the candle tax be applied to his new school. Of the 120 girls in his new school, 60 were Jewish. The ministry's office in Odessa was supportive of Khones's request.[44] The file does not contain Khones's own letter of request, and the Odessa overseer's is fairly brief. Thus we cannot know how Khones argued in favor of a mixed school. The fact that he was able to fill it so quickly suggests that there were few other opportunities for local non-Jewish girls. Perhaps the presence of a second school for Jewish girls made expansion impossible without relying on another population of girls. In any case, even if Khones had no strong ideological motivation but simply wanted to make his school larger, it is noteworthy that he was able to enroll such a large number of students in a religiously mixed educational setting.

Even more striking than the growth of schools where Jewish and Christian youth were taught together by design was the phenomenal growth in the number of Jewish children attending non-Jewish educational institutions. Whereas in 1841 fewer than 1,000 Jews had attended non-Jewish schools, by 1886 the number was up to 35,073.[45] This number represented nearly eleven percent of the school population, up from slightly over one percent in 1853.[46] Of course, these figures can only be understood in the context of the enormous growth of interest in modern education in the Jewish community and the expansion of education in the Russian empire. Nonetheless, it is significant that families were increasingly convinced by the benefits of education to send their sons and daughters not only to mixed educational institutions but more and more to non-Jewish ones.

That there was a contemporary awareness of this situation can be seen in two separate initiatives. First, Jews were asking for and receiving money to attend non-Jewish schools at all levels; and second, non-Jewish institutions were asking for and receiving money to educate Jews. Beginning already in the early 1860s, Jews in Odessa began requesting candle tax funds to send their children, male and female, to local pro-gymnasia and gymnasia. Here were families who wished to reap the benefits of merging with the surrounding population, who wanted to send their children to non-Jewish schools, but could not afford to do so. Finally, after a decade of correspondence, a number of subsidized slots were made available to Jewish students at certain local institutions.[47] Given the stated enthusiasm of the local and national government for educating Jews into Russian culture, it is telling that such a request took ten years to grant. Although a certain amount of the onus can be placed on bureaucratic incompetence, it is also clear that there was no articulated governmental policy on how to achieve the goal of acculturating the Jews, and thus each step came about slowly.

The Odessa Jews had originally asked for candle tax funds to spend on their children's education, but in the end the money was sent directly to the schools, to be spent on educating poor Jewish children. When a school in the nearby village of Kirch requested candle tax funds to support educating poor Jewish girls in 1864, its request was granted in a matter of months. The school was the only one in town catering to the poor, and nearly one-third of the students in its afternoon classes for girls were Jewish.[48] It is probably not coincidental that a request from a non-Jewish educator teaching Jewish girls was treated differently from a request directly from Jewish families seeking access to education.

Within the Jewish community, one of the early and ongoing activities of the Society for the Promotion of Enlightenment among the Jews of Russia was providing stipends for individual Jewish students. The records of the OPE can be viewed in detail in the archives but are also available in condensed versions in various published sources.[49] Perusing any of these reveals that a large number of Russian-Jewish university students studying in Russia as well as elsewhere in Europe were supported by the OPE. A smaller number of secondary students relied upon the funds as well. Of these groups, the majority was made up of male students, but female students were a significant minority.

By the 1870s, not only were both the MNP and the OPE providing money for Jews to attend non-Jewish schools, albeit in an ad hoc manner, but there was even an effort to increase the academic Jewish content in such schools. In December 1866 the ministry received a fascinating document from the Jewish community of Ekaterinoslav. In the letter, followed by numerous signatures of prominent local Jews, the authors stated that there were two local high-quality secondary educational institutions for girls. Twenty-five Jewish girls attended the more elite school and fifty the second school. However, these Jewish girls were being denied a fitting moral and religious education because they could not attend the religion courses on Christianity and had no equivalent courses of their own. The authors therefore suggested that two local teachers in government Jewish schools be hired, using candle tax funds, to teach the Jewish religion in the local girls high schools. Their request was granted and others followed suit.[50]

Beginning in the 1860s, we see the parallel growth of schools created expressly for Jewish and Christian children to study together and, more dramatically, of the number of Jewish children studying in non-Jewish schools. In terms of the schools designed to serve Jews and Christians together, all were for girls and most were connected in some way to the local private school for Jewish girls. Here again these fairly unencumbered institutions offered the only space for trying out new ideas. The entry of Jewish children into Russian schools required knowledge of the language of the land. Although more boys than girls took up positions in Russian schools, the number of Jewish girls was quite significant. The most likely setting for Jewish girls to have gained the necessary Russian skills to enter general schools was in the private schools for Jewish girls.

The End of the Beginning

The present study focuses on the theory and practice of education for Jewish girls, with special attention to private schools for Jewish girls during the second half of the nineteenth century. As described above, the first such school opened in 1831, but they began to appear at a rapid pace only after 1844. Educators continued to open private schools for Jewish girls in Russia well into the twentieth century. Nonetheless, this study takes into account primarily schools opened before 1881.

This is not because of any one specific event. I am not suggesting that the nature of schools for Jews in the tsarist empire changed overnight. Rather, the confluence of events led to profound rethinking. Historians have described how the pogroms, the legal backlash against Jews, and the perceived abandonment by the Russian liberal intelligentsia caused many Jews to explore new solutions to the difficulties of Jewish life in Russia from the mid-1880s.

The most important proponent of this position was undoubtedly Shimon Dubnow, considered the father of Russian Jewish historiography. Dubnow, who both lived through the period in question and wrote about it, presented 1881 as a major turning point.[51] More recently, scholars have called into question this strict periodization, pointing out, for example, that transformations associated with 1881 actually began earlier and even questioning the importance of some of the supposed turning points.[52]

While it is certainly true that strict periodization can obscure subtle changes and overdramatize more major changes, this need not lead to its abandonment. Jewish schooling began to change dramatically in the 1880s. Whereas in the past, various educators committed to the *Haskalah* or to a more vague goal of Russification had painstakingly experimented with modifications to the traditional *heder* curriculum or offered Jewish girls a primary education that was modern in certain aspects yet acceptable to traditionalists, they did so with a commitment to gradual change. By the late 1880s the idea of radical transformation became possible.

This contention is corroborated by Steven G. Rappaport's "Jewish Education and Jewish Culture in the Russian Empire, 1880–1914." In the introduction Rappaport explains his decision to begin his study in the year 1880, "because after decades of slow and sporadic development, this date marked a rapid increase in the establishment of reformed Jewish schools."[53]

At the same time, Russia itself was undergoing massive industrialization, millions of people were moving to the cities to find work, and new trends of thought were sweeping through the intelligentsia. High-minded theoretical discussions of the questions of the day gave way to immediate concerns about educating, feeding, and clothing the poor as well as harnessing their incipient political strength. Among the Russian intelligentsia, the answers to social problems were increasingly to be found in radical political solutions. This would erupt in 1905 and culminate in the revolutions of 1917.

As circumstances for Jews in the Russian empire gradually deteriorated, the majority of Jews retreated into their communities, hoping that eventually life would improve. These people pursued traditional educational paths for their children. Another large group began to look into leaving and put their energies and resources into what became a mass emigration. A far smaller number embraced new ideological solutions to the situation, from Zionism to Socialism.

The pain and frustration, as well as the faith in a new solution, are manifestly present in an article from 1888. The author, who signs himself "Ben-David," is supremely dismissive of Enlightenment strategies. He describes the schools for Jews in Odessa as "planted in nothingness and suspended from absence." According to Ben-David, the schools were never built for the students but for the teachers. The societies, such as the OPE, were created for "self-aggrandizement." Clearly in reaction to the harsh educational quotas instituted in the late 1880s, he questioned the wisdom of schools where "the girls learn embroidery, sewing, knitting, dance, at a time when all schools close the entrance to our sons, and the children of Israel in our city wander like lost sheep without finding aid to learn Torah or a trade."[54] For Ben-David the answer was to leave Russia for the Land of Israel.

Increasingly, Zionism, variants of socialism, and Jewish autonomism gained a following among Russian Jewry. One way that these groups sought to spread their message was education, including evening courses for adults and of course schools for Jewish children. The schools had clearly articulated goals that were manifest in their curricula. Zionist schools sought to create a generation of children fluent in Hebrew and prepared to settle the land. The Jewish Labor Bund built schools where Yiddish language and culture complemented socialist education. Many schools were opened specifically to provide poor Jews with a trade, as well as with literacy and some ideology.

Of course, new schools did not spring up out of nothing. In fact, as we have seen, to a large degree it was the private schools for Jewish girls that enabled their emergence. The private schools for Jewish girls discussed in this work offered educators the opportunity to experiment with change. As outlined above, these educators had varied levels of commitment to implementing change. Some saw training Russian-speaking Jews as the key to "improving" Russian Jewry. Others wanted to expose children to new and modern understandings of their religion. In either case, these specific goals had to be tempered by the reality of filling their classrooms.

Even the most ideologically motivated educator had to create a curriculum that would appeal to a broad spectrum of Jews in his or her local community. In the case of private schools for Jewish girls, this meant that the schools were moderate in character. In most schools, the parents could be assured that their daughters would come home knowing their prayers and such household skills as sewing and knitting.

Nonetheless, the schools allowed for some degree of experimentation. Some of the educators experimented with a more radical approach to Judaism, such as teaching a catechism. Other schools included high-level study of grammar and composition in either Russian or Hebrew. Still other schools moved away from the expectation of formal education belonging mainly in the upper classes by offering scholarship positions to poor girls. In some cases the idea of acculturation into the Russian culture was taken so far as to include mixed schools. Other educators experimented with teaching boys and girls together.

In essence, the period from 1844 to 1881 was one of experimentation and evolution in the education of Jewish girls, and indeed of Jewish children in Russia. At the beginning of the period, sending girls to school was still an anomaly. By the end, schools for Jewish girls existed across the Pale of Settlement. In the previous chapters I described what these schools had in common. However, they were far from static. Indeed, experimentation in educating girls was leading to the gradual adoption of new and different methods and content. There is no question that the schools were developing. However, it was the dramatic events of the 1880s that led to their being supplanted.

Had it not been for the tumultuous times—the pogroms, the legal backlash of the government, and the abandonment by the Russian liberals—private schools for Jewish girls might have continued to slowly evolve. But by the late 1880s and 1890s, educators were far less willing to create schools that appealed to a broad common denominator and espoused little clear ideology. Educators, and increasingly many Jewish families as well, wanted schools that promised some kind of answer to the dilemmas of the time.

In these three examples, trade schools for poor girls, schools for Jewish boys and girls, and schools for both Jewish and Christian girls, we can trace what would eventually become full-fledged educational movements in early experimentation. The flexible nature and desire for broad appeal that characterized the private schools for Jewish girls also made them ideal forums for implementing gradual change. Educators, whether for practical or political motives, pushed the boundaries of the possible. Once it became acceptable to open schools for Jewish girls and funding became available from time to time and place to place, educators began to experiment with schools specifically for the poor, schools for boys and girls, and methods of integrating Jews and Christians together in educational settings.

By the end of the period under examination, not only were there schools for Jewish girls in every province of the Pale of Settlement, but there were also new and innovative educational options. These included not only the three options traced above but also, increasingly, more ideologically motivated schools. All these trends were equally pertinent for boys and girls. The

Front cover of twentieth-anniversary brochure for D. Kupershteyn's school for Jewish girls in Vilna, 1912. (YIVO Institute for Jewish Research)

Jewish community of Russia was undergoing massive change. But just as the liberal Jewish press saw room for improvement, there were also other voices of dissent.

From the perspective of education, it is clear that many of the innovations around the turn of the century developed in the latter half of the nineteenth century, and specifically in the private schools for Jewish girls. The new ideologically motivated schools that proliferated in the early twentieth century would not have been possible without the groundwork laid by their predecessors. Nonetheless, it was the rapid upheavals, the political, economic, and physical uncertainty of Jewish life after 1881 that provided the stimulus to radical change. Had it not been for the pogroms and their backlash, there is every reason to believe that the schools would have continued to evolve gradually. As it was, evolution gave way to revolution.

After the early 1880s, no one opened private schools for Jewish girls along the old models. The new Jewish schools were Zionist or Socialist. Jews increasingly attended Russian institutions. And thus this story draws to a close.

CONCLUSION
Rediscovering Private Schools for Jewish Girls

The school that Shevel' Perel' opened in 1831 still served the Jewish community of Vilna in 1881. At that time, in addition to acting as the principal of the school, Vul'f Kagan, Perel's son-in-law, was also teaching Jewish religion in the local Russian gymnasium.[1] More and more Jewish students had begun to attend Russian institutions. Times had changed and Kagan pragmatically moved into a new growth area in the Jewish educational sphere. Although private schools for Jewish girls were no longer as popular as they had once been, they had helped to pave the way for Jewish attendance at Russian schools.

Something of the nature of Perel's vision, as well as the degree of change over fifty years, can be discerned in examining the location of the school. Perel' opened his new, modern institution on the street that Jews referred to as Daytsche gas and that non-Jewish Russians called Nemetskaia ulitsa. Until the first decade of the nineteenth century, this street, inhabited mainly by Germans, as the name suggests, had served as the border of the contained Jewish community.[2] In Perel's time it was opened up to Jewish residents. By placing his school there, on territory only recently open to Jewish residence, Perel' signaled his intentions. The school, existing at the very border between the Jewish community and the non-Jewish one, represented the cutting-edge of education and the possibility of Jews and their neighbors living together. By the end of the period of study, Daytche gas, like the school itself, had become a central thoroughfare of the expanded and now mixed Jewish community of Vilna.[3]

And beyond reflecting greater societal changes, Perel's school, and others like it, played a role in shaping Jewish society. Although Perel's school was the first modern private school for Jewish girls in the Pale of Settlement in 1831, dozens of educators followed him in opening girls' schools. Their schools, scattered throughout the Pale, made formal education available to Jewish girls for the first time. Thousands of Jewish girls passed through these institutions, learning basic literacy and numeracy as well as the fundamentals of their religion. These girls carried their knowledge with them back out into the community. Perel' himself had the pleasure of seeing his daughter Flora, after graduating from his school, go on to graduate from an elite women's secondary institution in Vilna before returning to her father's school to teach French and Russian.[4] She would later marry Vul'f Kagan, who would eventually run the school himself.

Despite the import of these schools for generations of Jewish girls, and despite the critical role they played in the Jewish community, after the 1880s members of the Jewish community were no longer opening or even looking for such schools. Indeed, if Vul'f and Flora Kagan or Markus Perel's children continued in the family business, it was not as teachers in private schools for Jewish girls. Kagan himself was by 1883 deriving part of his income from teaching Judaism to the throngs of Jewish students now attending the Vilna Men's Gymnasium. Jewish families increasingly sent their children to Russian schools or to more ideological Jewish schools. The need for moderately modern private schools for Jewish girls had passed.

More complete even than the disappearance of these schools from the Russian-Jewish street, however, has been the disappearance of their story. The chaotic turn-of-the-century politics ultimately not only made these schools obsolete, but also obscured them from historical inquiry. At this point it is imperative to rediscover their story.

A great deal has been written about the tumultuous turn-of-the-century period in Russian Jewish history. It was this era that gave birth to many of the streams of Jewish thought still relevant today, more than one hundred years later. Modern Zionism, Jewish Socialism, and vocal and organized Orthodoxy all took shape in the crucible of change wrought by the revolutionary period. For both of today's major centers of Jewish life, America and Israel, this was also an important turning point and source of immigrants. It is no wonder that contemporary historians have evinced enormous interest in this period.

However, tremendous change does not happen overnight. Recent historical work has shown that none of the movements associated with the post-1881 era actually began then. In fact, pogroms, emigration, proto-Zionism, and Jewish revolutionary activity all had roots in the previous decades.[5] This realization, important in its own right, also prompts the question of how these changes came about. If we cannot explain the seeming sea change in Jewish life with one momentous event, how can we account for it?

Answering a question of this scope is beyond the realm of any single study. Obviously the forces of modernity, occurrences in Russian and world history, and various political, economic, and intellectual trends and events must be considered. For the social historian, however, the answer must also lie in internal Jewish developments or in the interaction between internal and external forces. This work uses educational transformation to study communal transformation in the decades before 1881. It is only by examining these slow changes on a communal level that we can hope to make sense of the revolutionary changes that came later.

Jewish education underwent major changes in the course of the latter half of the nineteenth century. Perel's modern private Jewish school was only the third to open, and the second to stay open, in the Pale of Settlement. As we have seen, social and legal circumstances meant that between 1844 and 1873 most of the other modern private schools for Jews served girls. However, after the end of the government's experiment with state-sponsored Jewish education, these proportions would change. In 1883 there were 66 modern private schools for Jews, most of them still either for girls or mixed. By 1893 there were 232 such schools. Five years later, 338 private Jewish schools provided instruction to 6,534 boys and 8,710 girls.[6]

During these same years, more and more Jewish children of both sexes attended Russian educational institutions. In 1841 there were fewer than one thousand Jewish students studying in all Russian schools, private or public, including universities.[7] By 1886, immediately before the legal quotas on Jews went into effect, there were more than one thousand in higher educational institutions alone, with 26,639 Jewish students in general educational institutions throughout the Russian empire. Once the quotas came into effect, although more and more Jews continued to attend Russian educational institutions in pure numbers, their percentages changed. This was true due to the legal limits but also because Russian education was itself expanding at a rapid rate during this period. Thus, for example, although the number of Jewish men in university rose from 1,856 in 1886 to 3,602 in 1911, their percentage declined from 14.5 to 9.4. Jewish women, not included in the discriminatory legislation, continued to expand in both numbers and percentages. Whereas 5,213 Jewish girls attended Russian secondary schools in 1886, 8.11 percent of the total, in 1911 34,981 Jewish girls made up 13.5 percent of the girls' secondary school population.[8]

The private schools for Jewish girls that thrived for much of the nine-teenth century helped to bring about these impressive changes. They served as both a concrete representation of the changes afoot and a catalyst to fur-ther change. They also provided a unique forum for educational experimen-tation.

Shevel' Perel' and his school, and the many schools that followed, emerged when they did not just by lucky coincidence but due to a conflu-ence of new forces in the Russian Jewish community. The first generation of Russian-educated Jews, and of autodidacts who had absorbed sufficient Russian, wanted to put their new skills to a good use. They also wanted to encourage other Jews to learn the language of the land. But their personal and societal desires would have come to naught had the community not been ready.

Jewish families in the middle decades of the nineteenth century were surprisingly willing to go to effort and expense to provide their daughters with a modicum of formal education. For some this effort replicated the education offered to girls among their gentile business associates. For others it prepared girls for their expected role in family businesses. Still others may have wanted their daughters to be able to attend Russian schools, and used the Russian Jewish schools primarily as a gateway to further Russian school-ing. In all these cases, and the many more available options, we witness the inroads of modernity in the Jewish community.

The mechanisms of change within the Jewish community can perhaps best be illustrated in the development of the schools over time. From the introduction of the state Jewish school system for boys in 1844 until its demise in 1873, the only scope for creativity and experimentation in Jewish education was within the private schools for Jewish girls. Although there were certain minor amendments over time, the state schools were largely static and used standard curricula and textbooks. Opening other legal edu-cational institutions for Jewish boys was not feasible, as the state schools were officially mandatory. Thus innovative Jewish educators who wanted to experiment with new ideas had to do so within the girls' schools.

While Jewish boys in *heder* continued the traditional practice of using Hebrew texts, but never actually studying the Hebrew language, Jewish girls in private schools were studying Hebrew systematically. Their teachers origi-nally used textbooks from the German lands but over time developed their own teaching methods, and eventually their own texts as well.

Writing about the emergence of the *heder metukan,* or "reformed *heder,*" in the late nineteenth century, Jewish education historian Zevi Scharfstein describes how the spread of Zionist ideas in the Russian Jewish community led to the founding and increasing popularity of new *hadarim* with attention to hygiene, secular education, and especially Hebrew studies. Scharfstein goes on to say that these new institutions even welcomed Jewish girls: "Thus for the first time among the Jews could be seen girls who studied and knew sacred writings, and the history and language of their people."[9] In fact, Jewish girls' schools in the previous decades had provided the forum for the development of Hebrew pedagogy in Russian that enabled the emergence of the new Zionist schools.

A similar trend is apparent in the Yiddish and Socialist schools of the early twentieth century. H. Sh. Kazdan points out that the existence of the girls' schools outside the long religious tradition of the *heder* and *talmud torah* made it simpler to introduce reforms, in particular the teaching of Yiddish.[10] We have also seen that it was girls' schools, and often wealthy benefactresses, that first introduced serious training in crafts into Jewish schools. Both these innovations would be further developed in the Yiddishist and Socialist schools of the next generation.

In addition to serving as a fruitful source of pedagogical ideas and methods for the more ideological schools that came later, the private girls' schools provided a bridge to Russian education. Scholars have noted the preponderance of Jews in Russian educational institutions around the turn of the century. In particular, the number of Jewish women continues to confound. How is it that a traditional society, where Russian was not the spoken language in most homes, produced so many well-educated members of the Russian intelligentsia? Private schools for Jewish girls provide a key to understanding these issues.

As most Jewish children were not conversant in Russian, let alone literate, students needed to transition into Russian schools. In many cases they did so through the intermediary of Russian-language Jewish schools. The attendance records available suggest that a great many Jewish girls attended the private Jewish girls' schools for only a brief period. Although emigration, migration, and financial and other concerns go some way to explaining this trend, it is also clear that some families used the Jewish schools as a stepping stone to the promise of Russian schools.

And as greater numbers of Jewish girls attended both these institutions, they made it possible for other girls to do so as well. Iris Parush has suggested that it was Jewish girls' very exemption from religious study that made their rapid acculturation possible.[11] This is only one part of the story, but it is clear that over time it became socially acceptable, even in traditional circles, for Jewish daughters to attend general educational institutions. And of course it was this trend that helped to create the need for Sarah Schenirer's crusade several decades later.

A 1913 pamphlet for the progressive Jewish girls' school Yehudiah in Vilna described the educational evolution of Jewish girls as follows. Originally, Jewish girls received no formal education, but "the spirit of Torah suffused their cradle." Then, "European culture, with a bright light, catapulted into our lives" such that "a girl nowadays has no Jewish training what-so-ever." The author goes on to clarify that even when she attends a Jewish school, the girls will receive no meaningful Jewish education, only dry lessons in religion (*Za Kon Bozhii*).[12] In order to highlight the innovative and superior offerings at her own new school, this anonymous author explicitly contrasted them with those in the earlier generation of private schools for Jewish girls. For the purposes of advertising the new school, this was an effective strategy. For the purposes of the historian, it also shows the degree to which the new was indebted to the old.

In all these cases the private schools for Jewish girls serve as a missing link of sorts. While not providing the whole story, they help to explain some of the most important educational trends in the Jewish community in the later Imperial period. Brand new educational ideas, practices, and ideologies did not spring up ex nihilo but built upon models nurtured in an earlier period. The development of the private schools for Jewish girls was slow and evolutionary. Various educators tried out new ideas, within the limits of their abilities and the mores of the communities in which they functioned. Some of these ideas were adopted more widely and further developed by other educators. We have seen how the subjects of instruction, fee scales, pedagogical methods, and makeup of the student body changed over the years. These changes were gradual and contributed to later developments beyond the schools as well.

However, the educational institutions built on the foundations of these schools grew in revolutionary rather than evolutionary times. The final decades of the Russian empire demanded radical solutions to the so-called "Jewish Question." The conservative and evolving private girls' schools, serving the entire Jewish community, were no longer an attractive option. Jews sending their daughters and sons to Zionist, Bundist, and Russian schools was an ideological as well as an educational decision.

The creation of the new ideological schools became part of the founding myths of the new movements. For Zionists, the development of Hebrew-language schools helps to relieve some of the gloom and quiescence of the exilic experience. For Jews on the left, the existence of Socialist schools is a proud chapter in their collective history. Although for many years the topic of Russian integration was taboo in the West, the opening up of the former Soviet Union and the emigration of many of its Jews has mandated a greater understanding of this aspect of the Russian-Jewish experience. And for Orthodox Jews, the example of a Jewish woman who started out alone only to gain the support of the greatest rabbis of her generation is an attractive and important one. The stories of these groups are kept alive outside the academic community.

For Shevel' Perel' and those who followed his lead, however, there remains no contemporary constituency to retell the story. Moreover, the radical break with the past inherent in the other stories has led to the displacement of Perel's. Just as the exigencies of the turn of the century required radical educational solutions, the historians who came to make sense of that period were often also products of it. Writing from their own perspective as Zionists, Bundists, Autonomists, or other revolutionaries, they told the heroic, even mythical stories of their movements. Their interest was in the bold new beginning, not in the transitional period that preceded it. And thus this important chapter in Jewish history was lost.

The girls, however, were not lost. Even as the Jewish street was awash with ideological ferment, and later scholars have searched through the wreckage to make sense of the past, the girls found their way home. They may not have been world-famous revolutionaries or scientists, but they taught Russian and other subjects they had learned to their siblings, husbands, and children.

Even as the overblown pleas of *maskilim* sound patronizing to the modern ear, they also contain a grain of truth. Abram Iakov Bruk-Brezovskii was correct in stating that the Jewish community could only ultimately be changed through educating its daughters: "In their hands rests the fate of the next generation." Bruk-Brezovskii's own school in Kherson educated Jewish girls for more than twenty years. Anna Gertsenshtein, the first Russian Jewish woman to attend university abroad, may even have been one of his students.[13]

The hundreds of other Jewish girls he taught brought their newfound knowledge back to their homes with them. It was through these educated girls that the succeeding generations of Jewish children in Russia received their own early training and modeling. The exponential growth of Russian education over the course of the last decades of the nineteenth century can be seen as a direct consequence of these earlier schools, among other factors. As each subsequent generation of students graduated and turned to raising families of their own, they encouraged their own children to pursue formal Russian educational opportunities.

Bruk-Brezovskii and many other writers for the progressive Jewish press were correct that offering formal education to Jewish girls would ultimately transform the Jewish community. They could not have foreseen the directions that transformation would take, nor even less the terrible forces the twentieth century would unleash on the Russian Jewish community, but they recognized that teaching Jewish girls had consequences. The story of the girls, the schools they attended, and the educators who taught them must now be rediscovered and integrated into the larger story of Jewish life in late imperial Russia.

NOTES

Introduction

1. Abram Iakov Bruk-Brezovskii, "Iz rechi skazannoi soderzhatelem evreiskago devich'iago pansiona, v g. Khersone," *Sion* 20 (1861): 320.

2. Ibid.

3. Ibid., 321.

4. Klier, *Russia Gathers Her Jews*, 28–29.

5. The classic article on this period remains Richard Pipes, "Catherine II and the Jews."

6. See Klier, *Russia Gathers Her Jews*, chap. 5, for more on the statute.

7. Petrovsky-Shtern's *Jews in the Russian Army, 1827–1917* covers the development of the relationship between the military and the Jewish community.

8. On the crown rabbinate see Shohet, *Mosad "ha-Rabanut mi-ta'am" be-Rusyah*, 95–109.

9. For a treatment of this entire period see Stanislawski, *Tsar Nicholas I and the Jews*.

10. On the active public discussion of this period and the status of the Jews in the Russian press, see Klier, *Imperial Russia's Jewish Question, 1855–1881*.

11. Dubnow, *History of the Jews in Russia and Poland*, 2:379.

12. Krieze, "Bate-sefer Yehudiyim ba-safah ha-Rusit be-Rusyah ha-Tsarit," 126.

13. The work of Benjamin Nathans has recently demonstrated the importance of studying the Russifying elements of the Jewish community. See his *Beyond the Pale: The Jewish Encounter with Late Imperial Russia*.

14. In a book chapter titled "History or Education?," Gary McCulloch and William Richardson discuss the divide between scholars of history and education generally. Many of their findings have parallels within Jewish Studies. See *Historical Research in Educational Settings*, chap. 3.

15. Scharfstein, *Toldot ha-hinukh be-Yisra'el*.

16. Bramson, *K istorii nachal'nago obrazovaniia evreev v Rossii*, 68–69.

17. Greenberg, *The Jews in Russia*, 56.

18. See also Dubnow, *History of the Jews in Russia and Poland*, 1:121; Baron, *The Russian Jew under Tsars and Soviets*, 117; Levitats, *The Jewish Community in Russia, 1844–1917*, 50, 118, 124.

19. For one example of a popular treatment, see Benisch, *Carry Me in Your Heart: The Life and Legacy of Sarah Schenirer*. Recent scholarly work includes Weiss-

man, "Bais Yaakov: A Historical Model for Jewish Feminists," 139–46; Weissman, "Bais Ya'akov, A Women's Educational Movement in the Polish Jewish Community"; Weissman, "Bais Ya'akov as an Innovation in Jewish Women's Education"; and Bechhofer, "Identity and Educational Mission of Bais Yaakov Schools."

20. Katz's application of sociological methods and questions to Jewish history, most prominently in *Tradition and Crisis: Jewish Society at the End of the Middle Ages*, but in his many other contributions as well, ushered in a period of great creativity and innovation in the study of Jewish history.

21. Stanislawski, *Tsar Nicholas I and the Jews*; Zipperstein, *The Jews of Odessa*; Zipperstein, "Transforming the Heder."

22. Krieze, "Bate-sefer Yehudiyim ba-safah ha-Rusit be-Rusyah ha-Tsarit"; Rappaport, "Jewish Education and Jewish Culture in the Russian Empire, 1880–1914"; Nathans, *Beyond the Pale*; Zalkin, *Ba-'alot ha-shahar* and *El hekhal ha-haskalah*.

23. Stampfer, "Gender Differentiation and Education of the Jewish Woman"; Greenbaum, "Heder ha-banot, u-vanot be-heder ha-banim."

24. Hyman, *Gender and Assimilation in Modern Jewish History*, chap. 2, and Parush, *Nashim kor'ot*.

25. Krieze, "Bate-sefer Yehudiyim ba-safah ha-Rusit be-Rusyah ha-Tsarit."

26. For an early and excellent survey of the field see Olney, *Autobiography*.

27. See in particular Moseley, *Being for Myself Alone*, and Stanislawski, *Autobiographical Jews*.

28. For more on this collection see Cohen and Soyer, *My Future Is in America*.

Chapter 1

1. Klier, *Russia Gathers Her Jew*, 135.

2. McClelland, *Autocrats and Academics*, 29.

3. Alston, *Education and the State in Tsarist Russia*, 7.

4. Ibid., 35.

5. Eklof, *Russian Peasant Schools*, chap. 2.

6. Of particular interest in this regard is the lengthy debate over classical education in the gymnasia. Pedagogy and politics became hopelessly intertwined as a series of ministers of education sought to walk the fine line between the requests of students, educators, secondary schools, universities, the government, and the society at large. For more on this question see Darlington, *Education in Russia*, chap. 4, as well as Makowski, "The Russian Classical Gymnasium, 1864–1890."

7. Historians of the Jewish experience in Russia have typically viewed the quotas introduced in the wake of 1881 as specifically anti-Jewish. Deborah Howard, in her dissertation, points out that the crackdown had more to do with class than ethnicity, as can be seen by the infamous "Cooks Circular," also of 1887. Howard, "Elite Secondary Education in Late Imperial Russia, 1881–1905," 141–42.

8. See Sinel, *The Classroom and the Chancellery.*

9. Eklof, *Russian Peasant Schools*, 287.

10. Hutton, *Russian and West European Women, 1860–1939*, 47, 49.

11. For more on the Smolny Institute and eighteenth-century education see

Nash, "The Education of Women in Russia, 1762–1796," and part 1 of the first volume of Likhacheva, *Materialy dlia istorii zhenskago obrazovaniia v Rossii, 1086–1856.*

12. Stites, *The Women's Liberation Movement in Russia,* chap. 1.

13. Ibid., 51–52, and Satina, *Education of Women in Pre-Revolutionary Russia,* 44–50.

14. Johanson, *Women's Struggle for Higher Education in Russia, 1855–1900,* 22.

15. Stites, *The Women's Liberation Movement in Russia,* chap. 2.

16. Dudgeon, "Women and Higher Education in Russia, 1855–1905," 60–61.

17. Johanson, *Women's Struggle for Higher Education in Russia, 1855–1900,* 38–39.

18. Ibid., 51–53.

19. Ibid., 95–100.

20. A great deal has been written about the *heder* and its function in the Jewish community of Eastern Europe. For a survey of this literature, see Roskies, *Heder: Primary Education among East European Jews.* On the educational practices of the *heder,* see in particular Scharfstein, *Ha-Heder be-haye 'amenu*; and Roskies, "Alphabet Instruction in the East European Heder."

21. Kazdan, *Fun heyder un "shkoles" biz Tsisho,* 138.

22. For more on the *yeshivot,* see Stampfer, *Ha-Yeshivah ha-Lita'it be-hithavutah.*

23. On this topic, see Stampfer, "Heder Study, Knowledge of Torah and the Maintenance of Social Stratification," 271–89, and Parush, "Another Look at 'the Life of "Dead" Hebrew,'" 171–214.

24. See, for example, *Shulhan Arukh,* Yoreh De'ah 245:1, 4, 7.

25. For the most commonly cited early source, see Mishna Sotah 3:4.

26. Further information can be sought in the following works. For a partial list of pertinent sources, see Elinson, *Ben ha-ishah le-yotsrah,* chap. 13, and Ashkenazi, *Ha-Ishah be-aspaklaryat ha-Yahadut,* vol. 1, chap. 13. For explication of the sources, see Weissman, "Education of Jewish Women," or the introduction to Weissman's dissertation "Hinukh banot datiyot bi-Yerushalayim bi-tekufat ha-shilton ha-Beriti." For different perspectives, see also Zolty, *"And All Your Children Shall be Learned,"* chaps. 1–3; Wolff, "Teaching Women Torah"; and Biale, *Women and Jewish Law,* 29–41.

27. Byer, *Transplanted People,* 21.

28. YIVO RG 102, file 27, 3.

29. YIVO RG 102, file 27, 4.

30. Gottlober, *Zikhronot u-masa'ot,* vol. 1, 99.

31. Hilf, *No Time for Tears,* 25–26.

32. *'Arukh Ha-Shulhan,* Yoreh De'ah 246:19, as translated in Wolff, "Teaching Women Torah," 129.

33. For a nuanced treatment of R. Epstein's writing on women's issues, see Simcha Fishbane, "'In Any Case There Are No Sinful Thoughts.'"

34. Shmeruk, "Di Mizreh-Eyropeyishe nusahos fun der Tsenerene (1786–1850)," 334.

35. See Weissler, *Voices of the Matriarchs,* 25; see also 202n61. Recent scholarship on early modern Yiddish ethical and legal guidebooks for Jewish women has revealed another genre considered appropriate and acceptable for a female audience.

See *Meneket Rivkah: A Manual of Wisdom and Piety for Jewish Women* by Rivkah bat Meir, and Fram, *My Dear Daughter*.

36. Gottlober, *Zikhronot u-masa'ot,* 86.

37. See Immanuel Etkes, "Marriage and Torah Study among the *Lomdim* in Lithuania in the Nineteenth Century," and Glenn, *Daughters of the Shtetl*, chap. 1.

38. For more on these, see my "Educational Options for Jewish Girls in Nineteenth-Century Eastern Europe," *Polin* 15 (2002). Although many of these examples are taken from the turn of the century, some do come from earlier in the nineteenth century and all provide crucial qualitative data on Jewish life.

39. For more on German Jewish *Haskalah*, see Graetz, "The Jewish Enlightenment."

40. For a translation of the text of the edict, see Mendes-Flohr and Reinharz, *The Jew in the Modern World*, 36–40.

41. On Wessely, see Feiner, *The Jewish Enlightenment*, chap. 4, and Breuer, "Naphtali Herz Wessely and the Cultural Dislocations of an Eighteenth-Century Maskil."

42. Zinberg, *A History of Jewish Literature,* vol. 11, 21–26.

43. Levinsohn, *Bet Yehudah*, part 2, chap. 146, 148–50.

44. For more on maskilic writing and activism on education, see Moshe Avital, *Ha-Yeshiva veha-hinukh ha-mesorati be-sifrut ha-Haskalah ha-'Ivrit,* and Zalkin, *El hekhal ha-haskalah.*

45. Guenzburg, *Aviezer*, 8–34.

46. Levinsohn, *Te'udah be-Yisra'el.*

47. Levinsohn, *Bet Yehudah,* part two, chap. 146, 148–49.

48. See, for example, Gottlober, *Zikhronot u-masa'ot,* 245, and Lilienblum, *Hat'ot ne'urim*, 32–34. For more on maskilic autobiography, see Mintz, *"Banished from Their Father's Table,"* and Biale, *Eros and the Jews*, chap. 7.

49. For more on the embourgeoisement of the Western European Jewish family, see Kaplan, *The Making of the Jewish Middle Class,* and Baader, "Inventing Bourgeois Judaism."

50. Feiner, "Ha-Ishah ha-Yehudit ha-modernit," 467–99.

51. Cohen, "Reality and Its Refraction in Descriptions of Women in Haskalah Fiction," 144–65. For further scholarship on women in Hebrew fiction of the period, see Feingold, "Feminism in Hebrew Nineteenth Century Fiction," and Cohen, *Ha-Ahat ahuvah veha-ahat senu'ah.*

52. Balin, *To Reveal Our Hearts*, 29–30.

53. In particular, Benjamin Nathans's *Beyond the Pale* explores the growing phenomenon of professional, educated, Russified Jews in St. Petersburg. Frankel's classic *Prophecy and Politics* provides a comprehensive treatment of the entry of Jews into modern political movements.

Chapter 2

1. Beauvois, "Polish-Jewish Relations in the Territories Annexed by the Russian Empire," 84.

2. Beletskii, *Vopros ob obrazovanii russkikh evreev*, 18, citing Delo kantseliarii popechitel'stva Vilenskogo uchebnogo okruga, sviazka 427, no. 3619.

3. Examination of the enrollment data on the Vilna Gymnasium between 1808 and 1817 yielded no reference to Perel'. I was able to locate one Jewish student in the 1810/11 school year and what looked like two others in the 1809/10 school year. Lietuvos Valstybes Istorijos Archyvas (Lithuanian State Historical Archives, LVIA), f. 567, op. 2, d. 206, ll. 13 ob., 39 ob.

4. For a discussion of marriage ages and customs, see Stampfer, "Ha-Mashma'ut ha-hevratit shel nisu'e boser be-Mizrah Eropah," and Freeze, *Jewish Marriage and Divorce in Imperial Russia*, chap. 1.

5. Rossiisskii Gosudarstvennyi Istoricheskii Arkhiv (Russian State Historical Archive, RGIA), *fond* 733, *opis'* 97, *delo* 485, *listy* 2–4. The Standard Russian archival notation system is used hereafter: f. (*fond*), op. (*opis*), d., dd. (*delo, dela*), l., ll. (*list, listy*), ob. (*oborot*).

6. Zalkin, *Ba-'alot ha-shahar*, 197–98, 204. For more on the Odessa school, see Zipperstein, *The Jews of Odessa*, 44–55.

7. In a letter to the Ministry of Education in 1861, Perel' states that he invested his entire fortune of 1,600 rubles in the school (RGIA, f. 733, op. 98, d. 466, l. 8). The sum of 1,600 rubles was probably the dowry of his wife. It was at that time a substantial sum and enough to start a business but not enough to provide a living. ChaeRan Freeze suggests that dowries ranged from one hundred to several thousand rubles (Freeze, *Jewish Marriage and Divorce*, 30). For more contemporaneous examples of dowries, see Etkes, "Marriage and Torah Study among the *Lomdim* in Lithuania in the Nineteenth Century," 160, 161, 169. Perel' and his family were not among the wealthy elite of Vilna, but neither were they part of the struggling majority. They appear to have counted themselves among the emerging professional class.

8. RGIA, f. 733, op. 97, d. 295, l. 1.

9. For an excellent treatment of how the *maskilim* viewed women, see Feiner, "Ha-Ishah ha-Yehudit ha-modernit."

10. Krieze, "Bate-sefer Yehudiyim ba-safah ha-Rusit be-Rusyah ha-Tsarit," 23–24.

11. Lozinskii, *Kazennye evreiskie uchilishcha*, file 80623, 120.

12. RGIA, f. 733, op. 98, d. 466, l. 7–7 ob.

13. Iulii Gessen, "Prosveshchenie," *Evreiskaia entsiklopediia*, vol. 13, col. 45. Gessen is probably citing Beletskii (p. 9, citing Delo kantseliarii Popechitel'stva Vilenskogo uchebnogo okruga, sviazka 221, no. 2045), who names the principal of the school as Perel'.

14. Mordechai Zalkin presents an alternate explanation for the discrepancy over dates. According to Zalkin, Perel' took his state teacher's examination in 1830. Although he had applied to open a school, he may have had to wait for his results in order to do so (Zalkin, "Ha-Haskalah ha-Yehudit," 177). Israel Klausner suggests Perel's school for girls opened in 1826 (Klausner, *Vilnah, Yerushalayim de-Lita*, 208). Perel's brother-in-law, Yakov Lapin, praised Perel' for bringing maskilic education to both boys and girls (Lapin, *Keset ha-sofer*, 9).

15. A rough average of the number of students per year, based on the years for

which such information is available, is eighty-nine. As the school stayed open for over fifty years, even a conservative estimate suggests that over four thousand girls attended Perel's school. *Spiski chinovnikov i prepodavatelei Vilenskago uchebnago okruga*, 1859 (Vilna, 1859), 30 (115); RGIA, f. 733, op. 98, d. 466, l. 13ob (1861:77); YIVO RG 24, file 141, l. 20 (1869:50, 1870:85); RGIA, f. 733, op. 189, d. 581, l. 26 (1879:116).

16. RGIA, f. 733, op. 189, d. 241, l. 2.

17. Zalkin, *Ba-'alot ha-shahar*, 8, 10–11.

18. Lozinskii, *Kazennye evreiskie uchilishcha* 104, no. 80594.

19. RGIA, f. 733, op. 97, d. 295, l. 12 (list of Jewish schools in the region mentioned within correspondence regarding Perel's school).

20. Beauvois, "Polish-Jewish Relations in the Territories Annexed by the Russian Empire," 209.

21. Klier, *Imperial Russia's Jewish Question*, 73–74.

22. By the mid-nineteenth century major cities in the Hapsburg empire and in many German states had modern Jewish private schools. These were established by private initiative but with government permission. Most renowned among them was the Berlin Freischule (or *Hinukh Ne'arim*), established by David Friedlander in 1781. At the outset the school included only secular subjects, with the expectation that the boys would attend *heder* in addition. However, in 1784 the school announced the introduction of instruction in sacred subjects. More and more parents enrolled their sons in the Freischule such that within its first ten years, more than five hundred students obtained an education (Eliav, *Ha-Hinukh ha-Yehudi be-Germanyah*, 71–74). See also Feiner, "Programot hinukhiyot ve-idi'alim hevratiyim."

23. RGIA, f. 733, op. 97, d. 13, ll. 138 ob. 139. For more on Jewish schools in the Polish lands, see Levin, *Perakim be-toldot ha-hinukh ha-Yehudi be-Polin*. It is also worth noting that before 1832 Polish authority had extended into much of the Pale of Settlement. In the early years of the nineteenth century there were several failed attempts to establish state Jewish schools in the Vilna area. For more on this, see Beauvois, "Polish-Jewish Relations in the Territories Annexed by the Russian Empire," 82–83.

24. Krieze, "Bate-sefer Yehudiyim ba-safah ha-Rusit be-Rusyah ha-Tsarit," 20–26.

25. Stanislawski, *Tsar Nicholas I and the Jews*, 70.

26. The "learned Jew," sometimes translated as "Jewish Expert," was a post attached to some offices of the Ministry of Education, and later to other ministries as well, designed to provide the government with information about the Jewish community. See "uchenye evrei," in *Evreiskaia entsiklopediia*, vol. 15, cols. 147–48, for more. On the Rabbinic Commission, see Freeze, *Jewish Marriage and Divorce*, 83–95 and elsewhere.

27. Freeze, *Jewish Marriage and Divorce*, 91–96.

28. For more on the variant reports of the meetings, see Stanislawski, *Tsar Nicholas I and the Jews*, 79–82.

29. *Polnoe sobranie zakonov Rossiiskoi Imperii* (2) [henceforth *PSZ*], 19: 18,420 (13 November 1844).

30. Stanislawski, *Tsar Nicholas I and the Jews,* 98.

31. I. Cherikover, "Kazennyia evreiskiia uchilishcha," *Evreiskaia entsiklopediia,* vol. 9, cols. 111–12.

32. *Zhurnal Ministerstva Narodnago Prosveshchenie,* June 1856, as cited in Beletskii, *Vopros ob obrazovanii russkikh evreev,* 147.

33. See, for example, *PSZ* (2), 30: 29,276 (3 May 1855) and 31: 31,104 (5 November 1856).

34. *PSZ* (2), 37: 38,641 (6 September 1862).

35. *PSZ* (2), 48: 52,020 (16 March 1873).

36. Zipperstein, *The Jews of Odessa,* 50.

37. Ia. Tsitron, "Kazennoe evreiskoe devich'e uchilishche v Odesse," *Razsvet* 31 (23 December 1860): 499.

38. Levinsohn, *Bet Yehudah,* chap. 146, 148–50.

39. Lozinskii, *Kazennye evreiskie uchilishcha,* vol. 1, no. 80580, 79–80.

40. Kaufman, "'Al devar ha-hinukh," 50–51.

41. RGIA, f. 733, op. 97, d. 13, l. 47 ob.

42. Ibid., l. 50 ob.

43. RGIA, f. 733, op. 97, d. 308, l. 1–1 ob.

44. Ibid., ll. 3–4 ob.

45. RGIA, f. 733, op. 97, d. 868, ll. 3–12.

46. Ibid., ll. 5–9 ob.

47. For more on the Rabbinic Commission, see Freeze, *Jewish Marriage and Divorce in Imperial Russia,* esp. chap. 2.

48. RGIA, f. 733, op. 97, d. 868, ll. 26–28 ob.

49. RGIA, f. 821, op. 9, d. 2, ll. 2–8. I am grateful to ChaeRan Freeze for providing me with access to her notes on this document.

50. RGIA, f. 733, op. 97, d. 868, l. 29.

51. "Otchet chlena soveta Ministra Narodnago Prosveshcheniia Postel'sa po obozreniiu evreiskikh uchilishch s. 7 Maia po 7 sent. 1864," *Materialy otnosiashchiesia k obrazovanii u evreev v Rossii* (1865): 71–77, 92.

52. H. Gornberg, "Zametka o evreiskikh uchilishchakh," *Razsvet* 6 (1860): 86–87.

53. Lozinskii, *Kazennye evreiskie uchilishcha,* no. 83543, 245.

54. "Prosveshchenie," *Evreiskaia entsiklopediia,* vol. 13, cols. 57–58.

55. *Sbornik postanovlenii po Ministerstvu narodnago prosveshchenii* (1840–55), vol. 2, part 2 (St. Petersburg, 1876), 561.

56. *Sbornik* (1876), 562.

57. RGIA, f. 733, op. 97, d. 13, ll. 187–88 (outline for planned legislation regarding Jewish education, c. 1840s).

58. *Sbornik* (1876), 562–63. In practice, many applications never reached the central offices of the ministry in St. Petersburg. These institutions appear on internal MNP lists or lists published elsewhere but not in the files of the central archives. However, the vast majority of schools mentioned elsewhere are also to be found in the files of the Ministry of Education. Of those schools whose records were retained

in the archives, almost all were granted permission to open. This suggests either that the St. Petersburg central office nearly always followed the recommendation of the local offices or that unsuccessful applications were not retained. In either case it is fair to assume that some percentage of schools kept a low profile and do not appear anywhere in my records and that a certain number of others were unable to gain permission to open.

59. The *plan* and *programma* served to explain the workings of the new school. The *plan* was more general, outlining such issues as lodging, finances, and academics, with the *programma* providing details of the academic curriculum. In the text, I have left these words untranslated but italicized.

Chapter 3

1. Stanislawski, *For Whom Do I Toil?*, 68, 111.

2. Although there is no evidence from Gordon's tenure, an 1884 list of Jewish schools lists Khazanovich as the former vice-principal. This suggests that he had some role in the school before Gordon's departure. RGIA, f. 733, op. 189, d. 437, l. 3.

3. In an article from 1880, one correspondent even argued that Khazanovich was more effective than Gordon as principal. Z., "Tel'she," *Russkii evrei* 4 (1880): 129–30.

4. RGIA, f. 733, op. 189, d. 437, ll. 3–3ob [1884 Report on new principal].

5. Seregny, *Russian Teachers and Peasant Revolution,* and Ruane, *Gender, Class and the Professionalization of Russian City Teachers, 1860–1914.*

6. YIVO RG 24, file 141, ll. 139ob-140.

7. YIVO RG 24, file 141, ll. 17–17ob (1869 full report on school of Vul'f Kagan in Vilna).

8. Weisberg, *Igrot Yehudah Leyb Gordon*, 69.

9. Michael Stanislawski discussed the historical context of the poem in his *For Whom Do I Toil?*, 125–28.

10. Translation from Nash, "'Kotso shel Yud,'" 114.

11. *Ha-Olam* 38 (1936): 656. See also Weisberg, *Igrot Yehudah Leyb Gordon*, 133, 163–64. On Markel-Mosesohn, see Balin, *To Reveal Our Hearts,* chap. 1.

12. On Isaak Rumsh and his oeuvre, see Zalkin, "Itzhak Romash—Between 'Educating the Periphery' and 'Peripheral Education,'" 185–213. Abram Bruk-Brezovskii published two articles specifically on women's education: "Pansion dlia evreiskikh devits v Berdicheve," *Razsvet* 31 (1860): 204–6; "Iz rechi skazannoi soderzhatelem evreiskago devich'iago pansiona, v g. Khersone," *Sion* 20 (1861): 320. He may have published other pieces as well.

13. Gurvich, later Guriev, comes up in John Doyle Klier's chapter on the far more infamous apostate, Iakov Brafman (Klier, *Imperial Russia's Jewish Question, 1855–1881,* chap. 12).

14. Broido, *Memoirs of a Revolutionary,* 4.

15. Itah Yelin, *Le-Tse-etsa'ai,* 12.

16. RGIA, f. 733, op. 98, d. 214, ll. 2–2ob.

17. RGIA, f. 733, op. 98, d. 94, l. 1 ob. (1856 request to open school).

18. RGIA, f. 733, op. 189, d. 437, l. 3 (1884 discussion of fate of Gordon's school).

19. "Gurovich, Markus Solomonovich," *Evreiskaia entsiklopediia*, vol. 6, col. 852.

20. RGIA, f. 733, op. 189, d. 198, l. 1–1ob.

21. RGIA, f. 733, op. 97, d. 13, l. 189.

22. Lincoln, "Daily Life of St. Petersburg Officials," 97–98.

23. Shohet, *Mosad "ha-Rabanut mi-ta'am" be-Rusyah*, 14.

24. Y. L. Gordon, "Rech," *Ha-Karmel* (Russian) 6, no. 28 (1866): 121–22.

25. Feiner, "Ha-Ishah ha-Yehudit ha-modernit."

26. Rozenthal, *Toldot Hevrat marbe haskalah be-Yisra'el be-erets Rusya*, 170.

27. Lozinskii, *Kazennye evreiskie uchilishcha*, 297. Mordechai Zalkin suggests that Germaize actually switched his boys' school to a girls' school due to popular demand, but this is not in contradiction to my contention that it allowed him to maintain control of the school. Germaize would not have attempted to open a girls' school had he not been convinced of popular interest. Zalkin, *Ba-'alot ha-shahar*, 210.

28. RGIA, f. 733, op. 189, d. 570, l. 7 (file on Germaize school).

29. RGIA, f. 733, op. 189, d. 570, ll. 6–11.

30. RGIA, f. 733, op. 189, d. 130 l. 1 (request of members of Jewish community of Khoton for school to remain open).

31. RGIA, f. 733, op. 97, d. 419, ll. 2–2 ob.

32. *Pamiatnaia knizhka Vilenskago uchebnago ukruga na 1874*, 659, and *Pamiatnaia knizhka Vilenskago uchebnago ukruga na 1880/1 god*, 207.

33. RGIA, f. 733, op. 98, d. 214, l. 2 ob.

34. RGIA, f. 733, op. 189, d. 437, l. 3.

35. Krieze, "Bate-sefer Yehudiyim ba-safah ha-Rusit be-Rusyah ha-Tsarit," 319–20.

36. Parush, *Nashim kor'ot*, esp. chap. 4.

37. RGIA, f. 733, op. 189, d. 170, l. 40 ob. (1868 report on Berman schools, including staffing and expenses); f. 733, op. 189, d. 428, l. 2b. ob. (1871 request to open school).

38. RGIA, f. 733, op. 98, d. 300, l. 2 (1858 academic plan for school) and RGIA, f. 733, op. 98, d. 96, l. 11 ob.

39. *Pamiatnaia knizhka Vilenskago uchebnago ukruga na 1879/80 uchebnyi god*, 207.

40. RGIA, f. 733, op. 189, d. 474, l. 1–1ob. (1873 application of Sara Berman).

41. RGIA, f. 733, op. 189, d. 170 (file on the schools of Lazar and Anna Berman).

42. RGIA, f. 733, op. 98, d. 427, l. 20 (1860 letter from Kiev to St. Petersburg regarding new school).

43. RGIA, f. 733, op. 189, d. 481, ll. 1–1 ob. (inspection report, 1873); Rozenthal, *Toldot Hevrat marbe haskalah be-Yisra'el be-erets Rusya*, 110.

44. Kazenelson, *Mah she-ra'u 'enai ve-sham'u oznai*, 124.

45. Pinhas Kon pointed out a fascinating exception in his article on Jewish women in the Vilna midwifery program at the beginning of the nineteenth century. Although most Jewish families at this time had neither the interest nor the means to pursue professional education for their daughters, there were some wealthy and acculturated families with different goals. One of the documents he found introduces the Pines family in which two daughters were trained midwives, a son was in a gymnasium, and a third daughter had received permission to take the examination to become a teacher. Kon noted that this was the first record of a Jewish woman becoming a teacher legally ("Yidishe froyen in der akusherye-shul baym Vilner Universitet 1811–1824," 770).

46. Dudgeon, "The Forgotten Minority: Women Students in Imperial Russia, 1872–1917," *Russian History/Histoire Russe* 9:1 (1982): 16–17.

47. Rakowski, *Zikhroynes fun a Yiddisher revolutsonerin*, 39–54. See also the recent translation *My Life as a Radical Jewish Woman*.

48. Rakowski, *Zikhroynes fun a Yiddisher revolutsonerin,* 19.

49. RGIA, f. 733, op. 189, d. 428, l. 2b ob.

50. V-i, "Ekzamen v Dinaburge," *Ha-Karmel* (Russian) 24 (1863): 83.

51. RGIA, f. 733, op. 97, d. 288, l. 2–2 ob.

52. See, for example, RGIA, f. 733, op. 97, d. 336, l. 4 (1850 request from Ekert-Buchinskaia to MNP).

53. RGIA, f. 733, op. 98, d. 94, ll. 1–1 ob.

54. Thaden, *Russia's Western Borderlands*, 98, 196–97.

55. Bauer, Kappeler, and Roth, *Die Nationalitaten des Russischen Reiches in der Volkszahlung von 1897*, 93–95.

56. YIVO, RG 24, file 103, pp. 1–1 ob (also LGIA f. 567 op6 d. 853).

57. RGIA, f. 733, op. 98, d. 466, l. 14.

58. In his correspondence, Abraham Mapu, another important Hebrew literary figure, mentions his frustrated efforts to open a school for Jewish girls (Mapu, *Mikhteve Avraham Mapu,* xvii–xviii, 8–9). However, as I was unable to find a record of the school, I did not count him among the principals.

59. Gordon's lengthy entry in *Evreiskaia entsiklopediia* deals mostly with his literary output. His position as a government Jewish school teacher is mentioned, but not his work in private schools (VI, 690–96). Lazar Berman's entry includes his work as an editor, teacher, and author. Neither his short-lived private school in Dubno nor his wife Anna's educational career in the capital receive attention (vol. 4, cols. 281–81). A listing of major publications suffices for Bank and Rumsh, both minor writers (vol. 3, vols. 763–64; vol. 10, col. 517). Moisei Gurvich's claim to fame is as an apostate who wrote against Judaism. His work as a teacher in a government Jewish school previous to conversion receives brief mention (vol. 6, cols. 845–46). Only Markus Gurovich's work in women's education appears in his entry. Gurovich is credited with opening the first *pansion* for Jewish girls in Russia, in addition to his participation in other Jewish causes (vol. 6, col. 851–52).

60. Zalkin, "Itzhak Romash," 202.

61. Ben-Yehuda, *ha-Halom ve-shivro*, 60.

Chapter 4

1. Neither the MNP nor any other body kept track of all the private schools. Occasionally a local MNP office or Jewish communal organization would compile a list of schools open at that time (see, for example, the listings of Jewish schools open in 1880 in *Russkii evrei,* nos. 14, 21, and 23, pp. 558, 836, 916), but this is the most comprehensive list of the period to be published.

2. Likhacheva, *Materialy dlia istorii zhenskago obrazovaniia v Rossii, 1086–1856,* part 2.

3. RGIA, f. 733, op. 97, d. 128, ll. 1 ob. 2.

4. RGIA, f. 733, op. 97, d. 719, l. 18 (letter in favor of Gurovich's request for candle tax funding, 1856).

5. RGIA, f. 733, op. 98, d. 96, l. 6.

6. RGIA, f. 733, op. 98, d. 219, l. 2 ob.

7. This should be contrasted with the tuition usually paid by Jewish families for the *heder.* An 1843 report for the Ministry of Education estimates that the yearly cost per student was between 35 and 100 rubles, with each family paying between 2 and 10 rubles per month (RGIA, f. 733, op. 97, d. 20, l. 75 ob.).

8. RGIA, f. 733, op. 98, d. 214, l. 2 ob.

9. RGIA, f. 733, op. 98, d. 139, l. 5 [1854 advertisement for Perel's school].

10. B. Bertenzon, "Pis'mo v redaktsiu," *Sion* 40 (1862): 633. Bernard Bertenzon (1815–70) took part in Jewish politics and activism in the city of Odessa throughout his adult life (*Evreiskaia entsiklopediia,* vol. 4, col. 329).

11. Rozenthal, *Toldot Hevrat marbe haskalah be-Yisra'el be-erets Rusya,* 48, 50.

12. RGIA, f. 733, op. 189, d. 170, l. 12–12 ob. (1867 letter from Jewish Community of St. Petersburg to Ministry of Education supporting the Berman's request for candle tax funds).

13. RGIA, f. 733, op. 97, d. 13, l. 210.

14. RGIA, f. 733, op. 97, d. 13, l. 189–189 ob.

15. *PSZ* (2), 14, 12,808 (25 October 1839).

16. *Sbornik* (1876), no. 316, 651–60.

17. Sh. Z. Levin, *O korobochnom i svechnom sborakh,* 30.

18. For a local study of the candle tax, see Nadav, *The Jews of Pinsk, 1506–1880,* 356–59 and elsewhere.

19. *Sbornik* (1876), no. 640, 1334–36.

20. Stanislawski, *Tsar Nicholas I and the Jews,* 98.

21. *Zhurnal Ministerstva Narodnogo Prosveshcheniia* (June) 1856, cited in Beletskii, *Vopros ob obrazovanii russkikh evreev,* 147.

22. RGIA, f. 733, op. 97, d. 205, l. 12–12 ob. (1850 internal Ministry of Education document looking at schools for Jewish girls).

23. Ibid., ll. 9–10.

24. Ibid., l. 12.

25. RGIA, f. 733, op. 97, d. 308, ll. 1–2.

26. Lozinskii, no. 95330, 297.

27. RGIA, f. 733, op. 98, d. 96, ll. 1–2.

28. *Kol Mevaser* 36 (1863): 571.

29. Rozenthal, *Toldot Hevrat marbe haskalah be-Yisra'el be-erets Rusya*, 8.

30. RGIA, f. 733, op. 189, d. 170, l. 3–3 ob. (draft copy of listing clearly meant for internal use and stored haphazardly within the file on the Bermans' schools).

31. RGIA, f. 733, op. 189, d. 581, l. 26–26 ob.

32. *PSZ* (2) 38: 39, 157 (11 January 1863).

33. RGIA, f. 733, op. 189, d. 71, ll. 1–2.

34. See also RGIA, f. 733, op. 97, d. 189; op. 189, d. 189; d. 164.

35. See, for example, RGIA, f. 733, op. 189, d. 189, ll. 1–3 (1866 file on request of Jews of Ekaterinoslav to have funding for Jewish religion teaches in local women's schools).

36. RGIA, f. 733, op. 189, d. 581, l. 17 ob. 18.

37. Stanislawski, *For Whom Do I Toil?*, 110.

38. See, for example, Rappaport, "Jewish Education and Jewish Culture in the Russian Empire, 1880–1914"; Nathans, *Beyond the Pale*, 174 and chap. 6; and Horowitz, *Jewish Philanthropy and Enlightenment in Late Tsarist Russia*.

39. Rappaport, "Jewish Education and Jewish Culture in the Russian Empire, 1880–1914," 75–76, citing Tcherikower, *Istoriia obshchestva dlia rasprostraneniia prosveshcheniia mezhdu evreiami v Rossii*, 14–17.

40. Rozenthal, *Toldot Hevrat marbe haskalah be-Yisra'el be-erets Rusya*, 17; Tcherikower, *Istoriia obshchestva dlia rasprostraneniia prosvieshcheniia mezhdu evreiami v Rossii*, 206.

41. Rappaport, "Jewish Education and Jewish Culture in the Russian Empire, 1880–1914," 73.

42. Rozenthal, *Toldot Hevrat marbe haskalah be-Yisra'el be-erets Rusya*, 112.

43. Ibid., 167.

44. See, for example, ibid., 149. On Wengeroff, see his wife Pauline's memoir *Rememberings,* and especially the afterword by Bernard Dov Cooperman, "A Life Unresolved," 270–74.

45. Rappaport, "Jewish Education and Jewish Culture in the Russian Empire, 1880–1914," 74.

46. The ICA was founded by the prominent banker and philanthropist Baron Maurice de Hirsh in London in 1891, with the goal of helping European Jews to settle productively in more hospitable lands. In view of the harsh realities of life for many East European Jews, it also began to expend resources on local support ("Jewish Colonization Association," *Encyclopaedia Judaica,* vol. 10, col. 44).

47. Rappaport, "Jewish Education and Jewish Culture in the Russian Empire, 1880–1914," 83–86.

48. Horowitz, "The Society for the Promotion of Enlightenment among the Jews of Russia," 17, citing *Otchet OPE za 1881/1905–6 g.* (St. Petersburg, 1882, 1907).

49. Zalkin, *El hekhal ha-haskalah*, 64.

Chapter 5

1. Y. L. Gordon, *Ha-Karmel* (Russian): 6, no. 28 (1866): 121.

2. RGIA, f. 733, op. 189, d. 241, l. 2

3. RGIA, f. 733, op. 97, d. 206, l. 125 ob; see also f. 733, op. 98, d. 96, l. 3

4. See, for example, Beletskii, *Vopros ob obrazovanii russkikh evreev*, 8, and Krieze, "Bate-sefer Yehudiyim ba-safah ha-Rusit be-Rusyah ha-Tsarit," 21.

5. For more on the Jewish communities in Odessa and Vilna, see Zipperstein, *The Jews of Odessa*, and Cohen, *Vilna*.

6. *Sion* 8 (1861): 127–28.

7. RGIA, f. 733, op. 97, d. 295, l. 12 (internal MNP document relating to the question of funding Shevel' Perel's school in Vilna in 1850).

8. RGIA, f. 733, op. 189, d. 170, l. 3–3ob.

9. RGIA, f. 733, op. 189, d. 581, l. 26–26 ob.

10. The crossover between the terms is confirmed by Chekhov, *Tipy russkoi shkoly v ikh istoricheskom razvitii*, 6–10.

11. RGIA, f. 733, op. 98, d. 378, ll. 2–3 ob.

12. RGIA, f. 733, op. 98, d. 309, l. 4–4 ob.

13. RGIA, f. 733, op. 97, d. 13, ll. 187–88 (draft legislation for government Jewish school system, circa 1840).

14. For perspective on the massive success of Russification see Weeks, "Russification: Word and Practice 1863–1914," 471–89. For Perel's school as a model, see RGIA, f. 733, op. 97, d. 868, ll. 3–4, wherein the prospective founders of a new school in Mogilev specifically mention Perel's school as one of their curricular models.

15. Krieze, "Bate-sefer Yehudiyim ba-safah ha-Rusit be-Rusyah ha-Tsarit," 267.

16. Ibid., 271, 231.

17. RGIA, f. 733, op. 98, d. 378, l. 4.

18. The name of the principal is not given in this file; he is referred to simply as the principal of the school for Jewish girls. Although there are records for schools for Jewish girls in Berdichev opened in 1857 by Aron Frud (RGIA, f. 733, op. 98, d. 427, l. 4), in late 1860 or early 1861 by Mrs. Likhtenstein (RGIA, f. 733, op. 98, d. 427, l. 23–23 ob.), and in 1872 by Liuba Kenigsberg (RGIA, f. 733, op. 189, d. 481, l. 1), this is the only reference to a school that existed already in 1854. An 1860 article about the need to educate Jewish girls, with particular reference to Berdichev, mentions the existence of two *pansions* for Jewish girls but does not provide further information (H. Gornberg, "Zametka o evreiskikh uchilishchakh," *Razsvet* 6 [1 July 1860]). Perhaps the writer refers to the school of Frud and also that of the unnamed principal. It is less likely, but not impossible, that he is referring to the newly opened school of Mrs. Likhtenstein. Her school is referred to as "newly opened" in a letter of 1861, but it is difficult to date its exact opening. Another correspondent from Berdichev, S. Y. Abramovich, wrote rapturously of the first school for Jewish girls in the area in 1859. He refers to the principal in Hebrew as "Friede" (S. Y. Abramovich, "Mikhtav mi-Berdits'ev," *Ha-Magid* 44 [16 November 1859]). This is almost certainly the local pronunciation of Frud. Abramovich was a keen observer of progress

in his adopted city and it would be surprising if another school had opened that he did not know about. Either there was such a school that he somehow missed or perhaps the 1854 plan never reached fruition.

19. RGIA, f. 733, op. 97, d. 898, l. 2 (academic program for Jewish women's school in Berdichev, 1854).

20. RGIA, f. 733, op. 98, d. 96, l. 7–7 ob. (academic program for Jewish women's school in Kherson, 1856).

21. RGIA, f. 733, op. 98, d. 96, l. 4 (academic program for Jewish women's school in Odessa, 1856).

22. RGIA, f. 733, op. 98, d. 378, l. 5 (academic program for Jewish women's school in Mogilev, 1859).

23. Beer, *Toldot Yisra'el.*

24. Hecht, "Peter Beer—A Reformer of the Heder?" For more on Peter Beer, see Hecht, *Ein judischer Aufklarer in Bohem.*

25. RGIA, f. 733, op. 98, d. 96, l. 4 (program of school of Gringol'ts filed in 1856 but submitted sometime before that).

26. Berman, *St. Peterburgskiia Evreiskiia Uchilishcha*, 31.

27. RGIA, f. 733, op. 97, d. 686, l. 7.

28. See, for example, RGIA, f. 733, op. 97, d. 868, l. 7; d. 898, l. 2 and op. 98, d. 378, l. 2 ob.

29. RGIA, f. 733, op. 98, d. 177, l. 4 ob. (application materials for Anna Knristofov Val'tser's Vitebsk school, 1857). Much has been written on Homberg. For a recent reinterpretation, see Manekin, "Naftali Herts Homberg."

30. Petuchowski, "Manuals and Catechisms of the Jewish Religion in the Early Period of Emancipation," 48–62.

31. "Berman, Lazar Iakovlevich," *Evreiskaia entsiklopediia*, vol. 4, col. 282.

32. RGIA, f. 733, op. 189, d. 170, l. 139 (1884 Ministry of Education chart on the school of Anna Berman in St. Petersburg).

33. *Spravochnaia kniga po voprosam obrazovaniia evreev* (St. Petersburg, 1901), 138.

34. RGIA, f. 733, op. 98, d. 166, l. 2.

35. Russian does not offer a clear distinction between its terms for Hebrew and Yiddish. The term *evreiskii*, used in the academic plans, literally means "Jewish" and is ambiguous. Nonetheless, it is clear from context that the educators teaching *evreiskii* in their schools generally meant Hebrew and not Yiddish. In most cases where further detail, such as an academic program, is available, there can be no question that Hebrew was meant. For example, the term "ancient Hebrew language" (*derevnyi*) is often used in these more detailed documents . Other programs refer to the teaching of "points," namely, the system of Hebrew vocalization not used for Yiddish (see, for example, RGIA, f. 733, op. 98, d. 161, l. 5).

36. For more on the teaching and function of Hebrew in Eastern European Jewish society, see Stampfer, "What Did 'Knowing Hebrew' Mean in Eastern Europe?" and Stampfer, "Heder Study, Knowledge of Torah and the Maintenance of Social Stratification in Traditional East European Society," as well as Parush, "Mabat aher 'al haye ha-'Ivrit ha-metah.'"

37. RGIA, f. 733, op. 97, d. 233, l. 1.

38. RGIA, f. 733, op. 98, d. 378, ll. 4 ob. 5 (planned curriculum for school of David Shtern in Mogilev, 1859).

39. Gordon, *Razsvet* 52 (1861): 831.

40. For a sample curriculum for the government school system for Jewish boys, see Stanislawski, *Tsar Nicholas I and the Jews*, 101.

41. See, for example, the correspondence regarding the request of the Odessa government school for Jewish girls to replace a Hebrew textbook. RGIA, f. 733, op. 98, d. 716.

42. Bruk-Brezovskii, "Iz rechi skazannoi soderzhatelem evreiskago devich'iago pansiona, v g. Khersone," *Sion*, 322.

43. RGIA, f. 733, op. 98, d. 427.

44. Paperna, *Lehrbukh der Russishen shprakhe nakh Alendorfs metode.*

45. On Polish in the schools, see RGIA, f. 733, op. 97, d. 419; op. 97, d. 761; op. 97, d. 485; op. 98, d. 214; op. 98, d. 629; and "Minsk," *Razsvet* 19 (30 September 1860): 302. Of these schools, three were located in Minsk, one in Vilna, one in Rossieny, and one in Starokonstantin, all cities heavily influenced by Polish culture. These schools were founded between 1852 and 1860. There were no schools founded after the second Polish Uprising that list instruction in the Polish language. It is even possible that these schools had to abandon this subject after 1861, given the crackdown on Polish autonomy and culture. In May 1861 the curator of the Kiev educational circuit wrote to the MNP to ask about the policy toward a private Jewish girls' school with Polish listed in its 1855 plan (RGIA, f. 733, op. 98, d. 629, l. 1).

46. See, for example, RGIA, f. 733, op. 98, d. 139, l. 5 (1854 Advertisement for Shevel' Perel's school in Vilna); d. 177, l. 5 ob. (1857 plan for school of Anna Val'tser in Vitebsk).

47. For a listing of classes in the state schools for Jewish boys, see Stanislawski, *Tsar Nicholas I and the Jews*, 101. See also an advertisement for the twin schools of Anna and Lazar Berman in St. Petersburg. Girls had crafts and boys did not (*Ha-Karmel* [Russian] 6:28 [1866]: 220).

48. Gottlober, *Zikhronot u-masa'ot*, 165.

49. RGIA, f. 733, op. 97, d. 476, l. 2 (plan for school of Betti Shtern in Mitau).

50. RGIA, f. 733, op. 98, d. 161, l. 14 (program for Kishinev school of Sheinfel'd and Bliumenfel'd).

51. Porat, "Who Fired First?"

52. Jacobs, "What's Wrong with the History of American Jewish History?," 35.

Chapter 6

1. S. Y. Abramovitch, "Mikhtav mi-Berdits'ev," *Ha-Magid* 44 (1859): 175.

2. *Pamiatnaia knizhka Vilenskago uchebnago okruga na 1874*, 659; *Russkii evrei* 14 (1880): 558.

3. *Pamiatnaia knizhka Vilenskago uchebnago okruga na 1879/80 uchebnyi god*, 204.

4. Either of these estimates could exaggerate the number of students by count-

ing a student who stayed in school for three years as three separate students. However, many of the schools for which only one record exists undoubtedly remained open for more than one year, which would add to the number of students.

5. RGIA, f. 733, op. 189, d. 581, l. 27 (memo on Jewish schools in Kiev Educational District receiving candle tax monies, January 1880).

6. Eklof, *Russian Peasant Schools*, chap. 9.

7. Lishansky, *Mi-tseror zikhronotai*, 20–23.

8. YIVO, RG 24, file 141, p. 20 ob.

9. Khaim Funt, "Rech," *Minskiia gubernskiia vedomosti* 21 (1867): 117.

10. YIVO, RG 24, file 141, p. 24.

11. See, for example, YIVO, RG 24, file 141, 25–26 (1869 yearly report of Germaize school in Vilna).

12. Berman, *St. Peterburgskiia evreiskiia uchilishcha*.

13. RGIA, f. 733, op. 189, d. 170, l. 2 (1867 Request for government funding by Anna Berman).

14. Berman's original lists 113 pupils but number 44 is omitted. It is impossible to know whether this was simply a numbering error or if one student was inadvertently left off the list. In any case, we can only work with the 112 students listed.

15. Khaim Funt, "Rech," *Minskiia gubernskiia vedomosti* 21 (1867): 117.

16. YIVO, RG 141, l. 69 ob. (1869/70 yearly report of Schreiber school in Vilna).

17. Nadav, *The Jews of Pinsk*, 349.

18. On the makeup of the emigrants, see Simon Kuznet's classic article, "Immigration of Russian Jews to the United States."

19. Tidhar, *Entsiklopedyah le-halutse ha-Yishuv u-vonav*.

20. Hyman, *Gender and Assimilation in Modern Jewish History*, 78.

21. Hertz, *Doyres Bundistn*, vol. 1:130–31.

22. See, for example, Stites, *The Women's Liberation Movement in Russia*, 150, and Haberer, *Jews and Revolution in Nineteenth-Century Russia*, 274.

23. Berman, *St. Peterburgskiia evreiskiia uchilishcha*, 123–29. A feldsher was a sort of low-level medical professional common in rural Russia. For more on Jewish involvement, see Epstein, "Caring for the Soul's House," 102–6 and elsewhere.

24. I. Cherikover, "Prosveshchenie," *Evreiskaia entsiklopediia*, vol. 13, col. 57.

25. Bauer, Kappeler, and Roth, *Die Nationaliteten des russischen Reiches in der Volkszahlung von 1897*, 93–95.

26. Nathans, *Beyond the Pale*, 224. The work of Pinhas Kon revealed an even earlier experiment with higher education. As early as 1811 a midwifery program at Vilnius University accepted some Jewish women. However, this was a fairly marginal phenomenon and reflected more on the preceding Polish period than on the recently established Russian one. See Kon's "Yidishe froyen in der akusherye-shul baym Vilner Universitet, 1811–1824."

27. Balin, "The Call to Serve," 141.

28. Johanson, *Women's Struggle for Higher Education in Russia*, 62.

29. Ibid., 51–52.

30. Nikolai Rubenshteyn, "Pervaia evreika-studentka v Rossii," *Russkii evrei* 27

(1880): 1071.

31. RGIA, f. 733, op. 98, d. 96, ll. 1–1ob (report from Odessa office to MNP).
32. YIVO, RG 24, file 141, p. 74.
33. YIVO, RG 24, file 141, p. 17.
34. Khaim Funt, "Rech," *Minskiia gubernskiia vedomsti,* no. 21 (1867): 117.
35. *Pamiatnaia knizhka* (1879), 207.
36. Arnold, *The Metamorphosis of Heads,* 10, 99, and elsewhere.
37. This insight comes from El-Or, *Next Year I Will Know More,* 279.
38. Ibid., 272–74.
39. Vincent, *The Rise of Mass Literacy,* 144.
40. Stock, *Better than Rubies,* 12.

Chapter 7

1. D. Lazarev, "O vospitanii i stepeni obrazovannosti evreiskikh zhenshchin," *Uchitel',* 15/16 (1864): 559.
2. M. G. Gershfel'd, "K voprosu o zhenskom obrazovanii u evreev," *Russkii evrei* 6 (1880): 206.
3. "Grodno," *Ha-Karmel* 30 (1866): 233.
4. Ibid., 234.
5. Ia., "Kaments-Podol'sk, Ianvaria," *Razsvet* 39 (1861): 619–20. The important Russian doctor and controversial educational theorist oversaw the Kiev educational circuit from 1858 until 1861.
6. I. Tzedekh, "Ponevizh," *Russkii evrei* 31 (1880): 1214.
7. "Berdichev," *Sion* 42 (1862): 661–62.
8. I. Likub, "Chastnoe evreiskoe devich'e uchilishche v Simferopole," *Razsvet* 4 (1860): 54.
9. D.M., "Berdichev," *Razsvet* 28 (1860): 447.
10. Bruk-Brezovskii, "Iz rechi skazannoi soderzhatelem evreiskago devich'iago pansiona, v g. Khersone," *Sion* 20 (1861): 321.
11. L. Dreizin, "O vospitanii devits," *Ha-Karmel* (Russian) 1 (1864): 3–4.
12. Funt, "Rech," *Minskiia gubernskiia vedomosti* 21 (1867): 116.
13. Lazarev, "O vospitanii i stepeni obrazovannosti evreiskikh zhenshchin," 561.
14. Zeidler, "O zhenskom obrazovanii," *Razsvet* 40 (1861): 638.
15. B. Ts.-n, "Ekaterinoslav," *Razsvet* 11 (1860): 168.
16. "St. Petersburg," *Russkii evrei* 31 (1880): 1204.
17. M.S., "Nam pishut iz Peterburga," *Den'* 32 (20 December 1869): 517–18.
18. Lazar Berman, "Pis'mo k redaktoru," *Den'* 36 (4 September 1870): 591–93; *Den'* 40 (2 October 1870): 647.
19. Lifshits, *Mi-dor le-dor,* 102–3.
20. Salmon,"The Yeshiva of Lida," 113.
21. Reines, *Shene ha-me'orot,* part 2, p. 13.
22. See, for example, Sorski, *Toldot ha-hinukh ha-Torati,* 423, and Manekin, "Ha-Ortodoksyah bi-Krakov 'al saf ha-me'ah ha-20," 181–84.

Chapter 8

1. *Horodets: a geshikhte fun a shtetl,* ed. A. Ben-Ezra (Horodetz Book Committee, 1949), 132–33, quoted and translated in Kugelmass and Boyarin, *From a Ruined Garden,* 71–72 (emphasis added).

2. See Eklof, *Russian Peasant Schools,* esp. chap. 2.

3. RGIA, f. 733, op. 97, d. 848, l. 1ob. (letter of support for opening new school from Odessa Educational district).

4. RGIA, f. 733,. op. 97, d. 719, l. 18 (letter of support for stipend from Odessa educational district).

5. RGIA, f. 733, op. 189, d. 378, l. 2 (1858 plan for school).

6. RGIA, f. 733, op. 189, d. 170 (very large file on the Bermans' schools in St. Petersburg).

7. Stanislawski, *Tsar Nicholas I and the Jews,* 104–6, questions this assertion put forward by P. Marek, *Ocherki po istorii prosveshcheniia evreev v Rossii,* 80, among others.

8. H. Gornberg, "Zametka o evreiskikh uchilishchakh," *Razsvet* 6 (1860): 87.

9. Abram Iakov Bruk-Brezovskii, "Iz rechi skazannoi soderzhatelem evreiskago devich'iago pansiona, v g. Khersone," *Sion* 20 (1861): 321.

10. B. Bertenzon, "Pis'mo v redaktsiiu," *Sion* 40 (1862): 633.

11. There has been a good deal of scholarship on the development of professional education in a variety of countries and contexts. For a sampling of useful works, see Powers, *The "Girl Question" in Education,* and Klapper, "Jewish Women and Vocational Education in New York City, 1885–1925," 113–46.

12. Pannabecker, "Industrial Education and the Russian System," 19–31; Luetkemeyer, "Reaction to Pannabecker," 32–35.

13. RGIA, f. 733, op. 189, d. 461, ll. 1–5 ob. (correspondence between Ministry of the Interior and proposed society).

14. Saker is mentioned in Balin, *To Reveal Our Hearts,* 3, 203. I am grateful to Carole Balin for providing me with the following citations to Saker's published works: "O novoi sekte," *Nedel'naia khronika voskhoda* 8 (1882); "Zhenskii trud," *Razsvet* 15 (1879); "O neobkhodimosti . . . shkol zhenskie," *Odesskii listok* 38 (1883); "Ob evrei v zapadnom krae," *Den'* 7 (1879); "K evreiskie voprosi," *Den'* 24 (1869); and "Shakespeare," *Den'* 33 (1869). Steven Zipperstein also refers to both Saker and the literary circle in his *Imagining Russian Jewry,* 57, 81–82. See Dubnov-Erlich, *The Life and Work of S. M. Dubnov,* chap. 9, for a contemporary description of the Odessa Jewish literary scene, although with no mention of Saker.

15. "V to vremia kak . . . ," *Den'* 23 (1871): 351–52. It is interesting to note that Ms. Saker's powerful speech is preceded in written form by an undercutting introduction in which the editors question the wisdom of focusing on poor girls rather than both boys and girls.

16. Margulis, "O professional'nom obrazovanii evreev v Odesse," 394–95. For more on the curriculum, see also *Spravochnaia kniga,* 382.

17. Margulis, "O professional'nom obrazovanii evreev v Odesse," 396–98.

18. Ibid., 395–98.

19. Avraham Tsukerman, "Rusland, Kovno," *Ha-Magid* 29 (1872): 334.

20. "Kovno," *Russkii evrei* 9 (1880): 334–35.

21. *Russkii evrei* 3 (1884): 3–6.

22. *Russkii evrei* 31 (1880): 1201–06.

23. *Spravochnaia kniga*, 386.

24. "Soveshchanie Kommissii Obshchestva dlia rasprostraneniia prosveshcheniia mezhdu evreiami po professional'nomy obrazovaniiu," *Evreiskaia shkola* (January 1904): 42.

25. "Obshchestvo remeslennago i zemledel'cheskago truda sredi evreev v Rossii," *Evreiskaia entsiklopediia*, vol. 1, cols. 924–25.

26. Shapiro, *The History of ORT*, 47. See also Rader, *By the Skill of Their Hands*.

27. *Otchet obshchestva remeslennago i zemledel'cheskago truda za 1910* (St. Petersburg, 1911), 5, 27, 83–91.

28. *Trud* is mentioned in the introduction to Ms. Saker's speech, *Den'* 23 (1871): 351. See also Scharfstein, *Toldot ha-hinukh be-Yisra'el*, 1: 388.

29. *Evreiskaia shkola*, September 1905.

30. See, for example, Hirsz Abramowicz, *Profiles of a Lost World*, 221.

31. Wengeroff, *Rememberings*, 232.

32. I. O. Shul'kovskii, "Zhenskaia smena pri Orshanskoi Talmud-Tori," *Evreiskaia shkola* (January 1904): 40–41.

33. *Sbornik materialov ob ekonomicheskom polozhenii evreev v Rossii*, vol. 1 (St. Petersburg, 1904), table 68.

34. Stites, *The Women's Liberation Movement in Russia*, 60–63, 70–71, 110, and elsewhere. For more on prostitution in the Jewish community, see Weinberg, *The World of Our Mothers*, 78–79, and Bristow, *Prostitution and Prejudice*.

35. In fact, Maria Saker seems to hint at this danger in her article "Zhenskii trud i obrazovanie sredi russkikh evreev," *Razsvet* 15 (1879), col. 566.

36. Zalkin, "Ha-Haskalah ha-Yehudit be-Rusyah, 1800–1860," 193.

37. Scharfstein, *Toldot ha-hinukh be-Yisra'el*, 1: 363–69.

38. See Greenbaum, "Heder ha-banot, u-vanot be-heder ha-banim," 297–303.

39. Korngold, *Zikhroynes*, 33.

40. In 1877 Isak Germaize's school in Vilna was closed due to ongoing violations of the separation of the sexes. RGIA, f. 733, op. 189, d. 570, ll. 6–11.

41. RGIA, f. 733, op. 97, d. 673, ll. 1–3 ob.

42. "Vishtinets," *Ha-Magid* 5 (1879): 37–38.

43. RGIA, f. 733, op. 189, d. 164, ll. 1–3 ob.

44. RGIA, f. 733, op. 97, d. 189, ll. 1–1 ob.

45. "Prosveshchenie," *Evreiskaia entsiklopediia*, vol. 13, cols. 46 and 50.

46. Nathans, *Beyond the Pale*, 218.

47. RGIA, f. 733, op. 189, d. 435, ll. 1–3.

48. RGIA, f. 733, op. 189, d. 71, ll. 1–3.

49. See RGIA, f. 1532, as well as the Hebrew summary of the recording secretary L. M. Rozenthal, *Toldot Hevrat marbe haskalah be-Yisra'el be-erets Rusya*, and monthly updates published in various Jewish periodicals, including *Ha-Zefirah*.

50. RGIA, f. 733, op. 189, d. 189, ll. 1–3.

51. Dubnow, *History of the Jews in Russia and Poland*, vol. 3. See chaps. 21–27.

52. See, for example, Klier, "The Pogrom Paradigm in Russian History," in Klier and Lambroza, *Pogroms*, 13–38; Lederhendler, *The Road to Modern Jewish Politics*; Stanislawski, *Tsar Nicholas I and the Jews*; and Zipperstein, *The Jews of Odessa*. For another recent discussion of this issue, see Nathans, *Beyond the Pale*, 9–10.

53. Rappaport, "Jewish Education and Jewish Culture in the Russian Empire, 1880–1914," 17.

54. Ben-David, "Mikhtavim mi-Odesa," *Ha-Melits* 29 (1888): 293–94.

Conclusion

1. *Pamiatnaia knizhka Vilenskogo uchebnago okruga na 1881/2 god*, 10, 206.

2. Ran, *Yerushalayim de-Lita*, 1: 9.

3. *Vil'no i okrestnosti: putevoditel'*, 249.

4. YIVO, RG 24, file 141, p. 17.

5. See, for example, Klier, "The Pogrom Paradigm in Russian History," in Klier and Lambroza, *Pogroms*, 13–38; Lederhendler, *The Road to Modern Jewish Politics*; Stanislawski, *Tsar Nicholas I and the Jews*; and Zipperstein, *The Jews of Odessa*. For another recent discussion of this issue, see Nathans, *Beyond the Pale*, 9–10.

6. *Spravochnaia kniga po voprosam obrazovaniia evreev*, 644, 647–48.

7. Iu. Gessen, "Prosveshchenie," *Evreiskaia entsiklopediia*, vol. 13, col. 46.

8. I. Cherikover, "Prosveshchenie," *Evreiskaia entsiklopediia*, vol. 13, cols. 57–58.

9. Scharfstein, *Toldot ha-hinukh be-Yisra'el*, 1: 364–69.

10. Kazdan, *Fun heyder un "shkoles" biz Tsisho*, 203.

11. Parush, *Reading Jewish Women*, esp. pp. 5–7 and chap. 2.

12. *Froyen-shul "Yehudiyah" in Vilne*, 1–2.

13. Nikolai Rubinshtein, "Pervaia evreika-studentka v Rossii," *Russkii evrei* 27 (1880): 1071–72.

BIBLIOGRAPHY

ARCHIVAL SOURCES

Lietuvos Valstybes Istorijos Archyvas (Lithuanian State Historical Archives), Vilnius,
    Lithuania (LVIA)
        Fond 567   Upravleniie Vilenskogo uchebnogo okruga (Adminis-
                                        tration of the Vilna Educational Circuit)
Rossiiskii gosudarstvennyi istoricheskii arkhiv (Central State Historical Archives), St.
    Petersburg, Russia (RGIA)
        Fond 733   Department narodnogo prosveshcheniia Ministerstva
                                          narodnogo prosveshcheniia (Department of National
                                          Education of the Ministry of Education)
        Fond 1532   Obshchestvo dlia rasprostraneniia prosveshcheniia
                                          mezhdu evreiami v Rossii-OPE (Society for the Spread
                                          of Enlightenment among Jews in Russia)
YIVO Institute for Jewish Research, New York
        Record Group 24   Rabbinical School and Teachers' Seminary, Vilna
        Record Group 29   Vilna
        Record Group 52   Jewish State Schools in the Vilna School District
        Record Group 102 American-Jewish Autobiographies

PERIODICAL LITERATURE

Den'
Evreiskaia shkola
Grodnenskiia gubernskiia vedomosti
Ha-Karmel
Kievlianin
Kol Mevaser
Ha-Magid
Ha-Melits
Minskiia gubernskiia vedomosti
Nedel'naia khronika voskhoda
Odesskii listok
Odesskii vestnik
Ha-Olam
Razsvet

Russkii evrei
Ha-Shahar
Sion
Uchitel'
Vestnik russkikh evreev
Vilenskii vestnik
Voskhod
Zaria
Ha-Zefirah

BOOKS AND ARTICLES

Abramowicz, Hirsz. "A Jewish Teacher in Czarist Russia: Episodes from a Life." *YIVO Annual* 19 (1990).
———. *Profiles of a Lost World: Memoirs of East European Jewish Life before World War II*. Detroit: Wayne State University Press, 1999.
Adler, Eliyana R. "Educational Options for Jewish Girls in Nineteenth Century Eastern Europe." *Polin* 15 (2002).
———. "Private Schools for Jewish Girls in Tsarist Russia." Ph.D. diss., Brandeis University, 2003.
Adler, Ruth. "Dvora Baron: Daughter of the Shtetl." In *Women of the Word: Jewish Women and Jewish Writing,* ed. Judith Baskin. Detroit: Wayne State University Press, 1994.
———. *Women of the Shtetl: Through the Eyes of Y. L. Peretz.* Rutherford, N.J.: Fairleigh Dickinson University Press, 1980.
Ain, Abraham. "Swislocz: Portrait of a Jewish Community in Eastern Europe." *YIVO Annual of Jewish Social Science* 4, 1949.
Alston, Patrick L. *Education and the State in Tsarist Russia*. Stanford: Stanford University Press, 1969.
Arnold, Denise Y., and Juan de Dios Yapita. *The Metamorphosis of Heads: Textual Struggles, Education, and Land in the Andes*. Pittsburgh: University of Pittsburgh Press, 2006.
Ashkenazi, Shlomo. *Ha-Ishah be-aspaklaryat ha-Yahadut,* vol, 1. Tel Aviv: Jezriel, 1953.
Assaf, Simhah, ed. *Mekorot le-toldot ha-hinukh be-Yisra'el,* vol. 1. Tel Aviv: Dvir, 1954.
Avital, Moshe. *Ha-Yeshiva veha-hinukh ha-mesorati be-sifrut ha-Haskalah ha-'Ivrit.* Tel Aviv: Reshafim, 1996.
Azaryahu, Sarah. *Pirke hayim.* Tel Aviv: M. Nyuman, 1957.
Baader, Maria. "Inventing Bourgeois Judaism: Jewish Culture, Gender, and Religion in Germany, 1800–1870." Ph.D. diss., Columbia University, 2002.
Balin, Carole B. "Jewish Women Writers in Tsarist Russia, 1869–1917." Ph.D. diss., Columbia University, 1998.
———. *To Reveal Our Hearts: Jewish Women Writers in Tsarist Russia.* Cincinnati: Hebrew Union College Press, 2000.

Bar-Ilan, Meir. *Fun Volozin biz Yerusholayim.* New York: Oriam Press, 1933.

Baron, Dvora. *Parashiyot: Sipurim mekubatsim.* Jerusalem: Bialik Institute, 1968.

———. *The Thorny Path.* Trans. Joseph Shachter. Jerusalem: Israel Universities Press, 1969.

Baron, Salo W. *The Russian Jew under Tsars and Soviets.* New York: Macmillan, 1976.

Bartal, Israel, and Isaiah Gafni, eds. *Eros erusin ve-isurim: Miniyut u-mishpahah ba-historyah.* Jerusalem: Zalman Shazar Center for Jewish History, 1998.

Bauer, Henning, Andreas Kappeler, and Brigitte Roth, eds. *Die Nationalitaten des Russischen Reiches in der Volkszahlung von 1897.* Stuttgart: Franz Steiner, 1991.

Beauvois, Daniel. "Polish-Jewish Relations in the Territories Annexed by the Russian Empire in the First Half of the Nineteenth Century." In *The Jews of Poland,* ed. Chimen Abramsky, Maciej Jachimczyk, and Antony Polonsky. Oxford: Basil Blackwell, 1986.

Bechhofer, Shoshanah M. "Identity and Educational Mission of Bais Yaakov Schools: The Structuration of an Organizational Field as the Unfolding of Discursive Logics." Ph.D. diss., Northwestern University, 2005.

Beer, Peter. *Toldot Yisra'el.* Vienna: Schmid, 1810–31.

Beletskii, A. *Vopros ob obrazovanii russkikh evreev v tsartvovaniie Imperatora Nikolaia I.* St. Petersburg, 1894.

Benisch, Pearl. *Carry Me in Your Heart: The Life and Legacy of Sarah Schenirer, Founder and Visionary of the Bais Yaakov Movement.* Jerusalem: Feldheim, 2003.

Ben-Sasson, H. H., ed. *A History of the Jewish People.* Cambridge, Mass.: Harvard University Press, 1976.

Ben-Yehuda, Eliezer. *He-Halom ve-shivro: Mivhar ketavim be-'inyene lashon.* Jerusalem: Mosad Bialik, 1978.

Berman, Lazar. *St. Peterburgskiia evreiskiia uchilishcha: Otchet za pervyia piatnadtsat' let ikh sushchestvovaniia, 1865–1880.* St. Petersburg, 1885. Facsimile ed., Ann Arbor, Mich.: University Microfilms International, 1981.

Berman, Zehavah. *Be-darki sheli.* Jerusalem: Elisar, 1982.

Biale, David. *Eros and the Jews: From Biblical Israel to Contemporary America.* New York: Basic Books, 1992.

Biale, Rachel. *Women and Jewish Law: An Exploration of Women's Issues in Halakhic Sources.* New York: Schocken, 1984.

Borzyminska, Zofia. "Government-Sponsored Schools for Jews in the Kingdom of Poland, 1864–1870." *Gal-Ed* 13 (1993).

Bramson, L. M. *K istorii nachal'nago obrazovaniia evreev v Rossii.* St. Petersburg, 1896.

Bramson, L. M., and Iu. D. Brutskuy, eds. *Sistematicheskii ukazatel' literatury o evreiakh na russkom iazyke: So vremeni vvedeniia grazhdanskago shrifta (1708 g.) po dekabr 1889 g.* St. Petersburg, 1892.

Breuer, Edward. "Naphtali Herz Wessely and the Cultural Dislocations of an Eighteenth-Century Maskil." In *New Perspectives on the Haskalah,* ed. Shmuel Feiner and David Sorkin. London: Littman Library of Jewish Civilization, 2001.

Bristow, Edward J. *Prostitution and Prejudice: The Jewish Fight against White Slavery 1870–1939.* New York: Schocken, 1983.

Broido, Eva. *Memoirs of a Revolutionary.* Trans. and ed. Vera Broido. London: Oxford University Press, 1967.

Brooks, Jeffrey. *When Russia Learned to Read: Literacy and Popular Literature, 1861–1917.* Evanston, Ill.: Northwestern University Press, 2003.

Byer, Etta. *Transplanted People.* Chicago: Dr. M. J. Aron and other members of the Lider Organization of Chicago, 1955.

Chagall, Bella. *Burning Lights.* New York: Biblio Press, 1996.

Chekhov, N. V. *Tipy russkoi shkoly v ikh istoricheskom razvitii.* Moscow, 1923.

Cohen, Israel. *Vilna.* Philadelphia: Jewish Publication Society of America, 1943.

Cohen, Jocelyn, and Daniel Soyer, eds. *My Future Is in America: Autobiographies of Eastern European Jewish Immigrants.* New York: New York University Press, 2006.

Cohen, Rose. *Out of the Shadows: A Russian Jewish Girlhood on the Lower East Side.* Ithaca, N.Y.: Cornell University Press, 1995.

Cohen, Tova, and Shmuel Feiner, eds. *Kol 'almah 'Ivriyah: Kitve nashim maskilot ba-me'ah ha-tesha-'esreh.* Tel Aviv: Hakibbutz hameuchad, 2006.

———. "Reality and Its Refraction in Descriptions of Women in Haskalah Fiction." In *New Perspectives on the Haskalah,* ed. Shmuel Feiner and David Sorkin. London: Littman Library of Jewish Civilization, 2001.

Cohen, Tova. *Ha-Ahat ahuvah veha-ahat senu'ah: Ben metsi'ut le-vidyon be-te'ure ha-ishah be-sifrut ha-Haskalah.* Jerusalem: Magnes Press, 2002.

Darlington, Thomas. *Education in Russia: Presented to Both Houses of Parliament by Command of His Majesty.* London: Wyman and Sons, 1909.

Davar be-'ito: Berur devarim li-she'elat mekhes ha-basar. Pinsk, 1910.

Dawidowicz, Lucy S., ed. *The Golden Tradition: Jewish Life and Thought in Eastern Europe.* New York: Holt, Rinehart, and Winston, 1967.

Deich, Genrikh M. *Putevoditel'.* Ed. Benjamin Nathans. Moscow, 1994.

Dinur, Ben Zion, ed. *Mikhteve Avraham Mapu.* Jerusalem: Mosad Bialik, 1970.

Dinur, Bilhah. *Le-nekhdotai: zikhronot mishpahah ve-sipure havayot.* Arranged and edited by Ben Zion Dinur. Jerusalem: n.p., 1972.

Dubnov-Erlich, Sophie. *The Life and Work of S. M. Dubnov: Diaspora Nationalism and Jewish History.* Bloomington: Indiana University Press, 1991.

Dubnow, S. M. *History of the Jews in Russia and Poland from the Earliest Times until the Present Day.* Philadelphia: Jewish Publication Society of America, 1916–20.

Dubnow, Simon, ed. *Pinkas ha-medinah.* Berlin: Ajanoth, 1925.

Dudgeon, Ruth A. "The Forgotten Minority: Women Students in Imperial Russia, 1872–1917." *Russian History/Histoire Russe* 9:1 (1982): 16–17.

———. "Women and Higher Education in Russia, 1855–1905." Ph.D. diss., George Washington University, 1975.

Dukes, Paul. *A History of Russia: Medieval, Modern, Contemporary.* 2nd ed. Durham, N.C.: Duke University Press, 1990.

Eklof, Ben. *Russian Peasant Schools: Officialdom, Village Culture, and Popular Pedagogy, 1861–1914.* Berkeley: University of California Press, 1986.

El-Or, Tamar. *Educated and Ignorant: Ultra-Orthodox Women and Their World.* Boulder, Colo.: Lynne Rienner, 1994.

————. *Next Year I Will Know More: Literacy and Identity among Young Orthodox Women in Israel.* Trans. Haim Watzman. Detroit: Wayne State University Press, 2002.

Eliav, Mordechai. *Ha-Hinukh ha-Yehudi be-Germanyah bi-yeme ha-Haskalah ve-ha-emantsipatsyah.* Jerusalem: Sivan Press, 1960.

Elinson, Eliakim G. *Ben ha-ishah le-yotsrah.* Jerusalem: WZO Torah Education Department, 1983.

Encyclopaedia Judaica. 16 vols. Jerusalem, 1971.

Engel, Barbara Alpern. *Mothers and Daughters: Women of the Intelligentsia in Nineteenth-Century Russia.* Cambridge: Cambridge University Press, 1983.

Epstein, Baruch ha-Levi. *Mekor Barukh.* 4 vols. New York: Rabbi L. Goldman, 1954.

Epstein, Lisa Rae. "Caring for the Soul's House: The Jews of Russia and Health Care, 1860–1914." Ph.D. diss., Yale University, 1995.

Etkes, Immanuel, ed. *Ha-Dat veha-hayim: Tenu'at ha-Haskalah ha-Yehudit be-Mizrah Eropah.* Jerusalem: Zalman Shazar Center for Jewish History, 1993.

————. *Lita bi-Yerushalayim: Ha-'ilit ha-lamdanit be-Lita u-kehilat ha-Perushim bi-Yerushalayim le-or igrot u-khetavim shel R. Shemu'el mi-Kelm.* Jerusalem: Yad Izhak Ben-Zvi, 1991.

————. "Marriage and Torah Study among the *Lomdim* in Lithuania in the Nineteenth Century." In *The Jewish Family: Metaphor and Memory,* ed. David Kraemer. Oxford: Oxford University Press, 1989.

————. *Rabbi Israel Salanter and the Mussar Movement: Seeking the Torah of Truth.* Philadelphia: Jewish Publication Society, 1993.

Evreiskaia entsiklopediia. 15 vols. 1906. Reprint. Moscow: Obshchestva dlia nauchnykh evreiskikh izdanii i izdatel'stva Brokgaus-Efron, 1991.

Feiner, Shmuel. "Ha-Ishah ha-Yehudit ha-modernit: Mikrah-mivhan be-yahase ha-Haskalah veha-modernah." *Zion* 58, no. 4 (1993).

————. *The Jewish Enlightenment.* Philadelphia: University of Pennsylvania Press, 2004.

————. "Programot hinukhiyot ve-idi'alim hevratiyim: Bit ha-sefer 'Hinukh ne'arim' be-Berlin 1778–1825." In *Hinukh ve-historyah: Heksherim tarbutiyim u-politiyim,* ed. Rivka Feldhay and Immanuel Etkes. Jerusalem: Zalman Shazar Center, 1999.

Feingold, Ben Ami. "Feminism in Hebrew Nineteenth Century Fiction." *Jewish Social Studies* 49, nos. 3–4 (1987).

Fishbane, Simcha. "'In Any Case There Are No Sinful Thoughts'—The Role and Status of Women in Jewish Law as Expressed in the *Arukh Hashulhan.*" *Judaism* 42, no. 4 (1993).

Fishman, David E. *Russia's First Modern Jews: The Jews of Shklov.* New York: New York University Press, 1995.

Fishman, Isidore. *The History of Jewish Education in Central Europe: From the End of the Sixteenth to the End of the Eighteenth Century.* London: Edward Goldstein, 1944.

Fram, Edward. *My Dear Daughter: Rabbi Benjamin Slonik and the Education of Jewish Women in Sixteenth-Century Poland.* Cincinnati: Hebrew Union College

Press, 2007.

Frankel, Jonathan. "Assimilation and the Jews in Nineteenth-Century Europe: Towards a New Historiography?" In *Assimilation and Community: The Jews in Nineteenth-Century Europe*, ed. Jonathan Frankel and Steven J. Zipperstein. Cambridge: Cambridge University Press, 1992.

———. *Prophecy and Politics: Socialism, Nationalism, and the Russian Jews, 1862–1917.* Cambridge: Cambridge University Press, 1981.

Freeze, ChaeRan Y. *Jewish Marriage and Divorce in Imperial Russia.* Hanover, N.H.: Brandeis University Press, 2002.

———. "Making and Unmaking the Jewish Family: Marriage and Divorce in Imperial Russia, 1825–1917." Ph.D. diss., Brandeis University, 1996.

Freeze, Gregory L., ed. *Russia: A History.* Oxford: Oxford University Press, 1997.

———. "The *Soslovie* (Estate) Paradigm and Russian Social History." *American Historical Review* 91, no. 1 (1986).

Froyen-shul "Yehudiyah" in Vilne. Vilna, 1913.

Gessen, Iulii I. *Istoriia evreiskogo naroda v Rossii.* 2 vols. 2nd ed. Leningrad, 1925–27.

———. "K istorii evreiskogo sbora v Rossii." *Evreiskogo starina*, vol. 3. 1911.

Glenn, Susan A. *Daughters of the Shtetl: Life and Labor in the Immigrant Generation.* Ithaca, N.Y.: Cornell University Press, 1990.

Goodman, Zilla Jane. "Traced in Ink: Women's Lives in 'Qutzo shel Yud' by Yalag and 'Mishpachah' by D. Baron." In *Gender and Judaism: The Transformation of Tradition,* ed. Tamar M. Rudavsky. New York: New York University Press, 1995.

Gottlober, Abraham Baer. *Zikhronot u-masa'ot.* Jerusalem: Mosad Bialik, 1976.

Govrin, Nurit. *Ha-Mahatsit ha-rishonah: Devorah Baron—hayehah vi-yetsiratah, 1887–1923.* Jerusalem: Mosad Bialik, 1988.

Graetz, Michael. "The Jewish Enlightenment." *German-Jewish History in Modern Times,* vol. 1. Ed. Michael A. Meyer. New York: Columbia University Press, 1996.

Greenbaum, Avraham. "The Girls' *Heder* and Girls in the Boys' *Heder* in Eastern Europe before World War I." *East/West Education* 18, no. 1 (1997).

———. "Heder ha-banot, u-vanot be-heder ha-banim, be-Mizrah Eropah ba-tekufah she-kadmah le-Milhemet ha-'olam ha-rishonah." In *Hinukh ve-historyah: Heksherim tarbutiyim u-politiyim,* ed. Rivka Feldhay and Immanuel Etkes. Jerusalem: Zalman Shazar Center, 1999.

Greenberg, Louis. *The Jews in Russia: The Struggle for Emancipation.* New Haven, Conn.: Yale University Press, 1965.

Guenzburg, Mordecai Aaron. *Avi'ezer.* Vilna, 1863.

Haberer, Erich. *Jews and Revolution in Nineteenth-Century Russia.* Cambridge: Cambridge University Press, 1995.

Hadda, Janet. *Passionate Women, Passive Men: Suicide in Yiddish Literature.* Albany: State University of New York Press, 1988.

Halevy, Zvi. *Jewish Schools under Czarism and Communism: A Struggle for Cultural Identity.* New York: Springer, 1976.

Halperin, Israel. ed. *Pinkas va'ad arba' aratsot.* Jerusalem: Bialik Institute, 1945–46.

Hanover, Nathan. *Abyss of Despair.* Trans. Abraham J. Mesch. New York: Bloch, 1950.

Hartley, Janet M. *Alexander I.* London: Longman, 1994.

Hasanovitz, Elizabeth. *One of Them: Chapters from a Passionate Autobiography.* New York: Houghton Mifflin, 1918.

Hecht, Louise. *Ein judischer Aufklarer in Bohem: Der Pedagoge und Reformer Peter Beer (1758–1838).* Cologne: Libri Verlag, 2008.

———. "Peter Beer—A Reformer of the Heder?" Paper delivered at the thirty-second annual conference of the Association for Jewish Studies, Boston, 17–19 December 2000.

He-Hasid, Yehudah. *Sefer Hasidim.* Jerusalem: Mosad ha-Rav Kook, 1957.

Hertz, Jacob Sholem. *Doyres Bundistn.* New York: Farlag Unzer Tsayit, 1956–68.

Hilf, Mary Asia. *No Time for Tears.* New York: Thomas Yoseloff, 1964.

Horowitz, Brian. *Jewish Philanthropy and Enlightenment in Late-Tsarist Russia.* Seattle: University of Washington Press, 2009.

———. "The Society for the Promotion of Enlightenment among the Jews of Russia and the Evolution of the St. Petersburg Russian Jewish Intelligentsia, 1893–1905." *Studies in Contemporary Jewry* 19 (2003).

Howard, Deborah K. "Elite Secondary Education in Late Imperial Russia, 1881–1905." Ph.D. diss., Indiana University, 2006.

Howe, Irving, and Eliezer Greenberg, eds. *A Treasury of Yiddish Stories.* New York: Schocken, 1973.

Hundert, Gershon David, ed. *Essential Papers on Hasidism: Origins to Present.* New York: New York University Press, 1991.

Hutton, Marcelline J. *Russian and West European Women, 1860–1939: Dreams, Struggles, and Nightmares.* Lanham, Md.: Rowman and Littlefield, 2001.

Hyman, Paula E. *Gender and Assimilation in Modern Jewish History: The Roles and Representation of Women.* Seattle: University of Washington Press, 1995.

Jacobs, Benjamin M. "What's Wrong with the History of American Jewish Education?" *Journal of Jewish Education* 71 (2005).

Jazkan, Samuel Jacob. *Hinukh la-naar.* Vilna, 1894.

Johanson, Christine. *Women's Struggle for Higher Education in Russia, 1855–1900.* Kingston, Ont.: McGill-Queen's University Press, 1987.

Judge, Edward H. *Easter in Kishinev: Anatomy of a Pogrom.* New York: New York University Press, 1992.

Kahan, Arcadius. *Essays in Jewish Social and Economic History.* Chicago: University of Chicago Press, 1986.

Kaplan, Marion A. *The Making of the Jewish Middle Class: Women, Family, and Identity in Imperial Germany.* New York: Oxford University Press, 1991.

Katz, Jacob. *Tradition and Crisis: Jewish Society at the End of the Middle Ages.* Trans. Bernard Dov Cooperman. New York: Schocken, 1993.

Kaufman, Aharon. "'Al devar ha-hinukh." *Pirhe Tsafon* 2 (1844): 50–51.

Kazdan, Hayyim Solomon. *Fun heyder un "shkoles" biz Tsisho: Dos Ruslendishe Yidentum in gerangl far shul, shprakh, kultur.* Mexico: Shlomo Mendelson Fond, 1956.

Kazenelson, Judah Loeb Benjamin. *Mah she-ra'u 'enai ve-sham'u oznai: Zikhronot mi-*

yeme hayai. Jerusalem: Mosad Bialik, 1974.

Kelner, V. E., and D. A. El'iashevich. *Literatura o evreiakh na russkom iazyke, 1890–1947, knigi, broshiury, ottiski statei, organy, periodicheskoi pechati.* St. Petersburg: Gumanitarnoe agenstvo "Akademicheskii proekt," 1995.

Klapper, Melissa. "Jewish Women and Vocational Education in New York City, 1885–1925." *American Jewish Archives Journal* 53, nos. 1–2 (2001): 113–46.

Klausner, Israel. *Vilnah, Yerushalayim de-Lita: Dorot rishonim, 1495–1881.* Israel: Bet lohame ha-geta'ot, 1988.

Klier, John Doyle, and Shlomo Lambroza, eds. *Pogroms: Anti-Jewish Violence in Modern Russian History.* Cambridge: Cambridge University Press, 1992.

———. "1855–1894 Censorship of the Press in Russian and the Jewish Question." *Jewish Social Studies* 48 (Summer–Fall 1986): 3–4.

Klier, John Doyle. *Imperial Russia's Jewish Question, 1855–1881.* Cambridge: University Press, 1995.

———. *Russia Gathers Her Jews: The Origins of the "Jewish Question" in Russia, 1772–1825.* DeKalb: Northern Illinois University Press, 1986.

Kol Kitve Avraham Mapu. Tel Aviv: Dvir, 1939.

Kon, Pinhas. "Yidishe froyen in der akusherye-shul baym Vilner Universitet 1811–1824." In *Historishe shriftn.* Warsaw, 1929.

Korngold, Sheyna. *Zikhroynes.* Tel Aviv: Farlag Idpress, 1970.

Kositsa, Rohl. *Zikhroynes fun a Byalistoker froy.* Los Angeles: Schwartz Printing, 1964.

Kovets yagdil Torah: Likutim be-divre Torah, she'elot u-teshuvot ve-hidushe halakhot mi-maranan ve-rabanan more hora'ah be-Yisra'el ba-dor ha-zeh. Odessa: Moshe Eliezer Belinson, 1879.

Kramer, Sydelle, and Jenny Masur, eds. *Jewish Grandmothers.* Boston: Beacon Press, 1976.

Krieze, Simion. "Bate-sefer Yehudiyim ba-safah ha-Rusit be-Rusyah ha-Tsarit." Ph.D. diss., Hebrew University of Jerusalem, 1994.

———. "Bate-sefer Yehudiyim peratiyim: Gorem Rusifikatori o gorem Yehudi me-shamer?" In *Hinukh ve'historyah: Heksherim tarbutiyim u-politiyim,* ed. Rivka Feldhay and Immanuel Etkes. Jerusalem: Zalman Shazar Center, 1999.

Kugelmass, Jack, and Jonathan Boyarin, eds. *From a Ruined Garden: The Memorial Books of Polish Jewry.* 2nd ed. Bloomington: Indiana University Press, 1998.

Kuznets, Simon. "Immigration of Russian Jews to the United States: Background and Structure." *Perspectives in American History* 9 (1975).

Lang, Lucy Robins. *Tomorrow Is Beautiful.* New York, 1948.

Lapin, Jacob. *Keset ha-sofer.* Berlin, 1857.

Lederhendler, Eli. *Jewish Responses to Modernity: New Voices in America and Eastern Europe.* New York: New York University Press, 1994.

———. *The Road to Modern Jewish Politics: Political Tradition and Political Reconstruction in the Jewish Community of Tsarist Russia.* New York: Oxford University Press, 1989.

Levanda, V. O. *Polnyi khronologicheskii sbornik zakonov i polozhenii, kasaiushchikhsia evreev.* St. Petersburg, 1874.

Levin, Sabina. "Bate ha-sefer ha-elementariyim ha-rishonim li-yeladim bene Mosheh be-Varshah, ba-shanim 1818–1830." *Gal-Ed* 1 (1973).

———. *Perakim be-toldot ha-hinukh ha-Yehudi be-Polin: Ba-me'ah ha-tesha'-'esreh uve-reshit ha-me'ah ha-'esrim.* Tel Aviv: Tel Aviv University, 1997.

Levin, Sh. Z. *O korobochnom i svechnom sborakh.* Vilna, 1910.

Levinsohn, Isaac Baer. *Bet Yehudah,* vol. 1. Warsaw, 1901.

———. *Te'udah be-Yisra'el.* Photocopy of 1828 Vilna and Horodno ed. Jerusalem: Zalman Shazar Center, 1977.

Levisohn, Joshua Moshe. "The Early Vilna *Haskalah* and the Search for a Modern Jewish Identity." Ph.D. diss., Harvard University, 1999.

Levitats, Isaac. *The Jewish Community in Russia, 1772–1844.* New York: Columbia University Press, 1943.

———. *The Jewish Community in Russia, 1844–1917.* Jerusalem: Posner, 1981.

Lichtenstein, Haya (Weizman). *Be-Tsel Koratenu: Pirke Zikhronot mi-bet aba.* Tel Aviv: Am Oved, 1947.

Lieblich, Amia. *Conversations with Dvora: An Experimental Biography of the First Modern Hebrew Woman Writer.* Trans. Naomi Seidman. Berkeley: University of California Press, 1997.

Lifschutz, E. *Bibliography of American and Canadian Jewish Memoirs and Autobiographies In Yiddish, Hebrew and English.* New York: YIVO Institute for Jewish Research, 1970.

Lifshits, Tsevi Hirsch. *Mi-dor le-dor.* Warsaw, 1901.

Likhacheva, Elena. *Materialy dlia istorii zhenskago obrazovaniia v Rossii, 1086–1856.* St. Petersburg, 1899.

Lilienblum, Moses Leib. *Hat'ot ne'urim.* Vienna, 1876.

Lincoln, W. Bruce. "Daily Life of St. Petersburg Officials." *Oxford Slavonic Papers* n.s. 8 (1975).

———. *The Great Reforms: Autocracy, Bureaucracy, and the Politics of Change in Imperial Russia.* DeKalb: Northern Illinois University Press, 1990.

———. *Nicholas I Emperor and Autocrat of All the Russians.* Bloomington: Indiana University Press, 1978.

Lishansky, Shoshana. *Mi-tseror zikhronotai.* Jerusalem: Defus Merkaz, 1942.

Lowe, Heinz-Dietrich. "Poles, Jews, and Tartars: Religion, Ethnicity, and Social Structure in Tsarist Nationality Policies." *Jewish Social Studies* 6, no. 3 (2000).

———. *The Tsars and the Jews: Reform, Reaction and Anti-Semitism in Imperial Russia, 1772–1917.* Switzerland: Harwood, 1993.

Lozinskii, S. G., ed. *Kazennye evreiskie uchilishcha: Opisanie del byvshego arkhiva ministerstva narodnogo prosveshcheniia.* Vol. 1. Petersburg [*sic*], 1920.

Luetkemeyer, Joseph F. "Reaction to Pannabecker." *Journal of Industrial Teacher Education* 24, no. 1 (1986): 32–35.

Magnus, Shulamit S. "Pauline Wengeroff and the Voice of Jewish Modernity." In *Gender and Judaism: The Transformation of Tradition.* Ed. Tamar M. Rudavsky. New York: New York University Press, 1995.

Makowski, George Jerzy. "The Russian Classical Gymnasium, 1864–1890." Ph.D. diss., Indiana University, 1993.

Manekin, Rachel. "Ha-Ortodoksyah bi-Krakov 'al saf ha-me'ah ha-20." In *Krako-*

Kaz'imyez'-Krakov: mehkarim be-toldot Yehude Krakov, ed. Elchanan Reiner. Tel Aviv: Tel Aviv University, 2001.

———. "Naftali Herts Homberg: Ha-demut veha-dimui." *Zion* 71, no. 2 (2006).

Mapu, Avraham. *'Ayit tsavu'a.* Warsaw, 1881.

———. *Kol kitve Avraham Mapu.* Tel Aviv: Dvir, 1939.

———. *Mikhteve Avraham Mapu.* Ed. Ben Zion Dinur. Jerusalem: Mosad Bialik, 1970.

Marcus, Ivan G. *Rituals of Childhood: Jewish Acculturation in Medieval Europe.* New Haven, Conn.: Yale University Press, 1996.

Marek, P. *Ocherki po istorii prosveshcheniia evreev v Rossii.* Moscow, 1909.

Margulis, M. *Voprosy evreiskoi zhizni.* St. Petersburg, 1903.

Margulis, O. "O professional'nom obrazovanii evreev v Odesse." *Sbornik v pol'zu nachal'nykh evreiskikh shkol.* St. Petersburg, 1896.

McClelland, James C. *Autocrats and Academics: Education, Culture, and Society in Tsarist Russia.* Chicago: University of Chicago Press, 1979.

McConnell, Allen. *Tsar Alexander I: Paternalistic Reformer.* Arlington Heights, Ill.: Harlan Davidson, 1970.

McCullouch, Gary, and William Richardson. *Historical Research in Educational Settings.* Buckingham: Open University Press, 2000.

Mendes-Flohr, Paul, and Jehuda Reinharz. *The Jew in the Modern World: A Documentary History.* 2nd ed. New York: Oxford University Press, 1995.

Meneket Rivkah: A Manual of Wisdom and Piety for Jewish Women by Rivkah bat Meir. Ed. and with introduction and commentary by Frauke von Rohden. Trans. Samuel Spinner and Maurice Tszorf. Philadelphia: Jewish Publication Society, 2008.

Mintz, Alan. *"Banished from Their Father's Table": Loss of Faith and Hebrew Autobiography.* Bloomington: Indiana University Press, 1989.

Miron, Dan. *A Traveler Disguised: The Rise of Modern Yiddish Fiction in the Nineteenth Century.* New York: Syracuse University Press, 1996.

Mironov, Boris, with Ben Eklof. *The Social History of Imperial Russia, 1700–1917.* 2 vols. Boulder, Colo.: Westview Press, 2000.

Mohrer, Fruma, and Marek Web, eds. *Guide to the YIVO Archives.* New York: YIVO Institute for Jewish Research, 1998.

Moseley, Marcus. *Being for Myself Alone: Origins of Jewish Autobiography.* Stanford: Stanford University Press, 2006.

Nadav, Mordekhai. *The Jews of Pinsk, 1506–1880.* Ed. Mark Jay Mirsky and Moshe Rosman. Trans. Moshe Rosman and Faigie Tropper. Stanford: Stanford University Press, 2008.

Nash, Carol S. "The Education of Women in Russia, 1762–1796." Ph.D. diss., New York University, 1978.

Nash, Stanley. "'Kotso shel Yud' ('The Tip of the Yud')." *CCAR Journal: A Reform Quarterly* (Summer 2006).

Nathans, Benjamin Ira. "Beyond the Pale: The Jewish Encounter with Russia, 1840–1900." Ph.D. diss., University of California, Berkeley, 1995.

———. *Beyond the Pale: The Jewish Encounter with Late Imperial Russia.* Berkeley:

University of California Press, 2002.

Niger, Shmuel, ed. *A. M. Dik: Geklibene verk.* New York: Congress for Jewish Culture, 1954.

Niger, Shmuel. *Bleter geshikhte fun der Yidisher literatur.* New York: Congress for Jewish Culture, 1959.

Olney, James, ed. *Autobiography: Essays Theoretical and Critical.* Princeton, N.J.: Princeton University Press, 1980.

Orshanskii, I. G. *Evrei v Rossii. Ocherki ekonomicheskogo i obshchestvennogo byta russkikh evreev.* St. Petersburg, 1877.

———. *Russkoe zakonodatel'stvo o evreiakh.* St. Petersburg, 1877.

Pamiatnaia knizhka Vilenskago uchebnago okruga na 1879/80 uchebnyi god. Vilna, 1879.

Pamiatnaia knizhka Vilenskago uchebnago okruga na 1881/2 uchebnyi god. Vilna, 1881.

Pannabecker, John R. "Industrial Education and the Russian System: A Study in Economic, Social and Technical Change." *Journal of Industrial Teacher Education* 24, no. 1 (1986): 19–31.

Paperna, Abraham Jacob. *Lehrbukh der Russishen shprakhe nakh Alendorfs metode.* Warsaw, 1876.

Parush, Iris. "Mabat aher 'al 'haye ha-'Ivrit ha-metah.'"*Alpayim* 13 (1996).

———. "Another Look at 'the Life of "Dead" Hebrew': Intentional Ignorance of Hebrew in Nineteenth-Century Eastern European Jewish Society." *Book History* 7 (2004).

———. *Nashim kor'ot: Yitronah shel shuliyut ba-hevrah ha-Yehudit be-Mizrah Eropah ba-me'ah ha-tesha'-'esreh.* Tel Aviv: Am Oved, 2001.

———. "The Politics of Literacy: Women and Foreign Languages in Jewish Society of 19th-Century Eastern Europe." *Modern Judaism* 15, no. 2 (1995).

———. "Readers in Cameo: Women Readers in Jewish Society of Nineteenth-Century Eastern Europe." *Prooftexts* 14, no. 1 (1994).

———. *Reading Jewish Women: Marginality and Modernization in Nineteenth-Century Eastern European Jewish Society.* Hanover, N.H.: University Press of New England, 2004.

———. "Women Readers as Agents of Social Change among Eastern European Jews in the Late Nineteenth Century." *Gender and History* 9, no. 1 (1997).

Patterson, David. *Abraham Mapu: The Creator of the Modern Hebrew Novel.* London: Horovitz, 1964.

Petrovsky-Shtern, Yohanan. *Jews in the Russian Army, 1827–1917: Drafted into Modernity.* Cambridge: Cambridge University Press, 2009.

Petuchowski, Jacob J. "Manuals and Catechisms of the Jewish Religion in the Early Period of Emancipation." In *Studies in Nineteenth-Century Jewish Intellectual History,* ed. Alexander Altmann. Cambridge, Mass.: Harvard University Press, 1964.

Pipes, Richard. "Catherine II and the Jews: The Origins of the Pale of Settlement." *Soviet Jewish Affairs* 5, no. 2 (1975).

Plakans, Andrejs, and Joel M. Halpern. "An Historical Perspective on Eighteenth

Century Jewish Family Households in Eastern Europe." In *Modern Jewish Fertility,* ed. Paul Ritterband. Leiden: E. J. Brill, 1981.

Polnoe sobranie zakonov Rossiiskoi Imperii, 1649–1825. St. Petersburg, 1830.

Polnoe sobranie zakonov Rossiiskoi Imperii, second collection, 1825–81. St Petersburg, 1830–82.

Polnoe sobranie zakonov Rossiiskoi Imperii, third collection, 1881–1913. St. Petersburg, 1885–1916.

Polonsky, Antony, Jakub Basista, and Andrzej Link-Lenczowski, eds. *The Jews in Old Poland, 1000–1795.* London: I. B. Tauris, 1993.

———. "Warszawska Szkol Rabinów: oredowniczka narodowej integracji w Królestwie Polskim." In *Duchowosc Zydowska w Polsce,* ed. Michal Galas. Krakow, 2000.

Porat, Dan A. "Who Fired First? Students' Construction of Meaning from One Textbook Account of the Israeli-Arab Conflict." *Curriculum Inquiry* 36, no. 3 (2006).

Powers, Jane Bernard. *The "Girl Question" in Education: Vocational Education for Young Women in the Progressive Era.* London: Falmer, 1992.

Rabinowitz, Dan. "Rayna Batya and Other Learned Women: A Reevaluation of Rabbi Barukh Halevi Epstein's Sources." *Tradition* 35, no. 1 (2001).

Rader, Jack. *By the Skill of Their Hands: The Story of ORT.* Geneva: World ORT Union, 1970.

Rakovsky, Puah. *My Life as a Radical Jewish Woman: Memoirs of a Zionism Feminist in Poland.* Ed. Paula E. Hyman. Bloomington: Indiana University Press, 2002.

Rakowski, Puah. *Zikhroynes fun a Yiddisher revolutsyonerin.* Buenos Aires: Tsentralfarband fun Poylishe Yidn in Argentina, 1954.

Ran, Leyzer. *Yerushalayim de-Lita.* New York: Vilna Album Committee, 1974.

Rapoport-Albert, Ada. "On Women in Hasidism: S. A. Horodecky and The Maid of Ludmir Tradition." In *Jewish History: Essays in Honour of Chimen Abramsky,* ed. Ada Rapoport-Albert and Steven J. Zipperstein. London: Peter Halban, 1988.

Rappaport, Steven G. "Jewish Education and Jewish Culture in the Russian Empire, 1880–1914." Ph.D. diss., Stanford University, 2000.

Reines, Isaac Jacob. *Shene ha-me'orot.* Poland: Piotrkow Trybunaski, 1913.

Riasanovsky, Nicholas V. *A History of Russia.* 5th ed. New York: Oxford University Press, 1993.

Rogger, Hans. *Jewish Policies and Right-Wing Politics in Imperial Russia.* Berkeley: University of California Press, 1986.

Roskies, David G. "Ayzik-Meyer Dik and the Rise of Yiddish Popular Literature." Ph.D. diss., Brandeis University, 1975.

Roskies, Diane, and David G. Roskies. *The Shtetl Book.* New York: Ktav, 1975.

Roskies, Diane. "Alphabet Instruction in the East European Heder: Some Comparative and Historical Notes." *YIVO Annual for Social Science* 17 (1978).

———. *Heder: Primary Education among East European Jews: A Selected and Annotated Bibliography of Published Sources.* New York: YIVO Institute for Jewish Research, 1977.

Rozenthal, L. M. *Toldot Hevrat marbe haskalah be-Yisra'el be-erets Rusya.* St. Petersburg, 1885.

Ruane, Christine. *Gender, Class and the Professionalization of Russian City Teachers, 1860–1914*. Pittsburgh: University of Pittsburgh Press, 1994.

Sachar, Howard M. *The Course of Modern Jewish History*. New York: Vintage, 1990.

Sallis, Dorit, and Marek Web, eds. *Jewish Documentary Sources in Russia, Ukraine and Belarus: A Preliminary List*. New York: Jewish Theological Seminary of America, 1996.

Salmon, Yosef. "The Yeshiva of Lida: A Unique Institution of Higher Learning." *YIVO Annual* 15 (1974).

Satina, Sophie. *Education of Women in Pre-Revolutionary Russia*. Trans. Alexandra Poustchine. New York: n.p., 1966.

Sbornik materialov ob ekonomicheskom polozhenii evreev v Rossii, vol. 1. Evreiskago Kolonizatsionnago Obshchestva. St. Petersburg, 1904.

Sbornik postanovlenii po Ministerstvu narodnogo prosveshcheniia, vol. 2, part 2, 1840–55. St. Petersburg, 1876.

Schacter, Jacob J. "Haskalah, Secular Studies and the Close of the Yeshiva in Volozhin in 1892." *Torah U-Madda Journal* 2 (1990).

Scharfstein, Zevi. *Ha-Heder be-hayei 'amenu*. Tel Aviv, 1951.

———. *Toldot ha-hinukh be-Yisra'el ba-dorot ha-aharonim*. Jerusalem: R. Mas, 1960.

Schechter, Esther. *Di geshikhte fun meyn lebn*. Winnipeg: Dos Yidishe Vort, 1951.

Seeman, Don, and Rebecca Kobrin. "'Like One of the Whole Men': Learning, Gender and Autobiography in R. Barukh Epstein's *Mekor Barukh*." *Nashim: A Journal of Jewish Women's Studies and Gender Roles* 2 (Spring 5759/1999): 52–94.

Seeman, Don. "The Silence of Rayna Batya: Torah, Suffering, and Rabbi Barukh Epstein's 'Wisdom of Women.'" *Torah U-Madda Journal* 6 (1995–96).

Seidman, Naomi. *A Marriage Made in Heaven: The Sexual Politics of Hebrew and Yiddish*. Berkeley: University of California Press, 1997.

Seregny, Scott Joseph. *Russian Teachers and Peasant Revolution: The Politics of Education in 1905*. Bloomington: Indiana University Press, 1989.

Seton-Watson, Hugh. *The Russian Empire, 1801–1917*. Oxford: Clarendon Press, 1967.

Shapiro, Leon. *The History of ORT: A Jewish Movement for Social Change*. New York: Schocken, 1980.

Shatzky, Jacob. *Geshikhte fun Yidn in Varshe*, vol. 1. New York: YIVO Institute for Jewish Research, 1947.

Shavelson, Susanne Amy. "From Amerike to America: Language and Identity in the Yiddish and English Autobiographies of Jewish Immigrant Women." Ph.D. diss., University of Michigan, 1996.

Shmeruk, Khone. "Di Mizreh-Eyropeyishe nushaos fun der Tsenerene (1786–1850)." *For Max Weinreich on His Seventieth Birthday: Studies in Jewish Languages, Literature and Society*. The Hague: Mouton, 1964.

Shohet, Azriel. *Mosad "ha-Rabanut mi-ta'am" be-Rusyah: Parashah be-ma'avak-hatarbut ben haredim le-ven maskilim*. Haifa: University of Haifa, 1975.

Shtern, Yekhiel. *Heyder un beysmedresh*. New York: YIVO Institute for Jewish Research, 1950.

Shulzinger, Morris S. *The Tale of a Litvak*. New York: Philosophical Library, 1985.

Simon, Rachel. "Between the Family and the Outside World: Jewish Girls in the Modern Middle East and North Africa." *Jewish Social Studies* 7, no. 1 (2000).

Sinel, Allen. *The Classroom and the Chancellery: State Educational Reform in Russia under Count Dmitry Tolstoi*. Cambridge, Mass.: Harvard University Press, 1973.

Slutzky, Yehudah. *Ha-'Itonut ha-Yehudit-Rusit ba-me'ah ha-tesha'-'esreh*. Jerusalem: Mosad Bialik, 1970.

Sorski, Aaron. *Toldot ha-hinukh ha-torati*. Bnei Brak: Or ha-Hayim, 1967.

Sperber, Miriam. *Mi Berdits'er 'ad Yerushalayim: Zikhronot le-vet Ruzin*. Jerusalem: n.p., 1980.

Spiski chinovnikov i prepodavatelei Kievskago uchebnago okruga. Kiev, 1859.

Spiski chinovnikov i prepodavatelei Kievskago uchebnago okruga. Kiev, 1862.

Spiski chinovnikov i prepodavatelei Vilenskago uchebnago okruga. Vilna, 1858.

Spiski chinovnikov i prepodavatelei Vilenskago uchebnago okruga. Vilna, 1859.

Spisok uchebnykh zavedenii Iugo-zapadnago kraia. Kiev, 1874.

Spravochnaia kniga po voprosam obrazovaniia evreev. St. Petersburg, 1901.

Stampfer, Shaul. "Gender Differentiation and Education of the Jewish Woman in Nineteenth-Century Eastern Europe." *Polin* 7 (1992).

———. "Heder Study, Knowledge of Torah and the Maintenance of Social Stratification in Traditional East European Jewish Society." *Studies in Jewish Education* 3 (1988).

———. "Remarriage among Jews and Christians in Nineteenth-Century Eastern Europe." *Jewish History* 3, no. 2 (1988).

———. "Ha-Mashma'ut ha-hevratit shel nisu'e boser be-Mizrah Eropah." In *Studies on Polish Jewry: Paul Glikson Memorial Volume,* ed. Ezra Mendelsohn and Chone Shmeruk. Jerusalem: Magnes Press, 1987.

———. "What Did 'Knowing Hebrew' Mean in Eastern Europe." In *Hebrew in Ashkenaz: A Language in Exile,* ed. Lewis Glinert. New York: Oxford University Press, 1993.

———. *Ha-Yeshivah ha-Lita'it be-hithavutah*. Jerusalem: Zalman Shazar Center, 1995.

Stanislawski, Michael. *Autobiographical Jews: Essays in Jewish Self-Fashioning*. Seattle: University of Washington Press, 2004.

———. *For Whom Do I Toil?: Judah Leib Gordon and the Crisis of Russian Jewry*. New York: Oxford University Press, 1988.

———. "Jewish Apostasy in Russia: A Tentative Typology." In *Jewish Apostasy in the Modern World,* ed. Todd M. Endelman. New York: Holmes & Meier, 1987.

———. *Tsar Nicholas I and the Jews: The Transformation of Jewish Society in Russia, 1825–1855*. Philadelphia: Jewish Publication Society, 1983.

Stites, Richard. *The Women's Liberation Movement in Russia: Feminism, Nihilism, and Bolshevism, 1860–1930*. Princeton, N.J.: Princeton University Press, 1978.

Stock, Phyllis. *Better than Rubies: A History of Women's Education*. New York: G. P. Putman's Sons, 1978.

Stone, Goldie. *My Caravan of Years: An Autobiography*. New York: Bloch, 1945.

Tcherikower, Elias. *Istoriia obshchestva dlia rasprostraneniia prosviescheniia mezhdu evreiami v Rossii.* St. Petersburg, 1913.

Thaden, Edward C., with Marianna Forster Thaden. *Interpreting History: Collective Essays on Russia's Relations with Europe.* Boulder, Colo.: Social Science Monographs, 1990.

————. *Russia's Western Borderlands, 1710–1870.* Princeton, N.J.: Princeton University Press, 1984.

Thomashefsky, Bessie. *Mayn lebens-geshikhte.* New York, 1916.

Tidhar, David, ed. *Entsiklopedyah le-halutse ha-Yishuv u-vonav: Demuyot u-temunot.* Tel Aviv: Sifriyat rishonim, 1947.

Trunk, Yehiel Yeshaia. *Poyln: Zikhroynes un bilder.* New York: Farlag Unzer Tsayit, 1946.

Vil'no i obrestnosti: Putevodetel'. Vilna, 1883.

Vincent, David. *The Rise of Mass Literacy: Reading and Writing in Modern Europe.* Cambridge: Polity Press, 2000.

Weeks, Theodore R. "Rossification: Word and Practice 1863–1914." *Proceedings of the American Philosophical Society* 148, no. 4 (2004).

Weinberg, Sydney Stahl. *The World of Our Mothers: The Lives of Jewish Immigrant Women.* Chapel Hill: University of North Carolina Press, 1988.

Weisberg, Yitshak Ya'akov, ed. *Igrot Yehudah Leyb Gordon: Min shenat 618 'ad 652.* 4 vols. Warsaw: Ahim Shuldberg, 1894.

Weissler, Chava. "Prayers in Yiddish and the Religious World of Ashkenazic Women." In *Jewish Women in Historical Perspective,* ed. Judith R. Baskin. Detroit: Wayne State University Press, 1991.

————. "Traditional Piety of Ashkenazic Women." In *Jewish Spirituality from the Sixteenth-Century Revival to the Present,* ed. Arthur Green. New York: Crossroad, 1987.

————. *Voices of the Matriarchs: Listening to the Prayers of Early Modern Jewish Women.* Boston: Beacon Press, 1998.

Weissman, Deborah. "Bais Yaakov: A Historical Model for Jewish Feminists." In *The Jewish Woman,* ed. Elizabeth Koltun. New York: Schocken, 1976.

————. "Bais Ya'akov as an Innovation in Jewish Women's Education: A Contribution to the Study of Education and Social Change." *Studies in Jewish Education* 7 (1995).

————. "Bais Ya'akov, A Women's Educational Movement in the Polish Jewish Community: A Case Study in Tradition and Modernity." M.A. thesis, New York University, 1977.

————. "Education of Jewish Women." *Encyclopaedia Judaica Yearbook 1986–87.* Jerusalem: Keter, 1987.

————. "Hinukh banot datiyot bi-Yerushalayim bi-tekufat ha-shilton ha-Beriti." Ph.D. diss., Hebrew University, 1993.

Wengeroff, Pauline. *Memoiren einer Grossmutter.* Berlin: M. Poppelauer, 1913–19.

————. *Rememberings: The World of a Russian Jewish Woman in the Nineteenth Century.* Ed. Bernard D. Cooperman. Trans. Henny Wenkart. Bethesda: University Press of Maryland, 2000.

Wischnitzer, Mark. *A History of Jewish Crafts and Guilds.* New York: Jonathan David,

1965.

Wolff, Zvi. "Teaching Women Torah." *The Pardes Reader: Celebrating 25 Years of Learning.* Jerusalem: Pardes Institute of Jewish Studies, 1997.

Wolowelsky, Joel B., ed. *Women and the Study of Torah: Essays from the Pages of Tradition.* New York: Ktav/Rabbinical Council of America, 2001.

Yelin, Itah. *Le-Tse'etsa'ai.* Jerusalem: Ha-Ma'arov, 1928.

Zalkin, Mordechai. *Ba-'alot ha-shahar: Ha-haskalah ha-Yehudit ba-Imperyah ha-Rusit ba-me'ah ha tesha' 'esreh.* Jerusalem: Magnes Press, 2000.

———. *El hekhal ha-haskalah: Tahalikhe modernizatsyah ba-hinukh ha-Yehudi be-Mizrah Eropah ba-me'ah ha-tesha'-'esreh.* Tel Aviv: Hakibbutz Hameuchad, 2008.

———. "Ha-Haskalah ha-Yehudit be-Rusyah, 1800–1860: Hebetim hevratiyim." Ph.D. diss., Hebrew University, 1996.

———. "Itzhak Romash—Between 'Educating the Periphery' and 'Peripheral Education.'" In *Old World—New People: Jewish Communities in the Age of Modernization,* ed. Eli Tzur (Hebrew). Beer Sheva: Ben-Gurion University of the Negev Press, 2005.

———. "Kavim li-demut ha-moreh ba-haskalah ha-Yehudit be-Mizrah Eropah be-reshit ha-me'ah ha-tesha' 'esreh." *Ha-Moreh ben shelihut le-miktso'a.* Tel Aviv: Beit ha-sefer le-hinukh, 1995.

Zborowski, Mark, and Elizabeth Herzog. *Life Is with People: The Culture of the Shtetl.* 2nd ed. New York: Schocken, 1995.

Zinberg, Israel. *A History of Jewish Literature* 11, part 12. Cincinnati: Hebrew Union College Press, 1978.

Zipperstein, Steven J. *Elusive Prophet: Ahad Ha'am and the Origins of Zionism.* Berkeley: University of California Press, 1993.

———. *Imagining Russian Jewry: Memory, History, Identity.* Seattle: University of Washington Press, 1999.

———. *The Jews of Odessa: A Cultural History, 1794–1881.* Stanford: Stanford University Press, 1985.

———. "Transforming the Heder: Maskilic Politics in Imperial Russia." In *Jewish History: Essays in Honour of Chimen Abramsky,* ed. Ada Rapoport-Albert and Steven J. Zipperstein. London: Peter Halban, 1988.

Zolty, Shoshana Pantel. *"And All Your Children Shall be Learned": Women and the Study of Torah in Jewish Law and History.* Northvale, N.J.: Jason Aronson, 1993.

Zunser, Miriam Shomer. *Yesterday.* New York: Stackpole Sons, 1939.

INDEX

Abramovich, Sholem Yankev, 99
Alexander I, 3, 14
Alexander II, 3, 14, 34; Great Reforms
   of, 4, 14, 16, 64; 1864 statutes on
   education, 124
Alexander III, 4, 17
anti-Hasidic movement, 18
Aronovicheva, Simonia, 56–57
Arukh ha-Shulḥan, 20
Ashkenazi, Rabbi Ya'akov, 20

Bais Yaakov school for Jewish girls,
   Poland, 6
Balin, Carole, 26
Baltic Germans, position in tsarist
   Russia, 58
Beer, Peter: *Toldot Yisra'el,* 84, 87, 88
Bel'skiia, Nadezhda, 59
Ben-Yehuda, Eliezer, 61
Ben Ze'ev, Judah Lob, 84; *Yesode ha-
da'at,* 86, 88
Berdichev, 54, 62, 65, 71, 72, 81, 84,
   92
Berman, Anna, private school for girls,
   54, 75; advertisement for school,
   105; attacked in Russian-Jewish
   paper, 120; educational careers of
   students, 106–9; funding, 66–67;
   life paths of graduates,
   112; location in St. Petersburg,
   104, 106; primarily poor students,
   66–67, 104–5, 125; student
   retention, 109
Berman, Lazar, school for poor Jewish
   boys: advertisement for school,

105; attack on school in Russian-
   Jewish paper, 120; funding,
   66–67; *Osnovyi Moiseeva zakona*
   (Foundations of the Mosaic Faith),
   88, 89; *Sefer mosde dat Moshe,* 90
Berman, Sara, 54
Bertenzon, Bernard, 66
Bet Yehudah, 24
Birshenker, Anna, 54
Bramson, Leon, 5
Broido, Eva, 48
Bruk-Brezovskii, Abram Iakov, 1, 10,
   65, 84, 92, 118, 125, 150, 151
Byer, Etta, 19

candle tax funds, 9, 66, 67–73, 75,
   137; established to support major
   school system, 68; funds for non-
   Jewish schools, 70; for private
   Jewish girls' schools, 70, 71–72
Catherine II, Empress, establishment of
   Pale of Settlement, 3
co-education, 133, 134–35, 141
Committee for the Transformation of
   the Jews, 33
crown rabbis, 4

Daich, Iakov, 54
Derpt Educational Circuit, 41
Dikker, Mr., 117
Dreizen, L., 119
dual rabbinate, 4
Dubinskiis, 91
Dubno, Kiev province, 54
Dubnow, Shimon, 139

189

Uvarov, Count S. S., 14, 32, 33, 35, 68

Val'tser, Anna, 88
Vilna: center of rabbinic learning and
opposition to Hasidism, 79, 142;
center of Russian Jewish *Haskalah*,
79; Daytsche gas, 142; private
schools for Jewish students in,
32, 38–39, 45, 51–52, 54, 57; in
1830s, 29; Shevel' Perel' school for
girls in, 2, 28–31, 64, 69
Vilna educational circuit, 30, 38–39,
54, 71, 72, 73
Vilna Gymnasium, 28
Vincent, David, 113
Vitebsk province, 36, 86
vocational education: growing interest
in, 125. *See also* trade schools
Volhynia province, 19, 20, 80

Weissman, Deborah, 7
Wengeroff, Afanasii, 75
Wengeroff, Pauline, 129–30
Wessely, Naftali Herz: *Divre shalom
ve-emet*, 23

women's movement, education as
unifying goal, 16
World Fair of 1876, 126

Yelin, Itah, 48
yeshiva (pl. *yeshivot*), 18, 122
Yesodei ha-da'at, 84
Yiddish, 22
Yiddish schools, 148

Zak, Abram, 35
Zalkin, Mordechai, 6, 61, 75
Zalkind, Shlomo, 35
Zeidler, A., 119
Zel'verovich, Maksamilian, 59–60
zemstvo, 4, 14, 124
Zionism, 3, 99, 131, 140, 145
Zionists: embraced use of Hebrew, 132,
149; teaching jobs at *talmud torah*,
132
Zionist schools, 140, 142, 149
Zipperstein, Steven, 6
zogerke (women's prayer-leader), 21
Zolty, Shoshana Pantel, 7